NGOs in Himachal Pradesh

NGOs in Himachal Pradesh:
Organization, Issues and Challenges

Dr Raj Kumar Jishtu

KALPAZ

First Published, 2021

Published by

Kalpaz Publications
C-30, Satyawati Nagar,
Delhi – 110052
Ph.: 011-47034999, 9811692060
www.kalpazpublications.com
E-mail: kalpaz@hotmail.com

Printed at: G. Print Process, Delhi

Cataloging in Publication Data—DK

Courtesy: D.K. Agencies (P) Ltd. <docinfo@dkagencies.com>

Jishtu, Raj Kumar, author.

NGOs in Himachal Pradesh : organization issues and challenges / Dr. Raj Kumar Jishtu.

pages cm

ISBN 9789353242473

1. Non-governmental organizations—India—Himachal Pradesh. 2. Non-governmental organizations—India—Himachal Pradesh—Management. I. Title.

LCC JZ4841.J57 2020 | DDC 361.77 23

Contents

Foreword

Today the state has been relieved of many of its obligations by voluntary groups, organizations and collectivities that in one way or the other perform certain functions supposed to be performed by it. While the moralities and ethical values are left to be communicated by the society culture and traditions, the material task performance is done by the people through the agency of state and the backup supplementation by non-state associations, be they philanthropic, social, cultural or religious. The kinds are myriad and so is the performative narrative and the actors are none others than the non-governmental organizations. Harris argues that moral science does not imply an "Orwellian future" with "scientists at every door" rather it could be communicated through the mediation of science and literature as does happen with the other fields and the role of state and government, like any organization, should have limited power. The concentration of power in the hands of one person or few has always led to unprecedented suppression of human will and creativity resulting in enormous loss to human freedom, democratic spirit and the humanity as a whole. Hence, the power, the performance and the moral obligation to perform combined with the order and the law has also to assume a democratic character giving vent to different voices of man. In fact it is the imperative craving of a democracy to look for an informed, enlightened and active participant citizenry at the grass root level.

A Non-Government Organization is at best a human collectivity with organizational traits exempt from governmental control and ordination. While they have evolved as a ranked force of development world over in the last few centuries, these groups, both formal and informal, have been there since millennia. They assume different characters as per the socio-economic, cultural and political environment, at all local, national and international levels. There are references of such voluntary organizations during the times of wars and natural calamities in ancient India. The European conflicts and the two world wars saw the emergence of thousands of such groups with Red Cross emerging as the world's largest NGO in the twentieth century.

NGOs increased numerically manifold in the post-World War II era resulting in the evolution of the parallel welfarist and social service institutions Vis a Vis State. Today they play a significant role in different programmers and functions that help communities become more autonomous, self-reliant, empowered, and in the long run accomplishing sustainable development. Besides meeting out the numerous needs of the society on different accounts they also generate significant volume of employment, development narrative (education, health, agriculture) and improvised social participation in political activities and policy making. NGOs become instrumental in problem shooting, conflict resolution, capacity building such as ability, skill and knowledge of mobilizing resources, planning and evaluating community initiation and resolving the issues and problems in the society. They precipitate community participation in different programmers and plans, decrease conflicts and crime, and expedite the processes of social change, development and life standards of the people.

Non-governmental organizations (NGOs) have, over the decades, acquired huge consideration among social workers, volunteers, scholars, literary people and protagonists of human causes and welfare. Their role has become increasingly significant, holds Attack (1999), as the agents of the development process in the countries of the South, in all of their main areas of work such as humanitarian relief, long-term development, policy formation and political advocacy. Still for others like Straiten (1997), the NGOs provide a viable alternative to government as channels of development assistance, particularly in developing countries. Some of the NGOs' functions and major advantages include reaching and mobilizing the poor and remote communities; helping empowerment of the poor people to gain control of their lives, and they work with and strengthen local institutions; carrying out projects at lower costs and more efficiently than the government agencies and promoting sustainable development.

India has witnessed an enormous spate of NGO activity in the post-independence era, especially in the eighties and nineties. In the preliminary decades, the popular expectation was from the state to act as the chief liberator from social ills, poverty and underdevelopment, calamities, both natural and man-generated and work for the larger social transformation. However, steadily the scenario changed from the onus of the state in respect of the performance of these tasks towards the voluntary groups of civil society officially designated as NGOs.

The rise of NGOs is one of the central processes in the sphere of development since the 1980s. This period also coincides with the demise of developmentalism as a project of the nation-state and the rise of post developmentalist neo-liberal political economy (or what has also been described as market triumphalism). In what is often described as a move from inefficient states to efficient markets, NGOs hold a distinctive mediating position (Navistar 2001). Taking into account the role of NGOs in social reforms, economic development, water, forest, environment and sustainability and policy making and legislation, there is a great need to critically examine the changing relations between NGOs, State agencies, multilateral and bilateral funding institutions, and other social groups. This has great bearing on the way in which we conceive of the process of social change and the roles of different social actors within it.

Normally a layman notices little the presence of these organizations in society but we are connected with them in our routine activities as we experience them as part of our lives like social groups, clubs, youth associations, scouts and guides, salvation army, YMCA, and local festivals, temples, or places of worship etc. In many States they are called nonprofits or not-for-profits groups but mostly they are more commonly known as Non-Gormenrntal organizations (NGOs). India, a huge country with a population of 123 billion, according to the Times of India, boasts of having one NGO for every 600 people.

The history of NGOs in India is long as it has been at the core of Indian culture, the *Santa Tradition* to serve the poor, the suffering the helpless and the needy. Initially this happened on religious grounds as philanthropic acts but they steadily transformed into customs and traditions inspired by the objectives of spirituality and emancipation. However, the spirit of charity and altruism also guided the voluntary action of man in the past in diverse ways and forms even outside the formal established religious structures and channels rites. People believed that the service to the poor and deprived would be the service to God and, therefore, would be a means to attain spiritual salvation and sometimes atonement for any sinful act. Spirit of charity and altruism guided the voluntary action in the past, which had found expression in diverse forms even outside the formal established religious channels.

Many people including rulers have trod the path of service to their fellow beings and adopted it as their life mission. Floods, fires, earthquakes, epidemic outbreaks and other kinds of calamities were the occasions which motivated people to volunteer help to those who were trapped in disastrous situations. Community life was very strong and people were guided by the 'we' feeling and selflessness in extending their individual support. The help and support used to be individual, spontaneous and transitory. It is around the late 18th and early 19th century that associations and organizations were being formed to render such activities in a more organized and permanent profile (Punalekar 2004).

The tradition of service and donation has maintained continuity and it has further proliferated during the Raj, working to improve the conditions of the poor, increase the level of literacy and health and above all social good. The second half of the nineteenth century witnessed the emergence of nationalist consciousness all over India and self-help appeared as the primary focus of socio-political movements. Several groups or societies sprang up during the time including the *Friend-in-Need Society* (1858), *Parthian Samar* (1864), *Satyr Sheehan Samar* (1873), *Aria Samar* (1875), the *National Council for Women in India* (1875), *Indian National Conference* (1887) and the *Servants of India* in 1905. The British passed Societies Registration Act (SRA) long back in 1860 to confirm the legal status of the growing body of Non-Government organizations (NGOs). The SRA continues to be relevant legislation for NGOs in India even today although, most state governments have enacted amendments to the original version. It was with the foundation of *Servants of India* in 1905 that the missionary zeal got transformed into broader secular welfares programmers of the new organizations.

While Europe sagged in the blood of civil wars and ethnic conflicts in the nineteenth century, India while contesting the colonial narrative evolved a social reform movement of its own that with the instrumentality of the British government volunteered the eradication of several social evils and demand of civilian rights. It was the first organized voice from the social groups lending them a peculiar character. Most of these organizations were liberal and cut across the narrow lines of race, color, caste and community. During the freedom movement they served various purposes of service to the freedom fighters and their families and the poor and marginalized. Gandhi became a huge source of inspiration in effecting the mediatory role of them. In order to achieve these goals, several Voluntary Organizations were formed under the influence of the ideals of Gandhi Ji. A few of them are Sew, Elkay, Desha etc., which were instituted in Gujarat and some others might have been formed in other states also.

A significant growth of NGOs started after Indian independence when democracy led the people of the country to appreciate the terms like liberty, equality and the value of humanity and fraternity. The awareness about the civilian and human rights opened up parallel institutions of thought and service. While government launched programmers like Community Development Programme and Panchyati Raj there was a simultaneous emergence of voluntary organizations throughout the state. Today according to a CBI exercise about 31 lakh NGOs work in India (nonprofit, voluntary citizens' groups organized on a local, national, or international level) more than double the number of schools in the country, 250 times the number of government hospitals, one NGO for 400 people as against one policeman for 709 people (Indian Express Jan.7, 2020). This includes temples, churches, mosques, gurudwaras, sports associations, hospitals, educational institutions, and ganeshotsav mandals (temporary structures set up to house Ganesh festival celebrations), clubs, socio-economic and religious groups and so on. Most NGOs in India are small and dependent on volunteers. According to a survey conducted by society for Participatory research in Asia (PRIA), 73.4% of NGOs have one or no paid staff, although across the country, more than 19 million persons work as volunteers or paid staff at an NGO (ADB 2009). The NGO sector in India is characterized by tremendous diversity and heterogeneity. Ignoring this diversity, unfounded generalizations are often put forward and unfair comments and criticisms are offered. NGOs differ from one another in size, in funding, in functions; in the levels at which they operate; and in organizational structures, goals and membership (Fisher 1997). Therefore, NGOs have been performing a mammoth task of social reconstruction, welfare and service to the needy in India. The scenario of Himachal Pradesh also offers interesting issues covered up by the NGOs and this is the focus of the current study, a noteworthy exercise in the area.

The current work by Dr. Raj Kumar Jishtu that has been carried out on three levels i.e. *Himachal Pradesh Voluntary Health Association* (HPVHA), *Himachal Gyan Vigyan Samiti* (HGVS) and *Society for Participatory Research in Asia* (PRIA) offers tremendous insight into the organization, role and functioning of NGOs in the state of Himachal Pradesh. They have played a significant role in the socio-political and economic development of the state and the study underlines the major achievements and challenges faced by them. The work highlights certain drawbacks in NGOs like lack of internal democracy, dependence of governmental funding and lack of local resources, chances of misappropriation of funds due to absence of auditing, unskilled staff and poor quality on service. The work is first of its kind in Himachal Pradesh and would definitely benefit and inspire further research and interest in the area among the social workers, scholars and related officials.

Prof. Harish K. Thakur
Director
Centre for Canadian Studies &
Chairman Department of Political Science
H.P. University Shimla, 171005

Preface and Acknowledgements

Organizations are central to all the societies of the world and the large and complex organizations dominate every sphere of human activity irrespective of ideological and other differences. Organizations, as such have become very crucial and dominating factor affecting the quality of human life in the contemporary society. Organizations are not a modern invention, but are as old as human society itself. We are born with organizations, educated by organizations and most of us spend much of our lives working for organizations. We spend a good deal of our leisure time paying and praying in organizations. Modern civilization depends largely on organization as the most rational and efficient form of social grouping. By coordinating a large number of human actions, the organizations create a powerful social tool. It combines its personnel with its resources; it continually evaluates its performance, and tries to adjust itself accordingly in order to achieve its goals.

Human organizations constituted for the attainment of a common purpose are as old as human civilization and have been in existence in every part of the world. Such organizations which are also called Voluntary Organizations or Non- Governmental Organizations existed in India too, in the ancient past and medieval times. During foreign rule and subsequent national movement various reforms and demands for national freedom encouraged the growth of various non-governmental organizations.

After independence India was declared a 'Welfare State' and government undertook several welfare schemes under various plans and policies. It encouraged the Non- Governmental Organizations to undertake social welfare activities under the grant-in-aid programme of the government. With the passage of time, NGOs expanded their activities and government also recognized their importance and provided them greater space and scope in terms of social action. Governmental recognition helped in further proliferation of NGOs and they started emerging as developmental outfits not only supplementing governmental initiatives but also became provider of various services. Since liberalization of economy in India, government is gradually withdrawing from welfarism providing greater scope to NGOs, as such they have become an important part of developmental process in India. Now that NGOs are performing very important role in the socio- economic and political development hence their role, working and performance become very important subject matter of academic investigations. Hence, this study is a modest attempt to examine and analyse the performance, contributions and problems affecting the performance of NGO's in Himachal Pradesh.

The study of this nature cannot be all conclusive in itself as the NGOs are spread over the entire length and breadth of India. However, the issues raised in the current work may provide useful insight for further exploration by the scholars. During the current study I have benefitted from the advice, inspiration and support of many people. I extend my sincere thanks to Prof. Kamal Manohar Sharma and other faculty members of the Department of Political Science, Himachal Pradesh University, Shimla for their consistent guidance and counsel. I also thank Dr. L. N. Sharma, Associate Professor (Political Science- Retd.), and my colleagues at DAV College Kotkhai, Shimla, and the DAV College Managing Committee, New Delhi for permitting me to undertake the current study.

It is my duty to thank all the office-bearers, staff-members, social workers and beneficiaries of various NGOs who are the respondents and the source of primary information for this study. I am also grateful to the Librarian and the Staff members of the Himachal Pradesh University Library and Indian Institute of Advanced Study Shimla for providing me every help to consult all relevant study material.

Last, but not the least, my special thanks are reserved to my life partner, Ira Jishtu, and my beloved children Devansh and Apoorva who have been the source of inspiration and also for coping with my nonchalance during the study.

Dr. Raj Kumar Jishtu
DAV College, Kotkhai, Shimla

Abbreviations

3R's	-	Reading, Writing and Arithmetic
AP.	-	Per -Annual.
AIDS	-	Acquired Immune Deficiency Syndrome.
ANC	-	Anti natal Check-up
AUS AID	-	Australian Aid
AVARD	-	Association of Voluntary Association for Rural Association
CAPART	-	Council for Advancement of Peoples Action and Rural Technology
CLVA	-	Coordination Council of Voluntary Association
DPEP	-	District Primary Education Programme
GDP	-	Gross Domestic Product
HAQ	-	Health Assessment Questionnaire
HGVS	-	Himachal Gyan Vigyan Samiti
HIV	-	Human Immune deficiency Virus
HPSACS	-	Himachal Pradesh AIDS Control Society
HPVHA	-	Himachal Pradesh Voluntary Health Association
IIM	-	Indian Institute of Management
IIT	-	Indian Institute of Technology
IMF	-	International Monitory Fund
L.P.A.	-	Lakh per Annual
MNGO	-	Mother Non-Governmental Organization
NACO	-	National AIDS Control Organization
NGO	-	Non Governmental Organization
NREGA	-	National Rural Employment Guarantee Act
NRI	-	Non-Resident of India
PLWHA	-	People Living With HIV/AIDS
PRI	-	Panchyati Raj Institution
PRIA	-	Society for Participatory Research in Arial

RCH	-	Reproductive and Child health
STD	-	Sexually Transmitted Disease
U.K.	-	United Kingdom
U.S.A.	-	United States of America
Volga's	-	Voluntary Organizations
WB	-	World Bank
WTO	-	World Trade Organization
YAMC	-	Young Men's Christen Association
YWCA	-	Young Women Christen Association

List of Tables

Chapter - 1

Introduction

Organization as a structure is central to social sciences without which the conception of human activity both at individual and group level becomes unimaginable. Since times immemorable the group consciousness has shaped the patterns of relationships of man with man in society and also with environment and natural resources. However, with the process of scientization of the social sciences the role of groups or associations came to the fore in nineteenth century with the studies on social solidarity by Emile Durkheim that led to the sporadic waves of socio-political pluralism and group life. While Weber contributed towards neo-corporatist theory Robert Michel's focused on the life and processes of voluntary organizations implying elitist and populist elements within. Marx envisaged a special role to the organizations as part of class consciousness followed by the conception of integrative, performative roles by organizations in society by Talcott Parsons in twentieth century.

Thus our society is organizational, with large and complex organizations dominating every sphere of human activity all over the world, irrespective of ideological and other differences. Organizations, as such have become very crucial and dominating factor affecting the quality of human life in the contemporary society. Organizations are not a modern invention, but are as old as human society itself. We are born with organizations, educated by organizations and most of us spend much of our lives working for organizations. We spend a good deal of our leisure time paying, playing and praying in organizations. Modern civilization depends largely on organization as the most rational and efficient form of social grouping. By coordinating a large number of human actions, the organizations create a powerful social tool. It combines its personnel with its resources; it continually evaluates its performance, and tries to adjust itself accordingly in order to achieve its goals.[1]

All these characteristics allow organizations to serve the various modes of society and its citizens more efficiently than smaller and more natural human groupings such as families, friendship groups and communities. Organizations are not a modern invention. The pharaohs used them to build the pyramids. The emperors of China used them a thousand year ago to construct the great irrigation system. The first Pope created a universal church to serve a world religion. Modern society, however, has more organizations and they fulfill a greater variety of societal and personal needs, involve a greater proportion of citizens and affect a large segment of their lives. In fact, modern society has so many organizations that a whole set of second- order organization is needed to organize and supervise them.[2]

The modern organization is generally more efficient than their ancient or medieval species. Changes in the nature of society have made the social environment more congenial to organizations and their planning, coordinating and controlling has become more disciplined with the development of the study of administration.[3]

Now the question arises as to what is the organization? When any group combines for a given purpose, even if the group consists of only two persons or more, we have the psychic fundamentals of an organization, plus the principle which must underline all associated effort. Let us here employ the simplest illustration. Two men unite their strength to move some object that is too heavy or bulky to be moved by one. Here we have an associated effort, which is synonymous with organization and likewise coordination, the first principle that underlines all such effort[4]. "Organization is the form of every human association for the attainment of a common purpose".[5]

There are various types of organizations. Different classification schemes have been proposed by various writers on the basis of structure, size, ownership and the specific purpose served. The typologies provided by Balu and Scott (1963: 43) and quoted frequently by many writers seem to be quite relevant in the present analysis also. Based on the criterion "Who Benefits" in an organization, the authors identify the following four categories of organizations:- [6]

(i) Mutual Benefit Organization: of which the members are the primary beneficiary groups.

(ii) Business Concerns: of which the owners are the beneficiaries.

(iii) Service Organizations: of which clientele are the primary beneficiary groups

(iv) Common Wealth Organizations: of which public is the primary beneficiary group

Following are the general characteristics of the organization.[7]

(i) Division of labour, power and communication responsibilities that are not random or traditionally patterned but deliberately planned to enhance the realization of specific goals

(ii) The presence of one or more power centers to control the concerted efforts of the organization and direct them towards its goals, as well as review continuously the organization performance and re-pattern its structure where necessary, increase its efficiency; and

(iii) Substitution of personnel i.e. the removal of unsatisfied persons and the assignment of others to their tasks, as well as the recombination of personnel through transfer and promotion.

As the present study is on Non-Governmental Organization or Voluntary Organization an understanding of them seem to be imperative in this context. Generally, voluntary agencies and non- official organizations are treated as one and the same. This may not be so. All non-official organizations are not necessarily voluntary. Voluntary organizations are spontaneous in their origin whereas non-official agencies may be government sponsored. Although agencies like All India Women's Conference, Indian Council of Child Welfare etc. are voluntary, yet project implementing committees appointed by the Central Social Welfare Board to run welfare extension projects and committees for running after care homes appointed by the state governments, though constituted primarily of voluntary workers are not voluntary agencies but are known as non-official agencies, since these agencies do not come into existence voluntarily but are sponsored and substantially funded by the government. These organizations may not be able to arouse community's popular support, since they are not based on democratic foundations and should, therefore, not be equated with voluntary agencies.[8]

Voluntary organization has been defined by various writers in different words yet all carry the same notion. D. Paul Chowdhary has quoted, "A voluntary agency is a group of persons who have organized themselves as a legal corporate body to render social services or rural development through organized programmers. It is accountable to the community that it serves and from which it is supported. It is controlled and administered by an association of citizens, rather than by the government, although primarily financed by the contribution from the community."[9] David Sills defines voluntary organization as "a group of persons organized on the basis of voluntary membership without state control, for the furtherance of some common interests of its members."[10] N.R. Inamdar observes, "A Voluntary Organization in development to be of durable use to the community has to nurse a strong desire and impulse for community development among its members, to be economically viable to possess dedicated and hardworking leadership and command resources of expertise in the functions undertaken."[11]

Michael Banton, an anthropologist, characterized it as a group organized for the pursuit of one interest or of several interests in common. Usually, it is contrasted with involuntary groups serving a greater variety of ends, such as kin groups, castes, and social class's and communities.[12]

Norman John, who examined at length in his study the various definitions of voluntary social services, found their turning on four factors: (i) method of formation, which is voluntary on the part of a group of people; (ii) method of government, with self-governing of organization to decide on its constitution, its servicing, its policy and its clients; (iii) method of financing, with at least some of its revenue drawn from voluntary sources; and (IV) motives with the pursuit of profit excluded.[13]

Smith and Freedman considered voluntary association as a structure formally organized, relatively permanent, secondary grouping as opposed to less structured, informal, ephemeral or primary grouping[14]

As such Non-Governmental Organization or Voluntary Organization is an organization formed by persons to further some common interest of its members with voluntary membership without the direct control of the state.

In order to meet their objectives Non-Governmental Organization uses different strategies depending upon its ideology, capacity and experience. Generally, voluntary agencies follow four clear cut strategies, as pointed out by J.B.Singh[15] :-

(i) Simple charity, supplementing welfarism of the state.

(ii) Encouraging people's participation and implementing programmes launched by the government for larger benefit of the community or village.

(iii) Involving people in programme planning, raising resources, implementing activities and sharing fruits of development.

(iv) Conscience instilling and organizing people enabling them to demand and undertake planning and implementation of development programmes beneficial to them.

Again J.B. Singh in his study has classified non-governmental organizations into the following seven categories[16]

(i) Charity: Giving food, clothing, medicine, alms, in cash and in kind, land, building etc.

(ii) Welfare: Providing facilities for education, health, drinking water, roads, communication, etc.

(iii) Relief: Responding to call of duties during natural calamities.

(iv) Rehabilitation: Continuing and follow up of the work in areas struck by calamities and starting activities that are durable in nature.

(v) Services: Building up infrastructure in backward areas.

(vi) Development of socio-economic environment around human beings.

(vii) Development of human beings: Conscious raising, awakening, organizing, recording of priorities to suit social justice, redeeming the past and opening doors for opportunities to the oppressed and the exploited.

The bases for classification of organization generally have been structure, functions, size, support base, location, membership, status of control and the beneficiary activities.

Non-Government Organization does have some characteristics of their own and important among them are: [17]

(i) It is registered under an appropriate Act to give a corporate status to group of individual, so that they get a legal personality and an individual liability may give place to group liability.

(ii) It has an administrative structure, and a duly constituted managing/ executive committee.

(iii) It has definite aims and objects and programmes in fulfillment of these.

(iv) It is an organization initiated and governed by its own members on democratic principles without any external control.

Though the Non-Government Organizations are based on the above mentioned basic characteristics yet they are known for their virtues of human touch, dedication, flexibility, self-reliance and nearness to the community.[18] But these virtues of late are fast disappearing due to variety of problems social, economic and political which need further observation and investigations.

As such the Non- Government Organizations or Voluntary Organizations with the given categorization, classification, strategies and characteristics are global phenomenon affecting every sphere of human activity and India is no exception to them. Though voluntary action in India in the form of charity and reforms is continuing from ancient past yet the pre and post- Independence era has provided greatest space to it. Community development programmes, poverty alleviation programmes, reforms and various services in the health, education, and other social service sector have provided ample opportunities for the growth and action of Non-Government Organizations in India and they are influencing every region and sector in India. Therefore, the study of these organizations, their structure, working, role etc. becomes one of the most viable subject matter of academic probe. So, the researcher intends to investigate the structure, role, working, performance, contributions and problems affecting the Non-Government Organizations. Though these organizations are spread over the entire vast length and breadth of this county, yet the study at such a macro level is beyond the means of an individual investigator hence the study has been conducted at the micro level in one State of Indian Union i.e. Himachal Pradesh.

Significance of the Study

The historical retrospect and available literature unravel that India has got the tradition of voluntarism since ancient past and it operated freely and extensively in the fields of education, medicine, cultural promotion and even succor in crises like drought, epidemics and foreign invasions. The role and scope of voluntarism in development, evolved in ancient and medieval India was not affected even during the Muslim rule and norms evolved in voluntarism continued. During the British rule, voluntarism received a boost and in place of traditional sources new avenues of development provided greater space to self-help groups. Voluntarism played a significant role in education, health and social welfare development in India during the latter half of the nineteenth and the first half of the twentieth century. The spirit of voluntarism aroused and recognized during the British rule was further strengthened during the National Movement through independent institution building in education, industry, business, trade, and fostering of economic production particularly of industrial goods through *Swadeshi*. Mahatma Gandhi who played significant role during the National Movement believed that voluntarism was the solution for the reconstruction of India's economics and political organizations. To channelize the people's power at the grass- roots level Gandhiji founded many voluntary organizations such as *"Harijan Sevak Sangh,"* *"Gram Udyog Sangh", "Hindustani Talimi Sangh", "Sarv Seva Sangh"* etc.

After independence economic growth was assumed as the main engine of development, which was to be carried out by experts and professionals. The planning commission envisaged many schemes for the poor, laborers, farmers, for *Harijans*, for the *Adivasis*-indeed for all strata of population but the state machinery failed to implement the allocations.

The real state of affairs, whether in the political or in the economic arena or in the cultural arena or simply in respect of human dignity and life, was in sharp decline in the voluntary spirit in the arrangements of our affair and in the kind of collective ethos and sense of belonging and participation that can get generated through voluntarism, which can never get generated through states. To have thought that the democracy and the building of a just social order could do merely or largely through instrumentalities of the state was a serious mistake. The result was that with every move along the new model that we look rather unthinkingly, we not only centralized all initiatives, we also undermined the social function that entitles political parties and their various front organizations to perform, as we reduced democracy and political parties to electoral games.[19]

As a result of this looking to the state, to the government, to parliament and other central institutions for our freedoms, looking up in this manner, we overlooked the fact that the crux of a democracy consists in its social organizations and social base.

The key to democratic polity is a basic concept of social and political infrastructure. Politics needs an infrastructure, as much as the economy does, and without an infrastructure will be reduced to a mechanical solidarity. In other words, if a democracy is to function effectively, there has to be a whole lot of organizations other than merely electoral organizations.[20]

Even for the electoral system to become sensitive to the need of the people and to be rooted in the social structure there is need for social formations of a variety of kinds. The citizenry has to be awake, its groups have to be numerous, and multifaceted so that the individual belong to not just one set of organizations ordained by the logic of the state but a whole spectrum of organizations. Even for the limited task of making electoral democracy effective, there is need not merely of what today, in the new parlance that is emerging, we call 'voluntary agencies,' but agencies that are formed by larger and holistic spirit of social voluntarism.[21]

Organized forms of popular participation make development stable and the participation inculcates a feeling of community belonging and thereby vitalizes the whole process. When government functions are increasing in breadth and depth, popular participation becomes inevitable and the rise of popular associations natural. The planning commission stated that, 'properly organized voluntary efforts may go a long way towards augmenting the facilities available to the community for helping the weakest and the most-needy to a somewhat better life'. The where withal for that has to come from the time, energy and other sources of millions of people for whom voluntary organizations can find constructive channels suited through varying conditions in the country.[22]

Participation of voluntary association in the process of decision-making and decision implementing is necessary and obvious too. As a strategy, this partnership would help linking social action with state action.[23] Approach paper on the seventh plan looks at voluntary organizations as the eyes and ears of the beneficiaries, the weaker sections of the society, who have been left out of the mainstream of development benefits. As a strategy, voluntary associations would be associated more closely and critically to ensure that target groups receive development benefits meant for them, augment such programmers and, at the same time, use these associations as an alternative feedback mechanism.[24]

Participation of voluntary associations in the process of development has been an accepted part in our efforts of development. The Community Development Movement, in a sense, revolutionized the concept of administration and it is here that people from rural area were first associated with the administration of programmes intended for their own development. It is this participation, which elevated interest in individual gains to the faith in community benefits. The main problem in implementing programmes for the welfare of weaker sections is to reach the benefit to the real needy client. People lack information and knowledge about the services and there are built in limitations in the organization so the benefits do not flow smoothly.[25]

Information and knowledge is an extension function and voluntary organizations, more than bureaucratic structure, are best suited for the task. It is through continued activities and continued stay that voluntary associations get socialized with local surrounding and local identity. Regular interaction between agency authorities and beneficiaries would politicize them and through participation would organize them as partners in the process of development.[26]

Harold Laski, defined 'freedom of association' as 'a recognized legal right on the part of all persons to combine for the promotion or purposes in which they are interested.[27] Article 19(1) (c) of the Constitution of India confers on the Indian Citizens the right 'to form association or Unions.' This right includes the right to form associations for development but it has been found that in the country, besides local voluntary associations set up for the development of particular localities village/villages/town/towns/ cities, *talukas/tehsil*, districts etc. institution like cooperatives, industrial or trading corporate companies etc. have undertaken a development activity as an accessory or subsidiary function.

Pluralism in development instrumentalities in the form of various voluntary associations, institutions and groups, besides governmental mechanisms and public authorities, is essential to preserve democratic freedoms and way of life in the country enshrined in the Indian Constitution. Where alone individuals are helpless, voluntary organizations formed by these individuals can be effective in undertaking of the planned model of development. The planning in the country has a tendency to develop new areas and aspects of economic and social life and activity on account of various reasons. The unsatisfied wants and needs of the poor; the imbalance, conflicts and incompatibilities occurring within the economic and social processes due to development itself, urgency to reduce concentration of wealth and incomes and hence to curb monopolies; compulsions to catch up with galloping scientific and technological progress in the world and to maintain national security; and such other emergent reasons, have tended to widen the ambit of planned development. This tendency aggravates the trend of concentration of greater economic powers and political authority in the government which means bureaucracy and political persons. Governments are slow to innovate because they are too big and the informality and initiative are, by and large, lacking in them Great and path-breaking leadership in both political executive and bureaucracy is necessary to innovate in development. Voluntary associations, groups and institutions can innovate and set new paths in schemes and projects, and thus project comparative illustrations before the government and public authorities in the field of development. They can also modulate the details of a programme, scheme or project to suit the requirements of particular localities of clientele groups or changed circumstances.[28]

In the light of all these developments and thinking, the voluntarism and voluntary organization once again have assumed central place in the development process and rendering services, by and large to all sections and specifically to the excluded groups so that people may be benefited from the polices of the Government and have equal share in the power structure and inclusive development.

The details also clearly indicate that powerful forces of change and modernity have been operating in society for over a hundred years, however, after independence as India was declared to be a 'Welfare State,' they have become a part of policies pursued and initiated by the government. No region and social strata of society can isolate itself from the effect of these objectives forces of change like industrialization, urbanization and modernization. In fact, the very role of individual, community and minority groups has changed due to the impact of forces of transformation. In the modern time not only the government policies are taken into consideration for the process of nation building, but the role and contribution of individuals, community and groups are also being taken into account.

The present era is also known as an era of liberalization, privatization and globalization and India is also not an exception to this. In recent times, especially after 1991, the process of liberalization and privatization in India, took off at a pace of higher velocity. In this process the role of the state, by and large, is withdrawing from the welfare aspect of the society, giving more space to Voluntary Organizations or Non-Governmental Organizations. NGOs have come forward to fill the vacuum and take the responsibility of the state to ensure welfare of the society. This addition in the role and responsibilities of NGOs has made them a very significant subject matter of academic probe.

All this proves beyond doubt that Voluntary Organizations or Non-Government Organizations, which are now at the center stage of development process, makes them an important subject matter of study. As the state is withdrawing from welfarism due to globalization, liberalization and privatization, the role of Non- Government Organizations has increased tremendously, supplementing government initiatives and providing services in the field of education, health, rural development, environment, ecology, and prevention of crime, legal aid, development of scheduled caste, scheduled tribes and backward classes. As such these organization become an important and appropriate subject matter of investigation to research scholars, academics, policy planners and administrators. Investigations into the organizations, objectives, working and role of these Voluntary Organization or NGOs in the socio-economic and political fields escecially in the region where no studies have been carried out so far turns out to be an important and very significant area of academic investigations hence an humble attempt in this regard has been made in present study.

Organizations in the socio-economic and political fields especially in the region where no studies have been carried out so far turns out to be an important and very significant area of academic investigations hence a humble attempt in this regard has been made by the researcher in the present study.

Objectives of The Study

In view of the important role which the Non-Governmental Organizations have assumed at the present juncture, we have attempted to analyze the role, working, contribution and problems affecting the performance of the Non-Governmental Organizations in Himachal Pradesh. With this broad objective the study sets forth the following specific objectives:-

- To know and analyze the Organization, Working and Role performance of Non-Governmental Organizations in terms of their objectives and programmes in Himachal Pradesh.
- To know and analyze the contribution of Non-Government Organizations in socio-political and economic development.
- To know and analyze the problems affecting the performance of the Non-Government Organizations.
- To make suggestions to improve the organization, role and working of Non-Government Organizations.

The present study is based on empirical and analytical method hence inter-disciplinary approach i.e. historical, descriptive and analytical method have been applied.

Universe of the Study

Non- Governmental Organizations or Voluntary Organizations are a global phenomenon and India is no exception to this. Rather, India has a long tradition of voluntarism since ancient past, which has seen various changes from charity to inclusive process of development. There are countless non- government organizations working in India in various fields which need academic investigations into their different aspects, but the study of such a macro nature cannot be undertaken through an individual efforts hence the study, at the first instance has been limited to Himachal Pradesh. Total Universe of the study as shown in Table No. 1.1:-

Again in Himachal Pradesh hundreds of Non-Government Organizations have been established and registered under the Societies Resignation Act No. 21 of 1860 which are operating at the State, District and Block level but very few of them are effective and functional. To investigate, all of them are again beyond the means of individual efforts and as such at the second stage the study has been limited and focused on

Table No. 1.1

Universe of Study

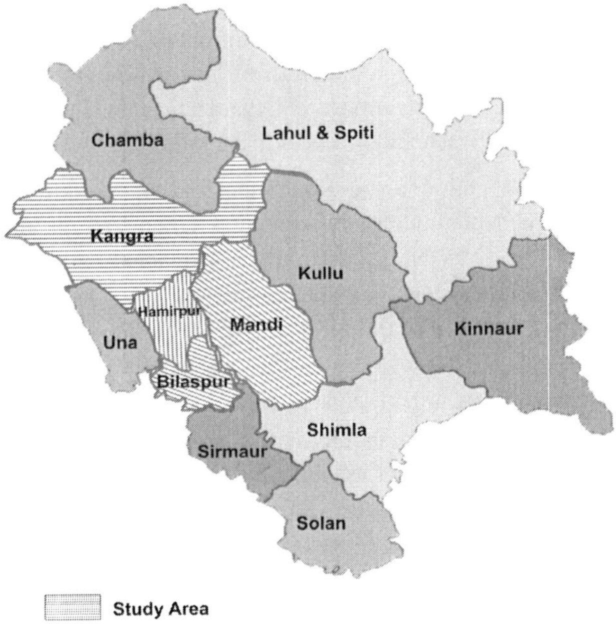

the State level Non-Government Organizations, which are operational and working effectively. At the Stale level also various Non-Government Organizations are working in different fields but in view of the physical and material resources at the disposal of the researcher, the study has again been limited to three Non-Government Organizations which are working in the field of rural Health, Education, rural self-governance i.e. *Panchayati Raj*. For the investigation and analyses in the present study the Non-Government Organizations are "Himachal Pradesh Voluntary Health Association" (HPVHA) "Himachal *Gyan Vigyan Samiti*" (HGVS) and "Society for Participatory Research in Asia" (PRIA). A humble attempt has been made to study the organization, objectives, programmes, working and contribution of these Organizations and also the problems affecting the performance being faced by these NGOs. Area of operation of these NGOs is shown below in Table No-1.2:-

Table No. 1.2
Area of Operation of the NGOs Himachal Pradesh

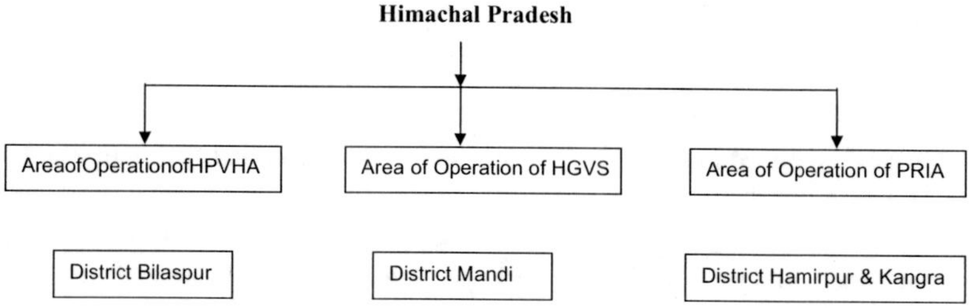

Data for the present study has been obtained from both the primary and the secondary sources. The secondary data obtained in the form of documents available with the organizations relating to their objectives, policies, programmers, and contributions. The primary data include the responses recorded through survey research from the office-bearers, staff, and social workers of the non-governmental organizations as well as beneficiaries.

The main focus of the study was to know about the organizational structure, working and role performance of the non-governmental organizations and their contributions in socio-economic and political development of Himachal Pradesh and thereafter to find out the amount of socio-economic and political development that had taken place due to the efforts of the non- government organizations. In view of nature of the present study the researcher decided to prepare a purposive representative sample of the respondents, to give varied representation on the basis of age, education socio-economic status etc. In all, 450 respondents constitute the sample (150 each NGO from the selected non-governmental organization's operational areas), to meet the requirements of the study. The ensuing chapters bring out the theoretical, historical, and literary details about the problem together with the role and performance of NGOs in Himachal Pradesh.

Notes

1. B. T. Lawani, *Non-Government Organization in Development,* Rawat Publications, Jaipur & New Delhi, 1999, p. 11.
2. op. cit. p. 11-12.
3. Edward Gross & Armitta E., *Organization in Society,* Prentice Hall Inc. Englewood elifts, New Jersey, 1971, pp. 1 - 2.

4. B. T. Lawaniop-cit. p. 12.
5. James D. Mooney, *the Principles of Organization,* Harper and Brother Publishers, New York, 1939 p. 1.
6. As quoted by B. T. Lawani op. cit. pp. 13-14.
7. *Ibid.*
8. B. T. Lawani, op. cit. pp. 17-18.
9. Escap- as quoted in 'Voluntary Efforts in Social Welfare and Development' by D. Paul Chowdhary, 1990, p. 31.
10. David L. Sills, *International Encyclopedia of social science* Vol- 16 , New York, the Mac Millan Co. and the Free Press London, Collier Mac Millan, 1968 p. 362-363.
11. N. R., Inamdar, 'Role of Volunteerism in Development' as Quoted in *Social Welfare Administration* by D. R. Sachdev, Kitab Mahal, Allahabad, p. 200.
12. Michal Banton, "Anthropological Aspects Voluntary Associations" in David sills (ed.) *International Encyclopedia of social science* Vol. 6, Op. cit. p. 357.
13. Norman Johnson, *Voluntary Social Services,* Oxford Basil Black- well & martin, Robertson, 1981 p. 14.
14. Constance Smith and Ann Freedman, Voluntary *Associations: Perspective on literature,* Cambridge (Mass) Harvard University Press, 1972 p. 8.
15. As quoted in Voluntary Agencies and Rural Development by I. S. Sandram, B. R., Publishing Corporation Delhi, 1986, op. cit. p. 67.
16. J. B., Singh, *Yojana,* November, 1984, p. 46 as quoted by I. S. Sandram in *Voluntary Agencies and Rural Development*, B. R. Publishing Corporation, Delhi, 1986, p. 66.
17. K. D. Gangrade, *Encyclopedia of Social Work in India*, Ministry of Information and Broadcasting, Govt. of India, New Delhi, 1987, pp. 220 - 221.
18. D. Paul Chowdhary, *Voluntary Effort in Social Welfare and Development, Sidhartha* Publishers, New Delhi, 1990, p. 3.
19. Rajni Kothari, 'Voluntary Organization in a Plural Society', *The Indian Journal of Public Administration,* Vol. XXXIII No. 3 July- Sept. 1987, p. 438.
20. *Ibid.*
21. Op. cit., 439.
22. *TheThird Five- Year Plan,* New Delhi Planning Commission Government of India, pp. 292-293.
23. V. G. Nandedkar, 'Voluntary Associations: A Strategy in Development', *The Indian Journal of Public Administration,* Vol. XXXIII No. 3 July- Sept. 1987, p. 469.
24. Op. cit., p. 470.
25. Op. cit., p. 478.

26. *Ibid.,* p. 479.

27 'Freedom of Association', *In Encyclopedia of the Social Sciences,* Vol. 6, New York Macmillan, 1931, p. 447.

28 Rajni Kothari, "Voluntary Organizations in a Plural Society", op. cit. p. 449.

Chapter - 2

Theorizing Organization

The State is the most universal and most powerful of all organizations. Wherever human beings have lived together for any length of time, there we find organization and authority and where we find organization and authority; there we have the nucleus of the State. The word 'State' has its origin in the Latin word 'status' which means standing or position of a person or a body of persons. The fact of the existence of the State is older than its name. The State as a word, 'Stato' appeared in Italy in the early part of the 16th century probably in the writing of Machiavelli. The meaning of the State in the sense of body-politic became common in England and France in the later part of the 16th century. The word 'steatskunst' became the German equivalent of 'rajionidi stato' during the 17th century and a little late the word 'steatstrecht' got the meaning of 'juspublicum'.[1]

The state is a geographically delimited segment of human society united by common obedience to a single sovereign. The term may refer either to the society as a whole or more specifically, to the sovereign authority that controls it [2]. A distinction is made sometimes between the descriptive and the normative theory of the state. But the latter can always be reduced to the former. Normatively, the concentration of coercive power in the hands of a single determinant authority is indispensable to the maintenance of public order, can be simply made descriptively state as the concentration of the excessive power to perform functions appropriated by it. Any one of the functions may not be adequately performed. The State thus cannot be merely defined in legal terms only. In other words it is more appropriate to define it jointly in terms of legal, coercive and functional.

Regarding role and functions of the state, the classical liberalist and contemporary liberalists have different point of view. The liberalist theory was developed in sixteenth century. The Classical liberalists also known as negative liberalists like Adam Smith, Jeremy Bentham and Herbert Spencer believe in the theory of laissez-faire which means that the state will not interfere in individual's life. The classical liberals call state as a necessary evil because the law and governance restrict the liberty of the individual, so it is a necessary evil. For development purposes, limited functions are given to the state like protection of life and property of the individual. To protect the rights, it is quite necessary to establish rule of law. To protect the citizens from foreign attack, establishment of judiciary, protection from illegal contracts, to encourage free competition including economic field, full respect to individual freedom, to establish peace and management, implementations of legal contracts for the state are other functions of the state according to the liberalists.

The Classical liberalists believe that state will not help unable and weak. They suggest the state will not support the 'industries' personally and the state will not impose taxes on export-import, will save all individuals from exploitation. Jeremy Bentham says that it is the functions of the state to provide maximum happiness to maximum number of people, which means state should do that activity which give maximum happiness to maximum number of people in that state. 'To talk, therefore, of the greatest happiness principle is to talk of the principle which proposes the maximization of pleasure and minimization of pain.[3]

From sixteenth to mid-nineteenth century the negative liberalists made their great effect and impact but in mid nineteenth century, the theory of laissez-faire came to an end because of economic inequality and exploitation of the working class. Now the state emerged as the institution of people's welfare. John Stuart Mill, T.H. Green, H. J. Laski, MacIver are treated as the main thinkers of contemporary liberalism. Thinkers belonging to this school of thought believe that the functions of state are to protect the natural rights like protection of life, property and liberty, to establish and manage law and order, to protect from foreign attacks, to establish judicial systems, to deal with foreign affairs in economic, social, political, strategic, scientific and technological fields, to establish and make treaties and contracts, to make management for education, to remove unemployment and poverty, develop agriculture and industries, to continue business, to provide social security, to develop natural resources and to remove all the obstacles from the way to good life.

The liberalists give more and more emphasis to removal of unemployment and poverty and to provide social security to the citizens of the state, which is clear from Laski's statement. For good it must be emphasized, is either social, or it is not good at all. If man is to live in community with his fellows it is necessary condition of his life that what he attains should, at least in the long run, involve benefit also to others[4].

At the other extreme is the Marxist theory, about functions of the state means the chief line of activity of the state lies in fulfilling the tasks that face it. The functions of the state break down into or are subdivided into directly dependent on the spheres or aspects of the country's life that are actively influenced by the given state internal functions, or on objects of a regional or global level that are influenced by the state external functions.

The functions of the state reflect its class nature and social significance. Their content come down chiefly to the organization of a new society and its system economic, social, political and cultural, stimulation of their progress and improvement, to the comprehensive development of the individual and defense of the gains of socialism.[5]

The chief internal functions of the state are economic organizational and cultural-educational. The state fulfills the function of control over the amount of labor and the amount of consumption, as well as that of protecting socialist property, law and order, the rights and freedoms of citizens. During the development of society and the state, some of these functions disappear such as suppression of the resistance of the class opponent, other emerge such as the function of managing scientific and technological progress, the function of protecting ensuring the rational use of natural resources, yet others are enriched to become more profound and capacious[6].

The nature and the character of the state as expressed in various forms of political power, functions of a economic redistribution and ensuring minimum social defense etc. are variety of inter- linked roles. Whether they add upto a holistic view or remain a mere conglomeration of fragments held together by the coercive power of the state is what distinguishes vitally one state or its definition from the other taken to its limit, the former version would make the state a vigorous entity, a matured totality to which all individual members belong. Some have equated the state with the nation and others with society and focused the process which produced the nation state embodying the spirit of the people, their culture, religion and above all their self-consciousness. This holistic view, if carried to its limits can justify both a democratic state as well as a totalitarian state. The Soviet Union was a totalitarian state built on the assumption of a holistic view of the socialist society and state. If it broke up, it was because it tried to reach the limits of this holistic view through its own anti-thesis, ignoring the democratic aspirations of the ethnic groups, cultures and nationalities.

Before that, Hitler had also a totalitarian, perversely ultra-holistic view which ultimately brought about a disaster on his nation.[7]

Neo- liberalism and globalization driven by the values of neo-liberalism have seriously harmed the anti-poverty and anti-exploitation struggle in the world today. The benefits to the few have not compensated for the increased poverty, inequality and uncertainty which very many have experienced. The idea of non-governmental as value-driven facilitators of change has been adversely affected by the decision of many to implement the welfare, social net programmes of institutions that are committed to economic liberalization and concerned to reduce its social cost[8].

Social services to be meaningfully provided to the general public need enormous resources. All along it has been the responsibility of the state to provide for these services. But a situation had arisen around the last quarter of the twentieth century due to which this responsibility became extremely difficult to be borne by the state alone in the face of ever shrinking resources. What became apparent was that unless production increased and wealth got created, services in social sector could not be provided. It also became obvious that people's dependence on the state for all such services could not continue to be entertained. The solution sought was to reverse the process reducing people's dependency by making them self-reliant in different aspect of their living, more particularly, in their economic life, as far as possible. This was possible only if people could be persuaded to get involved in the process of creating of wealth, management of that wealth and its distribution. In other words, people's entrepreneurship ability needed to be enhanced. where the state could not totally shirk its responsibility of providing basic services, it had to provide support to increase people's productivity by engaging them in various economic activities. Thus, the domain of social services sector transcended to economic productivity. It came to be recognized that the development endeavor should incorporate both social and economic sectors. While the former was a necessity, it could be in place only of it was backed by necessary economic support[9].

In the beginning of the 1980s, reversals developed and developing countries started thinking of privatization, liberalization and withdrawal of the state from the social sector programmers like education, health, nutrition, etc. because there was a movement that the state was incapable of tackling the problems of the neglected and the vulnerable groups of society[10]. Many Third World Countries, which were facing balance of payment problem, reduced their budget from social sector and started taking loan from International Monitory Fund (IMF) as well as the World Bank (WB) for the survival of the country's economy. The policy of the IMF and WB under the structural adjustment programmes was to give loan to the Third World Countries to 'help them adjust'. These money loans were tied to strict conditionalities. Loans were only granted when the countries agreed to the adoption of a compressive programme of macro- economic stabilization and structural economic reform[11].

During the implementation of IMF-WB's programme, an understanding was developed that investment in public sector was wasteful and therefore, the emphasis on NGOs was better. It was assumed where government failed to reach out to the marginalized sections and created a gap, NGOs could bridge it. NGOs were preferred because of their special characteristics like small size, more participatory, less bureaucratic, more flexible nature and cost effectiveness and soon[12].

The globalization process has brought neo-liberal economy or New Economy Policy in the developing countries. Though India embarked on a programme for economic liberalization in the late eighties, practically globalization process started in India in July 1991 when the country became a part of Structural Adjustment Programme. The New Economic Policy proposes removal of restriction on import-export know-how as well as forcing capital investment; lifting controls and restrictions on private enterprises and slowing free trade and commerce; privatization of economy of the country by disinvestment in public sector, selling out state holding to the national and international level private corporations, reduction of government subsidies on essential goods and services, retrenchment in the existing government employees etc. there is role back of the state and markets get importance. All these policy measures in the era of globalization have minimized the role of government and forced government to withdraw from the economic and social sector, which gradually created an adverse impact on various aspects of human life and survival. Due to some degree of effectiveness at the local level, then questions regarding the replacement of state, provision of NGO activities became acutely important, particularly in the light of continuing development trends.[13]

The present study revolves around some key words which are being used in the study time and again. These key words constitute the theoretical framework of the present study hence it is deemed appropriate to define these key words at the outset, to be clear about the actual meaning and the sense in which they have been used in the present study.

Organization

Organizations are as old as human society but their role and working has been changing with the time. The modern organizations are more efficient than their ancient or medieval species. Change in the nature of society has made the society environment more congenial to organizations, and their planning, co-ordination and controlling has become more disciplined with the development of the study of administration.[14]

Different scholars have defined the term 'Organization' differently. A top business executive defines an organization as 'a system of consciously coordinated personal activities or forces.[15] An economist uses the term organization as a short hand expression for the integrated aggregation of those persons who are primarily involved in managing risk and uncertainty, bearing, planning and innovation, coordination, administration and control, and routine supervision of an enterprise.[16] A social scientist describes an organization as 'a social form that achieves its goals through the co-ordinate efforts of individuals in offices,[17] and whereas others define an organization as 'a social group in which the members are differentiated as to their responsibilities for the task of a achieving a common goal.[18] Ganguli defines an organization is founded upon a 'basic system of stable expectations regarding differential responsibilities, and relationship among the members'[19], and Tagliere says that an organization is two or more persons interacting within a recognized power relationship for some common purpose[20].

When any group combines for a given purpose, even if the group consists of only two persons or more, we have the psychic fundamentals of organization, plus the principle which must underline all associated efforts. Organizations are social units or human groupings deliberately constructed and reconstructed to seek specific goals. There are, generally, two major reasons for the formation of any organization. First is social reason, because man is a gregarious being; he is always in search of relationship with other persons. The second is material reason. Man also organizes for impersonal material reasons. Through Organizations, he can do three things that he could not do alone: (i) he can enlarge his abilities; (ii) he can compress the time required to accomplish an objective through an organization; and (iii) he can take advantage of the accumulated knowledge of previous generations[21].

Organizations are characterized by: division of labor, power and communication responsibilities- divisions which are not random or traditionally patterned, but deliberately planned to enhance the realization of specific goals; the presence of one or more centers which control the concerted efforts of the organization and direct them towards its goals, these power centers must review continuously the organizations performance and re-pattern its structure, where necessary, to increase its efficiency and substitution of personnel i.e. unsatisfactory persons can be removed and others assigned their tasks. The organization can also recombine its personnel through transfer and promotion.[22]

Organizations are social units with purpose and specific goals; organizations reduce the service to their initial goal in order to satisfy their acquired needs, rather than adjust the service of their acquired needs, to that of their goals. Sometimes organization goes so far as to abandon its initial goals and propose new ones more suited to the organization's needs. An organizational goal is a desired state of affairs which the organization attempt to realize. The organization may or may not be able to bring about this desired image of the future. But if the goal is reached, it ceases to be a guiding image for the organization and is assimilated to the organization or its environment[23]. Organizational goals changes for three major reasons, the first is direct pressure from external forces, which leads to a deflection from the original goals, the second is pressure from internal sources, this may lead the organization to emphasize quite different activities than these originally intended and third factor is changed environmental and technological demands that lead the organization to redefine its goals.[24] Modern nations utilize organizations as a major tool in the development of their political, economic, social and military system. These organizations take many forms and represent the cross cutting and conflicting value systems within a society. In a period of rapid social change and evident social conflict, organizations are a major contributing factor both to change and conflict and resistance to change and conflict.[25]

Voluntary Organization

In the present study, organization refers to a Voluntary Organization, also known as Non- Government Organizations (NGOs) which are normally registered under the Societies Registration Act 21 of 1860 and are also redefined as service organizations. An analysis of the unique characteristics of service organizations seems to be imperative in this context. Some of the writers have explained candidly the difference between services organizations and other organizations.[26] According to them, in human service organizations, inputs and outputs are human beings and their mandate is to serve people with the ultimate aims of maintaining and improving the general welfare.

The strength of voluntary organizations in society has been the subject of research in social psychology and organization theory. Etzioni, using compliance as the major source of differentiation between organizations, offers a typology of organizations that places voluntary organizations in the category of a special type of formative organization. As he points out, when coercion is the basis of authority, compliance is alternative, when remuneration is the basis of authority, compliance takes a calculative turn; when authority has a normative, compliance is moral[27]. So, in organization' s theory voluntary organizations have thus been characterized as non-authoritarian, commitment- producing entities that rely basically on the formal and idealistic values shared by the organization members.[28]

The term 'voluntarism' is derived from Latin work 'voluntas' which means 'will'. The will assumes various forms of impulses, passions, appetites or desires. It is prior to or superior to the intellect or reason, all theories of voluntarism, whether Psychological, Ethical, Theological or Metaphysical which interpret various aspects of experience and nature in the light of the concept of the will, subscribe to the thesis.[29] It is the will that may produce miracles and thereby, some of the social evils, of which the unfortunate sections of the society are the victims, can be eradicated.

No comprehensive research efforts have been made so far to explore the motivating sources of voluntarism. Inequality among individuals is a perennial source of motivation for voluntary action in any society whatever is the stage of its development. Inequality may be in material, moral or intellectual terms. A. F. C. Bourdillon observed[30] that there is always an element of betterment of compensating inequality motivating individuals to volunteer their services. Social services are designed to help compensate for the inequality and to uplift the under-privileged. The minimum standard which the community can tolerate, he added for its citizens, is not static. It moves forward from one sphere of activity to another.

The term 'volunteer' is normally used to denote someone who offers unpaid service to a good cause. Bourdillon remarks that every voluntary organization is the product of the blood, sweat and toil of a few individual, who were known for their persistent efforts for achievement of their sincere aspirations.[31] One may identify five sources of voluntarism: religion, government, business, philanthropy and natural aid if the delivery system for human services is analyzed.[32]

The missionary zeal of religious organizations, the commitment of government organizations to the public interest, the profit-making urge in business, the altruism of the social superiors and the motive of self-help along fellowmen, all reflect in voluntarism. At the operational level, the above mentioned components may not differ much from one another but each of them is moved by an impulse with service as the common motivation.

G.D.H. Cole identified the problem of poverty as the point of focus in all types of associations. One essential element is that of philanthropy pure and simple- which has been always present, but it has been mingled, from time to time, with motives and impulses which have changed greatly from age to age, attributing the sufferings of the poor people either to religious or secular roots.[33] Some of the most ardent social reformers of the 18th century and early 19th century, who wanted to do many things, were insistent that it must keep its hand off education. They drew the line between physical welfare, which the state could legitimately arrange to promote, and intellectual and moral welfare, which was a matter outside the scope of political action.

William Beveridge put forward the idea of expansion of the social welfare cake by enunciating the concept of social insurance against the giant evils of want, disease, ignorance and squalor and the citizen's entitlement to welfare as of right kind of social security against misfortunes.[34]

Cole believed that although religion and social service have been most intimately inter twined in the early stages of voluntary organizations; there have been philanthropists at all times who were not moved by religious motives. Along with changing impulses, which removed the upper class philanthropists in doing good to their social inferiors' with the state, these inferiors began to play a significant part in looking after those and creating associations of their own, instead of receiving passively and as individuals, the benefaction of the well to do.[35]

With the acceptance of the obligation of the State to ensure for all its citizens a basic minimum standard of life, the state emerged as the major philanthropist. But the voluntarism and advocates of the right of the needy to be maintained at the hands of the state did not see eye to eye within the early stages of the new development. The voluntarisms were looked with suspicion in every thing done under their auspices.[36]

The term 'Voluntary Association' is variously indebted to different writers. Michael Benton, an anthropologist characterized it as a group organized for the pursuit of one interest or of several interests in common. Usually, it is contrasted with involuntary groups serving a greater variety of ends, such as kin groups, castes, social classes and communities.[37] Lord Beverage writes about the voluntary action and voluntary organization that a generation ago a voluntary worker was someone who gave unpaid service to a good cause, and the group which was formed for working for that good cause came to be known as a voluntary organization. He says, 'a voluntary organization, properly speaking is an organization which, whether its workers are paid or unpaid, is initiated and governed by its own members without external control.[38]

Marry Morris and Modeling Reff defines, 'a voluntary agency is a group of persons who have organized themselves as a legal corporate body to render social services or rural development through organized programmes. It is accountable to the community that it serves and from which it has support. It is controlled and administered by an association of citizens, rather than by the government, although primarily financed by the contribution from the community.[39]

Smith and Freedman defined voluntary organization as, 'structured, formally organized, relatively permanent, secondary groupings as opposed to less structured, informal, ephemeral or primary groupings, identified by the presence of offices filled through some established procedures; periodic, scheduled meetings; qualifying criteria for membership; and some formalized division and specialization of labor.[40]

David Sills, a sociologist, writes that definitions of the term "voluntary association" differ wildly but that they generally contain three elements.[41] A voluntary association is an organized group of persons: (a) that is formed in order to further some common interests of its members; (b) in whom membership is voluntary in the sense that it is neither mandatory nor acquired through birth; and (c) that exists independently of the state. He defines voluntary organization as "a group of persons organized on the basis of voluntary membership without state control, for the furtherance of some common interests of its members."[42]

N.R. Inamdar observes: 'A voluntary organization in development to be of durable use to the community has to nurse a strong desire and impulse for community development among its members, to be economically viable to possess dedicated and hardworking leadership and command resources of expertise in the functions undertaken.[43]

Organizations today, whether voluntary or government are an accepted fact of life. In fact in a modern society it is impossible to escape from the influence of organizations of one type or another. According to Bunker Roy, trade unions co-operatives, political parties, *Khadi* boards etc. are considered as non-government organizations; but not voluntary organizations. For voluntary organization, we need organizations which are indigenous, decentralized and non-statutory with direct participation of the programme.[44] Pat Young writes that non-profit motives and lack of state control are common features to all Voluntary organizations.[45] According to Shankar Pathaka voluntary organization is an association of people organized to meet the need of a section or the whole of that community. [46]

In his book, D. Paul Chaudhary has discussed some of the characteristics of a voluntary organizations[47] i.e. it is the result of the voluntary efforts, which though motivated by different factors is spontaneous in nature; it is an organization initiated and governed by external control; it is registered under an appropriate Act to give a corporate status to a group of individuals so that they get a legal personality and individual's liability may give place to group liability; it has general body and a regularly constituted Managing Committee representing all interests, men, women, professionals, public men, etc., it has definite aims and objects and a programme in socio-economic of community in which it is formed; it has considerable autonomy and flexible planning and management of its programmers and services; it has a sense of commitment to human development/ welfare; it undertakes people's needs and help to solve their socio-economic problems; it plans and implements its own programmes through its own voluntary and paid workers; and it raises its funds from the community.

The voluntary organizations are known for their virtues of human-touch, dedication, flexibility, self-reliance and nearness to the community.[48] The main feature of a voluntary organization is human-touch. Human-touch is a quality which is innate in a human being and can be developed with any amount of training or incentive. The second feature of voluntary organization is dedication. The sense of dedication is more important to volunteers whether they work individually or through a voluntary organization; without any sense of commitment and dedication, no voluntary organization could meet its destiny. The third feature of voluntary organization is the need of flexibility in the style of work. This is possible because voluntary organizations are capable of their operational designs. This is necessary because the essence of voluntary organization is to be open and non-bureaucratic. Therefore, flexibility is a virtue of a voluntary organization. The fourth important feature of voluntary organization is that it should be close to the community, having its roots in the community in which it is working.

Voluntary organizations should know the needs and problems of the community in which they are working. These organizations are not only familiar with such needs and problems but are also sensitive to them. The voluntary organizations at the community level are more close to the people than governmental organizations. One of the features of the voluntary organizations is innovation and self-reliance in their programmes and services. This is more often lacking in the governmental agencies.[49]

The choice of a strategy to be adopted by a voluntary organization differs from organization to organization and depends on the ideology, motivation, capability of the organization- experience of some voluntary agencies may act as catalytic bodies operating externally to the rural communities; others may emerge from within the rural communities serving as indigenous institutions. The voluntary agencies at present adopt a target group approach, but aim at self- reliance of the people they are serving. They want to dispel the prosperity of dependency development on the part of the beneficiaries. The voluntary agencies, once they have been able to assist a target group to become reasonably autonomous in their socio-economic status, move on to another target group still suffering from backwardness-economic and social. This enables them to serve large segment of the community.

Generally, voluntary agencies follow four clear cut strategies, as pointed out by J.B. Singh,[50] that are: simple charity, supplementing welfarism of the state, encouraging people participation and in implementing programmes launched by the government for the larger benefit of the community or village; involving people in programme planning, raising resources, implementing activities and sharing fruits of development; conscience instilling and organizing people enabling them to demand and undertake planning and implementation of development programmers beneficial to them.

S.P. Srivastava,[51] gives a classification of non-governmental organization: that are fully supported by state and or a foreign funding sources; that are partially supported by state agencies alone; that are supported by state and voluntary contributions and that do not receive grants- in aid from any source, national or international.

Sherwood Fix[52] based his classification after examining 5000 associations upon the distinction between majorly, mineral and medial organization. Majorly associations are those which serve the interests of the majority institutions of society, such as business, professional, scientific, educational, labor and agricultural associations. Mineral associations serve the interest of significant minority in the population, such as women's club, church organizations, hobby clubs and above all, ethnics. Medical associations mediate between major segments or institutions in the society. For example a parent-teacher association mediates between the family and the school system.

David L. Sills[53] developed a structural distinction between corporate type and federal type organizational structure and control in national organizations, while others have used other structural variables like accessibility or eligibility for membership as a basis for classifications.

Voluntary Action

The term 'Voluntary Action', literally interpreted, it only means community itself. In this interpretation, the identity of community is distinguished from that of public authority set up by statute or state directive. Very often voluntary action is equated with the work of non-official social service agencies operating in the community. This is only conventional usage of the term voluntary action.

In fact the term "Voluntary action" is equated with the concept of *Janashakti,* a phrase used by Vinobaji in his exposition of the philosophy of *Sarvodaya* (well-being of all). The form of operation is of secondary importance. So long as the activity is undertaken by an agency, organization or institution which is native to the people concerned and which works without interference or direction from outside, should be regarded as voluntary action. The *'Lok Semitis'* (People's Association) if they are organized by each community itself, without an executive or legislative compulsion and if they decide their own needs and priorities, they too could be rightly regard as voluntary. They can formulate their own constitution[54].

The expression voluntary actions usually related to social change of prevailing system or its parts. It has an element of discontent in its assumption and of protest in its expression. Sustained and enduring voluntary action, sensitive and responsive to the local needs and problems, cannot be carried out by a monolithic national body. Voluntary action needs organizations, which are indigenous, decentralized and non-statutory with direct participations of the beneficiaries of the target groups of the programme.[55]

William Beveridge regards voluntary action as is requisite and also a method of social advance in a free society. Voluntary action, according to him, covers all the undirected activities of individual citizens both private and public. However, in the post war period Beveridge's concern is reflected more in the action of individual citizen for a public purpose which is undertaken to improve the conditions of their lives or that of their fellow citizens.[56]

In India, quite a few professional social worker, educationists, practitioners and social scientists have addressed themselves to the theme of voluntary action and have used terms like voluntary efforts, voluntary organizations, non-governmental organizations, social actions or social activism interchangeably.

It can be said that different scholars and political thinkers have defined the voluntary efforts, voluntary organizations, non-governmental organizations differently. However, at the same time they have usually applied these types of terminology interchangeably for the same two types of organization i.e. voluntary and non-government organization. R. Renganathan has made it clear that in the United Nations Terminology, Voluntary organizations are called Non-Governmental Organizations.[57] The researcher also feels that there is hardly any difference between the voluntary organizations and non-governmental organizations, hence, has applied this concept accordingly.

Development

Non- government organizations working in different regions/parts of the country have an important role in development. By Development' means planned socio-economic change as well as 'Attitudinal' changes leading to distributive social justice and sustainable development. At the same time it needs to locate NGO's in terms of their linkages with the State and the neoliberal global economic regime. Thus, discourse on development must necessarily now address these ideological and political linkages between civil society and the state/market[58].

The term development has been used in a wider sense, it is a slow process of civilization, and the purpose of development is to provide increasing opportunities to all the people for a better life. It is essential to bring about more equitable distribution of income, wealth for promoting social justice and efficiency of promotion, to provide a greater variety of facilities like education, health service, nutrition, housing etc.

It would serve well to remember at the outset, what is now a well-known and widely accepted fact of social reality that the rise of the phenomenon of development including sustainable development has brought about the integration synthesis and unit of all social sciences into the social science[59] together with the integrated, inter-disciplinary, holistic systems approach as the social science method for study, research and analysis of all development issues. The multilayered and value laden[60] concept of development has both nomadic and empirical aspects. Some tend to see the former while others highlights the latter. But the fact is that, the normative and the empirical are interdependent and mutually reinforce each other. The concept of development involves economic, political, legal, administrative, social, material, spiritual, environmental, psychological, moral and cultural values on which depend the full development of the human personality and the dignity of man in society. Development is an umbrella concept; it is multi-dimensional, it is total, it is both quantitative and qualitative in nature. It has national and international, temporal and spatial aspects.[61]

The aims of development were spelled out in 1970's in the Preamble of the International Development Strategy for the Second United Nations Development decade. It involves 'humans' as distinct from material produce. It is defined as a process which involves improvement in the quality of life of the weaker sections and a greater participation and involvement of the masses in the process of decision making in the economic, social, political and cultural life of a society. In his book, 'Cruel Choice', Denis Goulet[62] has said, 'Development is not a cluster of benefits given to the people in need; it is rather a process by which a populace acquires a greater mastery over its own destiny'.

Schumpeter[63] defined development as only such changes in economic life as are not forced upon it from without, but arise by its own initiative from within. Dudley Scers,[64] said that development means creating conditions for the realization of human potential.

Development is an elusive concept and involves mobilization of natural resources, augmentation of trained manpower, capital and technical know-how and their utilization for attainment of constantly multiplying national goals, higher living standards and the change over from a traditional to a modern society. The essence of development is generally perceived as industrialization and modernization. Development is a multi-dimensional and multi linear process.

Development is also people-centered and citizen participation oriented. Citizens participation in the various interfaces of the developmental decision-making process, plan- formulation, implementation and monitoring and evaluation of development policies, plans, programmers and projects is the sine-quo-non of success, equity, economy, effectiveness and legitimacy of development administration. People's active involvement, co-operation and support to development efforts in general and their participation in the decision making process and sharing of the fruits of development in particular constitute the building-block– the 'heart beat and pulse rate' of development administration.[65]

Development is usually conceived as an aspect of change that is desirable, broadly predicated or planned and administered or at least influenced by governmental action. Thus the concept of development consists of (a) as aspect of change (b) a plan or prediction, and (c) involvement of the government for the achievement of that planned or predicted goal. The term Development is also used for the process of allowing and encouraging people to meet their own aspirations.[66]

The main aim of development is to increase national as well as per capita income and to raise the standard of living of the people and secure justice, freedom, equality and security for them in society. The focus of development is now increasingly on (a) equitable distribution of wealth and income, (b) full utilization of manpower; (c) better utilization of natural sources; and (d) protection of human environment etc.[67]

Hence development means change plus growth i.e.it includes growth modernization, increase in social facilities etc. Economic development is the process of securing a higher level of productivity in all the sectors of the economy which primarily depends upon the technological advances the community is able to make.[68] Economic growth with social justice is one of the most important goals of developing economy like India. Harmonious growth of inter sectoral income, trade and income distribution are prerequisites of accelerated economic development. In the process of growth, agriculture and industry depend on each other for raw materials and markets, besides it is often argued that declining output ratio of agriculture and industry increases the net domestic product and affects the income distribution pattern in the economy.[69]

The democratic approach to economic planning and implementation leads to equitable distribution of economic resources. One of the directive principles of economic planning in India has it in socialistic economic mode, which perhaps is more meaningful to achieving the political goal of making it impossible. This is possible by striving to attain the ideal of democratic socialism; the chances of attaining the orderly process of development are closely related to the effectiveness of measures to distribute the gains of development equitably or at least reasonably, among the income groups regions and sectors.

George Dalton[70] has vividly analyzed the different dimensions of the problem of development, what economists call development', political scientists call 'modernization', sociologists role differentiation and anthropologist cultural change'. These accompanying political and social changes make economic development processes even more complicated.

The institutions and structures through which people's participation can flow into development activities can be many and varied, formal and informal official and non-official such as people's local organizations local self-government units like *Panchayati Raj* Institutions in India, Municipalities, Municipal Corporations, Metropolitan City Councils, development authorities in rural or urban areas and above all, voluntary agencies, non-profit organizations, non- governmental organizations, cooperatives etc., these units of local self-government in rural or urban areas on the formal official side of the spectrum and voluntary associations on the informal-unofficial side both working at the grassroots level are considered to be the most essential institutional, mechanism for mobilizing people's support initiative, resources enthusiasm and cooperation for development purposes[71].

Development is defined as such the same as modernization- a far-reaching, continuous and positively evaluated change in the totality of human experience. Modernization theorists tended to equate modernization and development. The continuous process of industrialization, capitalist or socialist, is a clear example of modernization and for many, a key feature of development. They focused largely on the nation-states, and assumed that what has occurred in the west could be repeated, albeit with a little help in the way of capital, technology, expertise and rationality. Modernization theory emphasizes and approves of the trend towards western modernity[72].

Talcott Parsons has worked out a scheme for the analysis of behavior, comprising five pairs of 'pattern variables', each pair representing two polar types.[73] Hoselitz has adopted three of these namely, achievement versus ascription, universalism versus particularism, specificity versus diffuseness, for the analysis of action relevant to economic growth.[74] Action of the people in economically backward societies is marked by ascription. David C. Mc Clell has put forward a model of development which is predominantly psychological.[75] He has enunciated a type of mental readiness or preparedness which he sees as a precondition to development and modernization. The 'take off' of societies in history has been possible only when their members have been motivated by a will to act in a way which is more energetic, rational and organized. The growth of scientific knowledge in modern times has enabled us to adopt a safer and surer way to develop ourselves economically and socially without provoking the religious feelings of the communities of societies. Daniel Lerner has emphasized the role of international cooperation and communication in national development, particularly for the under developed countries of the third World.[76] He puts stress upon the fact that development in the countries of the Third World should proceed from within with the help of up-to- date ideas and techniques diffused through international cooperation, by improving human resources, by creating new consciousness for a better future, by liberating the dormant skill and creativity of the people and by matching the 'want-get 'ratio.

Dependency model, a key element of under development theory, arose from a growing disillusionment with economic strategies of development. It is indeed the case that under development theory is primarily concerned with economic structure but it was developed, in part, as a direct challenge to modernization theory. There is a variety of approaches, originating in classical Marxism and leading to a broad-based school of Neo- Marxist, where collective work has come to be known, at various t times, as dependency theory, world system theory and under development theory[77].

Baran asserted that ruthless exploitation is inherent in capitalism.[78] Under development in the third World countries was a direct result of capitalist development in the West. The only way Third World countries could escape from this economic impasse was to withdraw from the world capitalist system completely and introduce socialist economic planning. Frank[79] suggests that it is not poverty that has prevented under developed societies investing in their own future but the net out-flows of capital to the west. In fact, the Third World has subsidized the development of the First World. The Third World development has been further undermined by its declining share in world trade, through foreign control of its industries and through careful and restricted transfer of technology.

The Earth Summit in Rio de janeiro, 1992 and the Social Development Summit in Copenhagen luckily came up with two Alternative visions of development under the umbrella concepts of 'Sustainable Development' and 'Social Development' which provide centrality to non- economic dimensions of development and effectively challenge the supremacy of the economic growth model that held sway for long. These two alternative visions of development revolutionized the developmental thinking across the world and more so in the developing countries which were already getting disenchanted with pursing a materialist dream[80].

In India, development, definitionally and conceptually, denotes progress-social, economic, educational, cultural, scientific and technologies-brought about by planned/programmed efforts to inaugurate era of orderly and peaceful transformation of a society in a constitutionally desired direction. The unfortunate fact is that despite considerable progress, there have emerged marked disparities in income and in the poor people's access to resources, economic opportunities and social services. While everyone considers economic development as a priori condition and an essential instrument of social transformation and a desired vision of development. The social tensions that we are faced with are largely the result of our single-minded pursuit to economic growth model of development, putting the broader mandate of social transformation with social justice, equity, equality of opportunity and poor people's empowerment and participation in development efforts and its salient characteristics into the background. The much talked about model of economic development which outlined our development path provided an impression that the way we have gone about making development possible, is no longer suitable for the attainment of broader social and economic goals that are intended in the Directive Principles of State Policy[81].

In our context, what is desirable, indeed essential, is to dovetail economic growth with social growth; the development of social capital, to be precise. The peculiar inabilities of economic development, which essentially means economic growth, necessitate and underscore the need and significance of social development, emphasizing social justice, equity and an early end of the climate of discrimination, exploitation and oppression of the socially and economically marginalized sections of society. Given the social and economic inequalities and the unsatisfactory conditions of life for a substantially large section of society, the social science discourse on development paradigms conceives social development as a true indicator of human development. The preferred vision of development desires that human development should occupy a centre stage and should emerge as an ultimate goal of development planning[82].

The current development discourse in India voices extreme concern on the distortion of development especially concentrating upon environment degradation and development- displacement controversy. Herein, the need and significance of sustainable development has been emphasized. Environmental protection and sustainable use of natural resources seems to bathe current cry of the latest writings of development. The approach to intermix developmental considerations with environmental considerations has highlighted the need to preserve, protect environmental damage that hurts people, both today and in the future, and provides additional grounds for rethinking on our measurement of progress.[83]

In India, before independence, in terms of scope of coverage in development activities, laissez faire occupied the largest portion, voluntary action through philanthropy associational works and individual actions stood next, while state intervention came last. Here 'development' excludes the infrastructural activity, like laying out of ports, railways and roads, setting up of communications in the form of posts and telegraphic or building up of essentials for capitalist development in banks, insurance companies, etc. 'Development' here includes instituting or extending facilities for agriculture, health and medicine, education and allied human development or enrichment aspects. After independence, state intervention claims the largest amount of development activity, while laissez faire would come next and voluntarism would have the lowest share of development activity. Voluntarism has receded into a negligible role in development because people in general in need of help, succor or assistance expect it to come from the government through its plan outlay. The scope of developmental planning was expanded more and more, successively, in each of the seven five year plans and at long last, the Seventh Five Year Plan had to caution explicitly that hence forward voluntarism had to come forward to play a greater role in development-rural and urban.[84] It is in the context of these definitions and meaning that the various terms which constitute the theoretical framework of the study have been used in the present study.

Thus it emerges that during the process of inclusive development a new dimension of development like participatory development through voluntarism or non-government organization has grown. The content of which has to be decided by the law of dialogue and mutual give and take that emerges. Furthermore, a type of State policies must come up which consist in such production and distribution of powers that will prove compatible with social inclusiveness and growth beyond the narrow power field. Non- Government Agencies or Organizations must be encouraged in such a way and should not only be strengthened but also should not lose their cohesion. These organizations shall absorb other patterns of development within itself without losing their identity and continuous capacity for growth.

Notes

1. George H. Sabine, "State" selection of the Encyclopedia *of the Social Science,* Vol. XIV, New York. The Macmillan Company, 1956, p. 328.
2. David L. Sills (ed.) *International Encyclopedia of the Social Science*, Vol. XV, The Macmillan Company & The Free Press, 1968, p. 150-151.
3. Harrison, *The Greatest Happiness Principle, in* N. D. Arora, Theory *of State: A Short Introduction,* New Delhi: Social Sciences Research Publication 1983, p. 175.
4. Harold J. Laski, *A Grammar of Politics,* S. Chand & Company, New Delhi, 1984. p. 24.
5. Jane Sayer, *Theory of State and Law,* Moscow: Progress Publishers, 1987, p. 51.
6. *Ibid.*

7. J. D. Sethi, *Character of the Indian State: A Non - Marxist View,* New Delhi, Manohar Publications, 1992, p. 13.
8. Debrah *Eade, Development, NGOs and Civil Society,* Rawat Publications, Jaipur, 2005, p. 36.
9. Asok Kumar Sarkar, *NGOs and Globalization: Developmental and Organizational Facets,* Rawat Publications, Jaipur, 2008, p. 84.
10. C. P. Bhambhri, The Modern State and Voluntary Societies, *The Indian Journal of Public Administration,* Vol. XXXIII No. 3, pp. 395-398.
11. http:/www.phmovement.org/pubs/issuepapers/hong08.html.
12. M. Vahlhans, '*The New Popularity of NGOs: Will the Enthusiasm Last?', D+C Development and Co- operation,* May-June, pp. 20-22.
13. Komal Parmar, 'NGOs in Globalization and Sustainable Livelihoods', in Asok Kumar Sarkar (ed.) *NGO's and Globalization: Developmental and Organizational Facets,* op. cit. p. 37.
14. Edward Gross & Armitta E. *Organizations in Society,* Prentice Hall Inc., Englewood Cliffs, NewJersey, 197. pp. 1-2.
15. Chester I. Barnard, *The Functions of the Executive,* Harvard University Press Cambridge 1950, p. 72.
16. Frederick Harbison, *Entrepreneurial, Organization as a factor in Economic Development,* reprint No. 9 *Studies in Lower and Industrial Relations,* Princeton, New Jersey 1959. p. 365.
17. Robert S. Weiss *Processes of Organization,* Survey Research Center University of Michigan, An Arbor, 1956. p. 5.
18. RaplphN. Slogdell '*Leadership, Membership and Organization'* in Cartwright and Zander *Group Dynamics Research and Theory,* Row Peterson and company, 1954, p. 40.
19. H. C. Ganguli, *Structure and Process of Organization,* Bombay, Asia Publishing House, 1964, p. 5.
20. Daniel A, Tagliere, *People Power and Organization,* New York.' Amacom Publication, 1993, p. 3.
21. Herbert G. Hicks, *The Management of Organization,* Tokyo: Mc Grow Hill Book Company, 1967, pp. 7-16.
22. Amitai Etzioni, *Modern Organizations,* New Delhi; Printice Hall of India private Ltd., 1990. p. 3.
23. *Ibid.*
24. Richard H. Hall, *Organizations Structure and Process,* New Jersey. Printice Hall, Inc., Englewood Cliffs, 1972. p. 87.
25. Op.cit., p. 3.
26. Hasenfeld Yehesicel, Human *Service Organizations,* Engle wood cliffs N.J.: Printice Hall, 1983. p. l.
27. Amitai Etzioni, *A Comparative Analysis of Complex Organizations,* New York: The Free Press, 1975. pp. 43-44.
28. Mohit Bhattacharya, 'Voluntary Associations, Development and the State', *The Indian Journal of Public Administration,* Vol. XXXIII, No. 3 July-September, 1987.

29. Ricard Taylor, *The Encyclopedia of Philosophy,* Paula Edwards Editor- in- chief, Vol. 8, New York, Macmillan Free Press, 1967. p. 270.

30. A. F. C. Bourdillon (ed.) *Voluntary Social Services: Their Place in Modern State.* London, Collier Macmillan, 1967. p. 270.

31. Op.cit. p. 272.

32. M. A. Muttalib, 'Voluntarism and Development: Theoretical Perspectives', *The Indian Journal of Public Administration,* Vol. XXXIII, No. 3, July- September, 1987. p. 401.

33. G. D. H. Cole, 'Voluntary Social Services', in A. F. C. Burdillion ed. Op. cit. - pp. 11-12.

34. William Beveridge, *Voluntary Action in an Action in a Changing World,* London, Bedford square Press national Council of Social Services, 1979. p. 100.

35. G.D.H.Cole, op.cit, p. 16 Social Services, 1979. p. 100.

36. Op. cit. pp. 24-28.

37. Michael Benton 'Anthropological Aspects Voluntary Associations' in David L. Sills (ed.) *International Encyclopedia of Social Sciences,* Vol. 16 , New York, Macmillan Company and the Pre- Press, London, Collier Macmillan,1968. p. 358.

38. S.W. H. Beveridge, *Voluntary Action: A Report on Methods of Social Advances,* London, 1946 pp. 15-17.

39. Escarp- as quoted in *Voluntary Efforts in Social Welfare and development* By D. Paul Chowdhary, New Delhi Siddhartha Publishers 1990. p. 102.

40. C. Smith R. A. Freedom, *Voluntary Association; Perspective on the Literature,* Cambridge, Harvard University Press, 1972. p. 44.

41. D. L. Sills, 'Voluntary Association: Sociological Aspects'; *In International Encyclopedia of the Social Sciences,* Vol. 16, Collier- Mc Millan, 1968, pp. 363-367.

42. M. A. Muttalib, 'Volunteerism and Development; Theoretical Perspectives', *the Indian Journal of Public Administration,* Vol. XXXIII, No. 3 July-Sept. 1987. p. 402.

43. N. R. Inamdar, 'Role of Volunteerism in Development' as quoted in *Social Welfare Administration* by D. R. Sachdev, Allahabad, Kitab Mahal. p. 200.

44. Alka Srivastava, 'Non- Governmental Organization and Rural Development' *Social Action* Vol. 49. Jan-March 1999, pp. 28-29.

45. Pat Young, *Mastering Social Welfare,* London. Macmillan Education Ltd., 1985. p. 243.

46. Shankar H. Pathak, *Social Welfare, Health and Family Planning in India, New* Delhi: Siddhartha Publications, 1979. p. 29.

47. D. Paul Chowdhary, *Voluntary Efforts in Social Welfare and Development,* New Delhi: Siddhartha Publication, 1990. pp. 132-33.

48. *Ibid.*

49. Alfred de Souza, 'Some Social and Economic Determinants of leadership in India', in Alfred de Souza (Ed.) 1978 *The Politics of Change and Leadership Development,* New Delhi; Manohar Publications. p. 6.

50. As quoted in *Voluntary Agencies and Rural Development* by I. Sundram, Delhi: B. R. Publishing Corporation, 1986, p. 67.
51. S. P. Srivastava, 'Nature of Voluntary Action in India Today: A critique' *Social Action* Vol. 49, January-March, 1999. pp. 10-11.
52. M. A. Mattalib in 'Volunteerism and Development: Theoretical Perspective', *The Journal of Public Administration, op. cit.* p. 403.
53. Op.cit. p. 405.
54. B. L. Lawani, '*NGOs in Development : A Case study of Solapur District*, Rawat Publications, Jaipur and New Delhi, 1991 p. 31.
55. *Ibid.*
56. S. W. H. Beveridge, *Voluntary Actions: A Report on Methods of Social Advances,* London, 1946.
57. Dr. R. Renganathan, 'Role of Non-Governmental Organizations in Rural Reconstruction'. *Third Concept,* Vol. 15, No. 74, August, 2001.
58. Noorjahan Bava, *Development and the Social Science Method: An Inter-disciplinary and Global Approach,* New Delhi: Uppal Publishing, 1994, pp. 210-240.
59. Seymour Marlin, *Upset, Politics and the Social Sciences, New* Delhi: Anand R. Kundaji for weley Eastern Pvt. Ltd., 1972, pp. 13-14.
60. Op.cit. pp. 153-172.
61. Op.cit., pp. 169-171.
62. Quitted in R. P. Mishra (Ed.) *Local level Planning and Development,* New Delhi: Storing Publishers Pvt. Ltd. 1983. pp. 21-33.
63. Soumitra Sharma, *Development Strategy and the Developing Countries,* New Delhi. South Asian Publishers Pvt. Ltd. 1983.
64. Dudley Seers, 'What are we trying to Measure' The *Journal of Development Studies,* April 1972, p. 21.
65. Noorjahan Bava, *People's Participation in Development Administration in India: An Empirical Study of Tamil Nadu*. New Delhi: Uppal Book Publishers 1984.
66. Ashok Rajan Basu, *The Tribal Development Programm and Administration in India,* New Delhi: National Book Organization, 1985 p. 27.
67. The United Development Administration: *Current Approaches and Trends in Public Administration for National Development,* New York No. E 711 H- I, p. 8.
68. G. S. Kainth and R. S. Bawa, *Economic Development and Structural Changes: An Empirical Investigation,* Inter- India Publication, New Delhi. pp. 1-2.
69. Op cit. p. 34.
70. M. L. Patel, *Planning Strategy for Development,* New Delhi: Inter- India Publication, 1984, pp. 1- 2 John Kenneth Galbraith, Economic Development, London; Hayward University Press 1969, p. 2.
71. *Ibid.*
72. Jag Mohan Singh Verma, 'Models of Development: A Critique', in S. P. Srivastava (ed.) *Development Debate: Critical Perspective,* Rawat Publications, Jaipur and New Delhi, 1998, p. 48.

73. Talcott Parsons, *The Social Systems,* Glencoe, I II, Free Press, 1951.
74. B. Hoselitz, *Sociological Aspects of Economic Growth,* New York, Free Press, 1960.
75. David C. Mc Cleland, *The Achieving Society,* New York, Dvan Nostrand, 1961.
76. Daniel Lerner, *The Passing of Traditional Society, London*, The Free Press, 1964.
77. Jag Mohan Singh Verma, 'Models of Development: A Critical' in S. P. Srivastva (ed.) The *DevelopmentDebate: Critical Perspectives,* op. cit. p. 53.
78. P. Baran, *The Political Economy of Growth, New* York, Monthly Review Press, 1973
79. Op. cit. p. 56.
80. S. P. Srivastava (ed.) *The Development Debate: Critical Perspectives,* Rawat Publications, Jaipur and New Delhi 1998, pp. 7-8.
81. *Ibid.*
82. Op. cit., p. 13.
83. Op. cit., p. 14.
84. Seventh Five year Plan 1985-90, Vol. II Delhi Government of India, Planning Commission, 1985. pp. 68-70, 295, 298-300.

Chapter - 3

NGOs: Glimpses of the Past

In ancient and medieval India, voluntarism operated freely and extensively in the fields of education, medicine, cultural promotion, and even succor in crises like droughts, floods, epidemics and foreign invasions or depredations by robbers and criminals. Pluralism played a great role in development, though restricted in scope, both by default of wide communication and transport network and the sway of the concept of *'Dharma'*. People's conception of functions of State was limited to maintenance of law and order and observance of good behavior. Each unit of social organization and government in the social and territorial hierarchy, viz., the individual, the family, the caste, the village, the temple, the guild, the town or city, the region and the highest level of government, owed certain responsibilities in development in the above restricted sense inherent in the conception of its own *'Dharma'*. A general statement of a historian that the ancient Indian State sought to promote the moral, material, aesthetic and spiritual progress of the whole community is to be construed with the above parameters of the social and political organization in the country in ancient and medieval times[1]. The poor and the destitute, the sick, the distressed and the disabled, the widows and the orphans, the jobless and the old, were provided succor by different social organs. The agriculturists, the artisans and artisans, trader, businessmen, the bankers and the professionals were helped out of difficulties by their colleagues in the occupation or profession. Philanthropy was widespread and the state came to the rescue of the community in extreme contingencies of helplessness. Kautilya's *Arthasastra* might have depicted the expended bureaucratic hierarchies of a central government of the Maurya Empire[2], indicating exceptional conditions of developed welfare statism. The Gupta Empire also represented another instance of developed welfare statism, though, incomparable in scope to the Maurya Empire. The paragon of the Mauryan welfare statism was missed from the government of Harsna which followed a laissez-faire policy.[3]

The large scope of voluntarism in development during ancient and medieval India, however, did not mitigate the social inequities of the rigid caste system, particularly heaped on the lower castes, especially the untouchables. The large- scale distress of and ravages on the people resulting from droughts, folds pestilences, robberies, crime, foreign invasions or excessive exploitation by the monarch, the aristocracy or government officials could not be saved by voluntarism, howsoever beneficent was its role in normal times.[4]

The above delineation of the role of voluntarism in development in ancient and medieval India was not affected much by the inroads of the Muslims and the establishment of their rule in different parts of the country, including the Mughal Empire at Delhi and Agra. In Muslim society also, the above mentioned norms of voluntarism were applied. Barring the benevolent regimes of rules like Shershah and Akbar, the super imposition of another government, however, tended to entail heavier taxation and other levies on the peasants other sections, which tended to depress their standard of life.[5]

India as such has a great tradition of voluntary service and in spite of rapid changes, the urge to serve fellowmen is still strong and widespread. Right through the ages, this tradition has been accepted as social obligation on the part of the individual towards his less fortunate brethren. Religion emphasized the virtue of *dan* i.e., free gift, which encompassed different forms of social service. Giving cash assistance to the needy, imparting knowledge, providing food and shelter to pilgrims, care of the sick and the destitute were considered to be righteous acts. Institutions like *Math's* and temples were responsible for the religiously inspired forms of service, and social institutions like caste and the joint family were concerned with the care of the handicapped, the destitute, the widow and the aged. Religious considerations, by and large, motivated acts of charity and service to please God and acquire *punya;* they also generated an honest desire in a large number of people to help the needy. In the long historical process the Indian social system developed many tendencies and practices which were by no means healthy and desirable.[6]

With the impact of the west, these accretions came to be sharply identified and seriously questioned. A strong opposition grew to the practice of *sati*, the treatment given to widows, the evils of child marriage and the caste system. There was a wave of social reform movement in the nineteenth and early twentieth century which marked the emergence of new phase of social work in India.[7]

India has got a unique tradition of social work. The social workers who have contributed a lot to the welfare of the vulnerable people created a history of social work. In fact the personalities involved in charity and philanthropic social work did an excellent job. Rather, they became the moving institutions and organizations of social work. Social reform by way of social action was the main focus of social work during the ancient period. The following discussion would help to know the historical development of voluntary action in India.

The dawn of the 19th century can rightly be said to be the beginning of the social reform movement in India. Raja Ram Mohan Roy (1772-1833), Ishwar Chandra Vidyasagar (1820-1891), SasiPada Banerjee (1842 -1925), Keshab Chandra Sen (1838-1884), Swami Dayanand Saraswati (1824 - 1883), Swami Vivekanand (1863-1902), Mahatma Phule (1827-1888), Pundit Ramabi (1858-1922), Maharishi Karve (1858-1962), Sir Sayyad Ahmed Khan (1817 -1898), Behramji Malbari (1853-1912), are the persons, who brought about social change in India through voluntary agencies. *Brahmo Samaj* was established by Raja Ram Mohan Roy in the year 1828 with the object of the opposing belief of orthodox Hindus and opposing child marriage, and propagating widow remarriage. Ishwar Chandra Vidyasagar also supported widow remarriage. He started a campaign in favor of widow remarriage and could draw the attention of Government of India, which passed the Hindu Widow Remarriage Act, 1856. Another social reformer, Keshab Chandra Sen, strongly advocated intercaste marriage, widow remarriage, and removal of *purdah* system. The enactment of the Civil Marriage Act of 1872 goes to his credit. Another important landmark in the reform movement was the *Arya Samaj* founded by Swami Dayanand Saraswati in Bombay in 1875 and was established to fight against idol worship. Sir Sayyad Ahmed Khan took interest in higher education of Muslim girls and supported modern education and social reforms for the community. Swami Vivekanand, the disciple of Ramakrishna Paramahansa, made lasting contributions to the making of modern India by propagating his views and ideals of service.

As a sequel to the reform movement of the 19th century a number of voluntary institutions, especially for the welfare of women, were started towards the end of the century. These institutions were, by and large, the work of certain individuals totally dedicated to the cause of social welfare. The establishment of the Servants of India Society, founded by Gokhale (1866-1915) in 1905 is a landmark in the history of social work of the early 20th century. The society was started to promote a spirit of nationalism and feeling of brotherhood. The Servants of India Society marks the beginning of an organized effort for enlisting the co-operation of a band of dedicated volunteers recruited and trained for a specific purpose. Relatively a larger number of people were involved in carrying out its mission than in the case of earlier institutions which were started and managed by one or two individuals who fought against heavy odds for a cause for which they had total devotion.

During the British rule, voluntarism in development received boost in new religious, cultural and social surroundings, though traditional sources of voluntarism lost the leaven and intensity. The laissez-faire policy of the British government in economic, and apparently in religious and social matters left another avenue of development open to the 'Natives' then resort to self-help, another term of voluntarism. The Christian missionary educational institutions and hospitals and dispensaries set an example to the non-convert majorities both Hindus and Muslims to emulate. School and colleges were established by educational societies set up by English-educated natives and affluent businessmen, *zamindars* and members of aristocracy to impart western education to the native children and youngsters. Libraries and lecture series were another source of social renaissance that ushered in cultural development of a novel kind of voluntary associations. A new religious awakening was aroused by voluntary associations stabilized in due course in institutional form. Some of these kindled and generated sentiments of religious and social reforms and the associations were funded by them. Voluntarism played a significant role in educational, health and social welfare development in India during the latter half of the nineteenth and the first half of the twentieth century. Not that the extent of development achieved was such as to solve the problem of development altogether, but a spirit of voluntarism was aroused which gained a wide recognition as an avenue of development during the British rule.

Historically speaking, voluntary organizations have proliferated and have actively taken part in various fields of social action during the British Rule. The first known voluntary organization according to the records maintained in the National Archives of India was the "Friend- in-Need Society" of Madras which applied for financial assistance to the Governor General in the year 1858-1859 through the Governor of Madras. The society was able to get financial assistance with the approval of the Governor General within one month of submission of the proposal to the Governor of Madras. The enactment of the Societies Registration Act of 1860 is a landmark in the history of voluntary organization in India. The Act is still operative with minor amendments and adoption by the Central and State Governments. The Christian missionaries have played a significant role in the growth of voluntary organizations in India. Some of the educational and medical institutions particularly in the south were started by Foreign and Indian Christian missionaries, who demonstrated a good deal of commitment to the causes they were striving to serve. Besides, other voluntary organizations in the field of education, health, welfare of the destitute, handicapped, chronically ill, etc. came into being and started working in the community.[8]

During the British period voluntary action had four sources:

(i) Initiative for social service by the wives of the British and later Indian officers through their clubs;

(ii) Caste based social welfare service by the Indians;

(iii) Social welfare service sponsored directly or by agencies created by foreign missionaries; and

(iv) Contributions by wealthy persons for welfare work.

During the days of the National Movement, with the growth of voluntarism in social and welfare development, new movements were initiated in rural areas, including agricultural development except the cooperative credit movement, in a few provinces. In the Industrial fields, managing agency and other forms of legalized voluntary modes helped industrial and ancillary activity including banking and development in the country.

The national movement breathed a spirit of strengthening the normal fiber of the people through self-help and autonomy through independent institution building in education, industry, business and trade, and fostering of economic production, particularly of industrial goods through *Swadeshi*. The triad creed of National Education, *Swadeshi* and Boycott were advocated by *Tilak*, Aurobindo and other during the first decade of the 20th century to bolster *Swarajya*. Gandhi propagated the creed in the course of the Non-Cooperation Movement and the national reconstruction on the basis of *Swadeshi*, village self-government and village self-sufficiency. Voluntarism secured fresh leases in the national movement. Gandhi based it on the philosophy of spiritualism, on the soul force or love force,[9] which to him marked the Indian culture from the Western.

Gandhi considered *Swaraj* to be the freedom of every individual and each individual to be the master of the means of his livelihood.[10] He was opposed to centralization of the means of production and reinforced the strength of voluntarism in the economic aspect of national life by decentralization of political authority down to the *Gram-Panchayats* which were to be completely independent of provincial or central government and his concept of trusteeship would apparently make the capitalists hold the laborers in ransom. Vinoba Bhave has interpreted trusteeship to mean *Vishwastabhava,* i.e., a feeling of mutual confidence, not only between the propertied and the laboring classes, but also between the rulers and the ruled so that the rulers with all the democratic checks and balances and the government's accountability to the people would discharge authority with a sense of responsibility towards the ruled[11]. Gandhi wanted each agriculturist to own and operate the spinning wheel, *'Charkha'*, to supplement his meager income from land and keep himself fully employed and he wanted different village crafts and industries to process the produce of the village farmer and he desired the agriculture cattle to serve the man rather than the man being servile to the machine[12]. Voluntarism was the core of Gandhi's thinking on the reconstruction of India's economic and political organization.

It was in the beginning of the 20th century that, Gandhiji came on the Indian political scene and started the movement for India's freedom. A large number of dedicated workers inspired by Gandhiji's leadership started constructive work. Gandhiji's contribution in the development of voluntary organizations is of a great importance. His approach to voluntary organization was unique. For example, Gandhiji wanted the Indian National Congress to be converted into *Lok Seva Sangh* (People's Service Association) to lead, organize and channelize people's power at the grassroots. To channelize the people's power at the grassroot level Gandhi founded the following organizations:[13]

(i) *Harijan Sevak Sangh* (Association for the Service of the Un-touchables).

(ii) *Gram Udyog Sangh* (Association for Promotion of Village Industries).

(iii) *Hindusthani Talimi Sangh* (Association forEducation of Hindusthani).

(iv) *Sarva Seva Sangh* (Association for Welfare of All).

Most of these organizations were located at places where Gandhiji used to stay such as *Wardha* (*Sewagram*), Ahmadabad (Sabarmati), etc. Gandhiji not only started voluntary organizations himself but also motivated and helped others to start some voluntary organizations. Some *Gandhian* workers and others were also associated with the establishment of Vidyapeeths (Indigenous Universities) such as *Kashi Vidyapeeth*, Gujarat *Vidyapeeth*, and Rural Development Institutes at *Shantiniketan*, *Wardha, Gandhigram*, etc.[14]

After independence voluntary action changed in its approach and structure, the issues covered by the voluntary activist during this period were also of different type. Event he parties involved in the voluntary sector were different. After independence India was declared to be a "Welfare State". The government undertook welfare schemes under various plans and policies. Besides, it also encouraged voluntary organizations to undertake social welfare programmers under the grant-in-aid programme and set up autonomous bodies like Central Social Welfare Board, Indian Council of Social Welfare etc.

Some of the institutions started by Mahatma Gandhi and by the wives of the officers with the support of the British Government and those started by the Indian philanthropists, Christian missionaries, Ramakrishna Mission, etc. continued to function. Although national organizations like Indian Red Cross Society, Young Men's Christian Association (YMCA), Young Women Christian Association (YWCA), *Harijan Sevak Sangh*, etc. were functioning, yet it was around this time that several all-India level voluntary organizations such as Kasturba Gandhi National Memorial Trust, Indian Council of Social Welfare, Indian Council of Child Welfare, Youth Hostel Association, Association of Social Health. etc., were setup.

Voluntary Organizations or NGOs increased in number since independence, especially since 1960. They have entered increasingly into 'development' fields, spanning different sector and social segments, both in rural and urban areas. Some among them are very much active in the tribal areas also. Secondly most of these NGOs are markedly different from the earlier organizations which were either motivated by sheer philanthropic or charity goals or as an appendage to the mainstream political movement, essentially freedom movement spearheaded by Gandhi, and the Congress Party. Gandhian principles underlying voluntary action received a short shrift in the post-independence era and hence fossilization of Gandhian institutions in most parts of our country.[15]

The decade that followed India's independence marked a phenomenal increase in the number of voluntary agencies in the country; they expanded their activities to cover practically every field of social welfare. They not only undertook programmers with their own resources but also organized projects sponsored by the State.

Provision of welfare services, since the beginning of the first plan has been a co-operative venture between the state and voluntary organizations. The planners in India have all along emphasized the role of voluntary agencies and have recognized services rendered by them in various fields.

The First Five Year Plan said: "A major responsibility for organizing activities in different fields of social welfare like the welfare of women and children, social education, community organizations, etc., falls naturally on private voluntary agencies. Any plan for social and economic generation should take into account the services rendered by these agencies and the state should give them maximum co-operation in strengthening their effort. Public co-operation through these voluntary social service organizations is capable of yielding valuable results in channelizing private efforts for the promotion of social welfare."[16]

Having recognized the importance of voluntary organizations the government took concrete steps to assist voluntary agencies. During the period of the First Five Year Plan, the Central government established the Central Social Welfare Board in 1953 with the main object of assisting voluntary agencies in organizing welfare programmers for women and children and for the physically handicapped. The Central Social Welfare Board in collaboration with the State Government organized State Social Welfare Advisory Boards in each state and union territories.[17]

With the establishment of the Central Social Welfare Board, the voluntary organizations got an unprecedented support from the government on a systematic basis. It has so far given grants over ten cores of rupees and as many as 6,000 voluntary agencies all over the country have benefited from its grant-in-aid programmes. The Board, besides giving assistance to the already existing agencies, helped in establishing many new ones. It is reported that about 3,500 voluntary agencies were started between 1951- 1960 and a majority of them (about 2,000) were established between 1954- 1955. Further, a study of the growth of voluntary agencies reveals that among 6,000 agencies aided by the Board, as many as 3,000 were started after the Board was set up. Very few agencies have been started after 1960 because the Board decided to continue its aid only to those agencies which had received its grants up to 1960 and did not favor the idea of giving grants for starting new agencies for organizing welfare work. The growth and development of voluntary agencies during the post-independence period was rather molded by the government schemes meant for these voluntary organizations. While the state sponsored programmers gave a great push to the work of voluntary agencies, they also gave rise to a feeling that they are making voluntary agencies less dependent on community support. Since the sponsored programmers made provision for the staff, the efforts of welfare agencies to mobilize volunteers to man their programmes got somewhat diluted. Further, the financial assistance given to voluntary agencies based on the system of matching contributions made them more conscious of raising funds but not of raising volunteers. All this had a restrictive effect, to some extent at least, on the growth of voluntary agencies in the true sense of the term.[18]

Voluntary action in India, thus, is the product of social, ethical, economic, political, democratic, cultural and religious values and considerations. Its recorded history is around 150 years old. Today the number of voluntary agencies working in different fields of social services, social welfare and rural development may be more than 25,000. If rural *Mahila Mandals,* youth clubs and other small voluntary groups are added to this, the total number might exceed three lakhs. According to the information available with the Ministry of Rural Development, there were in the seventies around 60,000 *Mahila Mandals*, 90,000 youth clubs working in rural areas. The states of West Bengal, Maharashtra, Tamil Nadu and Rajasthan had the largest number of rural development agencies in the seventies, and benefited from it. This was primarily due to availability of grants- in aid from Central Social Welfare Board and PADI (now CAPART). In addition, there may be many more agencies which are unregulated, not receiving any grant, are in the nature of kinship group, based on mutual aid, self- help, private and public trusts and ventures promoted by business houses. Voluntary action in India is of great historical, importance for it lit the spark for political, social, and economic freedom.[19]

By the 1990s, the politico- economic context has changed substantially in India and across the globe. A key change was the liberalization, globalization and privatization of the economy and the restructuring of economic growth, as a key strategy for poverty alleviation on the part of national governments and the World Bank.

However, the strategy now being promoted for enhancing growth is quite different from that advocated in the 1970s. It is led by the market rather than the state export oriented, rather than its import substitution oriented, labor- intensive rather than the capital intensive and women inclusive rather than women exclusive. Under the new scenario, the role envisaged for NGOs by the Indian government and the World Bank is quite different from that of 1980s. They are now being called upon to provide 'delivery services' that is to implement local development programmers rather than supplement a government programmes in the area of operation[20] As such the role and importance of NGOs have increased to a greater extent at the present juncture.

Thus the tradition of voluntarism in India is quite old which certainly has undergone various changes with the passage of time. Form the charitable arena it has moved to developmental process and today Voluntary Organizations or Non-Governmental Organizations are at the centre stage of developmental activities. The post-independence era provided ample scope for these organizations to flourish and serve the community especially the deprived sections of the society. The national planning process and implementation of various governmental programmes provided ample scope and opportunities to NGOs as the government could not undertake all developmental activities itself at the ground level. Earlier, whereas it was the welfarism which allowed the NGOs to step in but after 1991 it is the policy of liberalization, globalization and privatization wherein the state is gradually withdrawing itself from the welfarism and NGOs are stepping in a great manner to serve the cause of community especially the depressed and the deprived sections, so as to bring out the socio-economic and political change in the society. All this leads to the conclusion that NGOs are at the center-stage-of developmental process at the present juncture, hence the study of their organization, objectives, working and contribution are certainly a very significant subject matter.

Notes

1. A. S. Altekar, *State and Government in Ancient India*, Delhi: Motilal Banarsi das, 1958 , p. 384.
2. N. R. Inamdar, *The Pattern of Public Administration in Kautilya's Arthasastra,* Orient though Nasik, 1956.
3. A.S.Altekar, op.cit. p. 355.
4. N. R. Inamdar, 'Role of Voluntarism in Development' *The Indian Journal &Public Administration.* Vol. XXXIII No. 3, July- September 1987, p. 422.
5. R. C. Majumdar, H. C. Raychaudhari and K. K. Dutta, An *Advanced History of India,* London. Macmillan, 1948. pp. 560-563, 571, 576-77.
6. B.T. Lawani, op-cit p. 30.
7. *Ibid.*
8. D. Paul, Chowdhary, *Voluntary Efforts in Social Welfare and Development,* Siddharth Publication, New Delhi, 1986, p. 8.
9. M. K. Gandhi, *Hind Swaraj or Indian Home Rule, Ahmadabad*, Navajivan publishing 1939, reprints 1982.
10. *Young India,* November 15, 1928, p. 281.
11. Vinoba Bhave,' Introduction' in K. G. Mashruwala, *Gandhi and Marx,* Ahmadabad, Navajivan Publishing House, 1951, pp. 24-26
12. The Third Five-year Plan, New Delhi: Planning Commission, Governmen of India, pp. 292-293.
13. B.T.Lawani, op. cit. p. 41.

14. *Ibid.*
15. S. P. Punalekar, 'Tree and the bark: On Dialectics of Voluntary Organizations and social change', in by S.N. Pawar & others, *NGOs and Development: The Indian Scenario (eds.*), Rawat Publications. Jaipur and New Delhi-2004 p. 36.
16. Planning Commission, Government of India, *The First Five Year Plan*, p. 607.
17. *Ibid.*
18. D. Paul Chowdhary, *Voluntary Social Welfare in India, op*. cit. pp. 54-55
19. Op. cit., p. 46.
20. Komal Parmar, 'NGOs in Globalization and sustainable Livelihoods 'in Asok Kumar Sarkar (ed) *NGOs and Globalization: Development and Organizational Facets,* Rawat Publication, New Delhi. 2008. pp. 37-38.

Chapter - 4

NGOs in Himachal Pradesh: Organization, Role and Performance

An attempt is being made in this chapter to sketch out the profile of Non- Governmental Organizations under investigation in the present study viz-a-viz their organizations, working and performance with special reference to the state of Himachal Pradesh where these organizations are working. However, before the NGOs are profiled, it is worth while to outline a brief history of Himachal Pradesh, where these NGOs are operating.

Himachal Pradesh: A Background

Himachal literally means land of snowy mountains. Himachal Pradesh is a small world in itself, which is entered from the plains of Punjab, or *Shivalik* hills or through beautiful meandering valleys of hills of Shimla, covered with pine and typical temperate mountain flora. It is bound between 30^{0}22to 30012 North latitude and 75^{0}47 to 79^{0}4 east longitude. To the east, it forms India's border with Tibet, to the north lies state of Jammu and Kashmir, *Uttarakhand* in the south-east, and Haryana in the south and Punjab on its western side. The entire territory of Himachal Pradesh is mountainous with altitude varying from 350 to 7000 meters above the mean sea level and is a hilly and mountainous tract. The total area of Himachal Pradesh is 55,673 square kilometers which is divided into twelve administrative districts.[1]

Himachal Pradesh came into being as a Chief Commissioner' s province of the Indian Union on April 15 , 1948 as a result of merger of 30 erstwhile princely states of Punjab and Shimla Hills into the Union. All the areas at that time constituted into four districts viz. *Chamba, Mahasu, Mandi* and Sirmour with an area of 27, 169 square kilometers. In 1951 it was made a part 'C' state and on 1st July 1954, the neighboring part 'C' state of *Bilaspur* was integrated with Himachal Pradesh, thereby adding one more district with an area of 1,068 squarekilometers.[2]

Himachal Pradesh maintained its status of a part 'C' state of the Indian union till 1956, when the State Reorganization Commission led by Justice Fazil Ali and two members i.e. H.N. Kunzru and, K. N. Panikar submitted its recommendations to abolish the categorization of states as part A, B, C, etc. and recommended the merger of all part 'C' states or to maintain these independently as union territories for a specified period and as such Himachal Pradesh was formed as a union territory. In 1960, the border *tehsil* of *Mahasu* district- *Chinitehsil* was carved as a separate administrative unit and district *Kinnaur* was formed raising the total number of district to six. In 1963, 'Territorial Council' was provided to the state. On 1st November 1966, the Punjab state was reorganized with the formation of Haryana, as a separate state and merger of *Kullu, Kangra, Shimla and* some hilly areas of *Hoshiarpur* district and Dalhousie of Gurdaspur district into Himachal Pradesh constituting four new district viz. *Kullu, Lahaul-Spiti, Kangra* and *Shimla*, raising the total number of districts to 10. Status of Himachal Pradesh, as union territory continued till the award of a full statehood on 25th January, 1971[3]. On 1st September 1972, two districts viz. *Hamirpur* and *Una* were created by trifurcation of *Kangra* and *Mahasu* and *Solan* district were reorganized as *Shimla* and *Solan* districts[4]. Presently there are twelve districts, forty five sub-division, sixty seven *tehsils* and thirty seven sub-*tehsils* in Himachal Pradesh. Himachal Pradesh which is the 18th state of the Indian Union with the present population of 68, 64, 602 lakh is also known as fruits bowl of India. In this State, in addition to governmental organizations, various other Non-Government Organizations are also working and providing various services to the people. Out of them we have selected three state level NGOs, for the present study which are being profiled and analyzed in the present chapter.

Non-governmental Organizations

NGOs in India have long historical legacies, as voluntary action has been an integral part of our national life and character." It (voluntary action) has been in existence through centuries. Many rulers and many people in the past trod the path of service to their fellow beings and adopted it as a life mission" (Gangrade and Soorynoorthy 1996) But, the source of voluntary action was mainly religious, inspired by the desire for spiritual salvation and sometimes for atonement of guilt and inner anxieties. Spirit of charity and altruism guided the voluntary action in the past and it had found expression in diverse forms even outside the formal established religious channels. Calamities or disasters at local or regional levels stirred some motivated people into action and they helped the needy and distressed without the consideration of caste, creed, relation or language. Instances of support and help to the famine-ravaged communities by the group of social workers and philanthropists in the 16th and 17th centuries remind us of the presence of such communitarian values and sentiments.[5]

During the 19th century, voluntary action was stimulated by the need for social reforms in India's ubiquitous social structure, where rigidities of caste system held sway over the lives of rural communities. Even nascent urban areas of late 19th century were not totally free from caste prejudices and its invisible violence.

Thus the focal force for voluntary action during these times was reform movements spearheaded by the liberals, reforms-oriented Hindus and Christian Missionaries. Freedom movement gave further fill lip to voluntary action and there was complementary relationship between the two. [6] After independence the strategy of development not only provided greater spaces to NGOs but also turned them as development outfits. The contribution of NGOs in India has been substantial in the areas of education-both formal and non-formal, health and medical services, social welfare services, youth development etc. The NGOs have been known for their virtues of human touch, dedication, flexibility, self-reliance and nearness to the community. The Seventh Five Year Plan document (1985-95) envisaged a greater role of the voluntary agencies and the NGOs in implementation of development. These are expected to;-

(i) supplement government efforts so as to offer the rural poor choices and alternatives;

(ii) to be the eyes of the people at the village level;

(iii) set an example, it should be possible for the voluntary agency to adopt simple, innovative, flexible and inexpensive means with its limited resources to reach a large number with less overheads and with greater community participation;

(iv) activate the delivery system and to make it effective at the village level to respond to the felt needs of the poorest of the poor;

(v) disseminate information;

(vi) make communities as self- reliant as possible;

(vii) to show, how village and indigenous resources could be used, how human resources, rural skill and local knowledge grossly under-utilized at present could be used for their own development;

(viii) demystify technology and bring it in a simple form to the rural poor;

(ix) train a cadre of grass-root workers who believe in professionalizing voluntarism;

(x) mobilize financial resources from within the community with a view to making communities stand on their own feet;

(xi) mobilize and organize the poor, generate awareness to demand quality services and impose a community system of accountability on the performance of village-level government functionaries.[7]

India witnessed a rapid growth in numbers and areas of activities of Non-Government Organizations or Voluntary Organizations in many parts of the country. Increasingly the term 'Non-Government Organizations' encompasses a large variety of organizations of different origins, sizes, purposes, approaches and structures. Among them, few exist only on paper and are predominantly self-serving. However, among them genuine organization have acquired vast experiences in the areas of grassroots development processes, people's participation, empowerment strategies and organization building etc.[8]

Himachal Pradesh is no exception to Non-Government Organizations and a large number of them have been constituted and registered under the Societies Act. Some of them exist only on papers but some are actively working amongst the people of this Pradesh with the active participation of the people themselves. Here in this chapter we are presenting and analyzing the organizations, working and role performance of three such Non-Government Organizations which are effectively working in Himachal Pradesh.

Himachal Pradesh Voluntary Health Association (HPVHA)

Two to four million Non-Government Organizations (some of these will legally qualify to be called NGOs due to their incorporation under the relevant Act) in India are engaged in various social sector activities helping the poor, deprived, disadvantaged and destitute. (McCann and John Stone 2006) Increasing fund flow to Indian NGO sector in recent years has led to a vast proliferation of NGOs. (Biswas 2006) These NGOs are largely operating as service providers with concentration in the area of education, health, nutrition for mother and child, income generation, small loans for self-employment and environmental activities (Desai 1999) NGOs play an important role in linking communities and the Government. NGO's especially those working to provide various services such as health, education, nutrition and rural development, act as a buffer between the state and people.[9]

One such Non- Governmental Organization which is working in the health sector in Himachal Pradesh is, 'Himachal Pradesh Voluntary Health Association' (HPVHA) which was established in 1987, as a registered nonprofit making society having a secular constitution, which aims at improving the health of the people, irrespective of the caste, creed, sex and region. It is a State level federation of Voluntary Organizations engaged in health and development activities. The Organization works in the field of community health and helps the grassroot level voluntary organizations to plan, implement and evaluate their development programmes. The Himachal Pradesh Voluntary Health Association, liaisons for the grassroot non-profit organizations with the State government, the National Government, and the International Agencies, with commitment to promote social justice in the provision and distribution of health services in Himachal Pradesh.[10]

The geneses of HPVHA can be traced to the national level 'Voluntary Health Association Movement' started in the late1960's. The Bangalore Meet of leaders of Voluntary Hospitals and Health Association held in July, 1969 called for co-ordination and collaboration for promoting community health and an association known as Co-ordination Agency for Health Planning was formed,[11]. Dr. James Tong then Director of Catholic Hospital Association of India and Dr. James McGillivray, Director of CMC, World Council of Churches, Geneva were two inspiring forces and pioneers in the movement. Later on, in a national convention held in the city of Madras in September 1974, a federation called 'Voluntary Health Association of India' was formed; replacing the Co-ordination Agency for Health Planning and Himachal Pradesh Voluntary Health Association (HPVHA) is a part of it. The membership of HPVHA is open to all health and development non-profit making registered organizations, who believe in the ideology and objectives of the association. At present HPVHA is involved in health related project such as Reproductive Health, Promotion of Low Cost Primary Health Care through alternative systems of medicine, prevention and control of STD/ HIV/AIDS, disability, child health and rights, capacity building of NGOs, advocacy and information dissemination. The organization is registered under the Societies Registration Act XXI of 1860 and Foreign Contribution Registration Act 1976 vide registration No. 5947 and 182510014 respectively,[12] with the mission to make 'Health A Reality' to the people of Himachal Pradesh.

Organizational Structure

HPVHA's organizational structure,[13] as given below Table No. 4.1, is broadly divided into two levels, the Management Team and the Administrative Staff. The designated Executive Director is the one who creates a bridge between the both levels. The policy decisions are taken at the managerial level and Executive Director implements and conveys the same down the line of command. The Executive Director foresees that the policy matters are conveyed properly at all the levels and results/objectives are as decided by the management, achieved.

Table No. 4.1: Organizational Structure of HPVHA

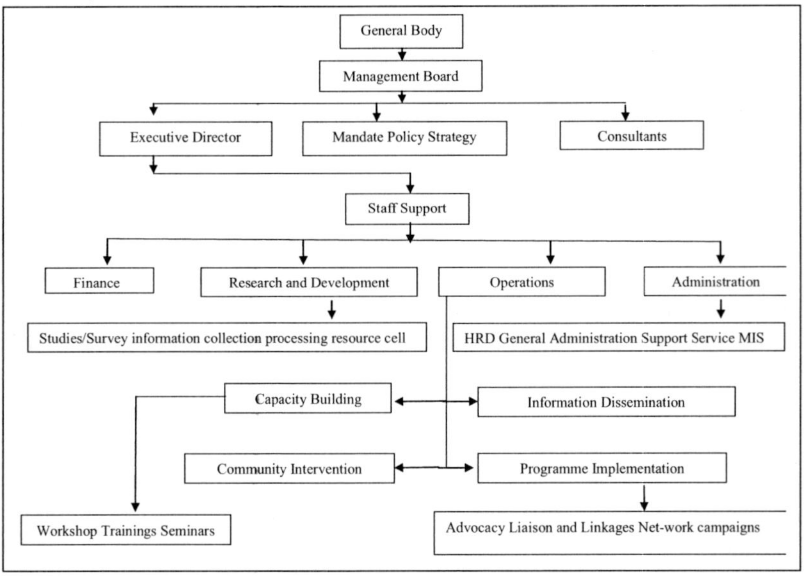

Resources

HPVHA gets financial support from foreign as well as Indian,[14] agencies. Prominent among them are:

Foreign Support

- American Cancer Society, USA.
- Council for Social Development, New Delhi.
- HAQ- Centre for Child Rights, New Delhi.
- IGSS, New Delhi.
- La Mansion des Himalaya (MDA) France.

- Room to Read India Trust, New Delhi.
- MISERERO, Germany.

Indian Support

- Child line India Foundation, Mumbai.
- Ministry for Health and Family Welfare, New Delhi.
- VHAI, New Delhi.
- Hriday Shan, New Delhi.
- Help Age India, New Delhi.
- Gram Niyogan Kendra, Ghaziabad.
- Department of Social Justice and Empowerment, Himachal Pradesh.
- HPSACS, Shimla.
- SCSTE, Shimla
- District Rural Development Agency, Solan, Bilaspur and Hamirpur.

Income and Expenditure statement of HPVHA as shown in the Annual Reports is given in the following Tables No. 4.2:-

Table No. 4.2: Income and Expenditure Statement of HPVHA

Year	*Income*	*Expenditure*	*Balance*
2002-2003	4,777,876	4,777,876,	Nil
2003-2004	7,64,650	3,01,565	4,63,085
2004-2005	1108484	723421	385063
2005-2006	766091	282652	485439
2006-2007	477397	102809	374588

Goals and Objectives of HPVHA

The objectives of the HPVHA are:[15]

(i) Justice in healthcare leading to self-reliance in community health with community participation;

(ii) To fulfill the needs of the community with optimum utilization of natural or other available resources;

(iii) To create the environment for building up people's health movement through effective networking, campaigning and public affair related activities.

(iv) To help into evolution of low cost, appropriate and people oriented health programme in harmony with the traditional knowledge and skills of community;

(v) To provide support services to community health programmers taken up by the grassroots level voluntary organizations;

(vi) To conduct research and studies on various aspects of primary healthcare and provide consultancy services;

(vii) To provide training and education to people concerned through their participation;

(viii) To strengthen voluntary organizations in the area of health and development;

(ix) To enhance the collaboration between government and voluntary organizations;

(x) To play a major role in the larger areas of social justice, environment and sustainable development.

Keeping in view the health and development status of Himachal Pradesh, there are several health issues and vulnerable sections of the population, which are of concern for HPVHA. In spite of governmental programmers and infrastructure in place, there still remains vulnerable, unreached and remote locations which need to be focused on HPVHA strategy paper has been developed to give future direction, capacitate and to enable HPVHA address priority issues envisioned, keeping in view the changing scenario of health and development and the public and voluntary movement in the state.[16]

The objectives of HPVHA vision 2010,[17] are to:

(i) To identity priority areas for interventions in health and development;

(ii) To identity dark un-served and underserved voluntary geographical locations for interventions;

(iii) To develop strategies, future line of action and resource planning;

(iv) To streamline own systems and to make them adequately dynamic to meet the challenges.

Programmed Undertaken by HPVHA

To initiate evidence based advocacy and policy intervention HPVHA undertook the Children Budget Analysis in collaboration with HAQ- Centre for Child Rights, New Delhi, and the study involves analysis of the Himachal Pradesh State Government budget for five-year Period i.e. 2000 to 2005 from children perspective. The major objectives of the study were: to analyze the direct budgetary provisions and expenditure for child health, education, development and protection in the state; generation of public debate on the rights of the children and the budgetary allocations made to child related programmes; to advocate increased transparency in budgeting and policy of the government with respect to child related programmers, to ensure increased commitments to children and increased focus on children in budgeting process and budget debates.[18]

As a large share of the allocations and expenditure for child related schemes and programmers are done in the states, a study of the state budget became necessary for holistic understanding. HPVHA completed the preliminary first year analysis for 2003- 2004 of the state government budget. The study in its first year gave an insight of status of allocations and implementation of programme for children in the state of Himachal Pradesh. While analyzing the state government budget and schemes it did learn the whole process of budgeting and also identified the gray areas related to child health and rights which needs to be strengthened.[19]

HPVHA was accorded the status of MNGO under RCH programme by the Ministry of Health and Family Welfare, Government of India, initially for five districts of Himachal Pradesh namely *Bilaspur, Hamirpur, Kullu, Mandi* and as a special case district of *Lahaul-Spiti*, where HPVHA itself carried out the intervention. After wards as per the policy guidelines of the Ministry of Health, Government of India, all mother NGOs were allotted two districts each and *Bilaspur* and *Mandi* district were retained by HPVHA and this project is being implemented in five block of *Mandi* and two block of *Bilaspur* district. The scheme focused on addressing the unmet-reproductive child health needs in un-served and underserved areas of the two selected districts. HPVHA is moving from exclusive awareness generation to actual delivery of Reproductive Child Health services. This is done through the utilization and strengthening of existing government infrastructure and effective use of human resources.

The objectives of the project are: to promote 100 percent early registration of pregnant women in project areas, ensure at least three ANC check-ups; promote institutional deliveries; guarantee 100 percent immunization of 0-6 year's children; ensure reduction in the unmet need for spacing; promote/disseminate information on availing services incentives under '*Janani Suraksha Yojna.*'[20]

HPVHA in collaboration with AUSAID is implementing project tit led, 'Perspective building to improve reproductive health of women in Himachal Pradesh'[21]. In 40 pockets of all the twelve district consisting of 120 *Gram Panchayats* covering approximately 2,40, 000 population for a period of three years, which aims at designing a comprehensive strategy and plan to achieve basic health and development for maternal and child care in the state of Himachal Pradesh.

Healthy Highway project *Barmana*[22], a wing HPVHA has been implementing STD/HIV/AIDS prevention and control targeted intervention on transporters support by HPSACS-NACO. The intervention is operational on Chandigarh-*Kullu*-National Highway No- 21 in district *Bilaspur* that is having second highest number of detected HIV$^+$cases after district *Hamirpur*. The project has made significant contributions in prevention and control of STD/HIV/AIDS among truck drivers and community in the area. The key elements of this intervention project were: Behavior changes communication: STD cases identification and treatment; Condom Promotion and Creation of Enabling Environment. The Methodology of the project was: One to one and focus group discussion, exhibitions, awareness camps cum health checkup camps on STDs; Establishing condom depots and peer educators, creation of enabling environment; celebration of important days and community mobilization involving PLWHA and creation of self-help groups.[23]

As such HPVHA has got a very specific health related programmers targeted on the vulnerable sections of the society. In order to know the reality of the working of HPVHA, an investigation was carried out in villages of *Bilaspur* district where the NGO is actively working. In order to assess the performance of the organization a survey was carried out, in which 150 selected respondents answered to the querries relating to the working of HPVHA. The respondents were administered the interview schedule. The profile of respondent as well as the information collected from them on the working and performance of HPVHA is being presented and analyzed in the following pages through different Tables:

Age-wise Distribution of the Respondents

Age-wise all the age- groups should be included in the samples as to know the views of the respondents about the various querries to the study. In the present study an effort has been made to give representation to all the age groups. Age- wise distribution of respondents is as given below in Table No. 4.3:-

Table No. 4.3: Age-wise Distribution of the Respondents

18-35 years	36-55 years	56-75 years	Total
73	53	24	150
(49)*	(35) *	(16) *	(100)

**Figures in parenthesis in all the tables denote a percentage which has further been rounded off.*

As the Table No 3.3 shows, 49 percent of the respondents are from 18-35 years age- group, 35 percent form 36-55 years age- group and 16 percent from 56-75 years age- group. The majority of the respondents are from 18-35 age- groups which are young, dynamic and active age-group to be benefitted with the activities of the NGO, though other age-groups do get the benefit of the services of NGOs.

Sex-wise Distribution of the Respondents

All the sections of the society, male as well as female, are getting the benefit of the services being rendered by HPVHA, hence the sample study include both the sexes and their distribution is as given in Table No. 4.4:-

Table No. 4.4: Sex-wise Distribution of the Respondents

Male	*Female*	*Total*
73	77	150
(49)	(51)	(100)

As the Table No. 4. 4 shows, among the total respondents 49 percent are male, and 51 percent are female which clearly indicates that proper representation and opportunities have been given to both the sexes of the society so as to make out the representative sample.

Education-wise Distribution of the Respondents

Education is the most important factor to awaken an individual. Education provides competence to understand the structure, nature and role of the society and the various organizations working within. Educated people are more vigilant about the happenings around and they can analyze the things in a better way. Educated people can not only take benefit of services of the NGOs but they can also guide others also and analyze the working and performance of the organization. Education- wise the sample study includes different groups which are given in Table No. 4.5:-

Table No. 4.5: Education-wise Distribution of the Respondents

Illiterate	*Primary/ Middle*	*Matric.*	*+2*	*Graduate*	*Post - Graduate*	*Total*
30	51	48	7	8	6	150
(20)	(34)	(32)	(4)	(6)	(4)	(100)

As the Table No. 4.5 shows, among the total respondents, 20 percent are illiterate, 34 percent are educated up to primary/ middle level, 32 percent are matric pass, 4 percent are + 2, 6 percent are graduates and only 4 percent are postgraduates, which indicate that education- wise the respondents belong to different backgrounds. Though majority of the respondents are literate enough to understand and analyze the working and performance of the NGOs yet illiterate section also constituted the sample that needs and utilizes the service of the NGO.

Marital Status of the Respondents

It is believed that married people are more responsible in comparison to unmarried and they can analyze the things more objectively and responsibly as they have to share the burden of their families. In the present study both the groups have been given due representation and the marital status of the respondents is as given in Table No. 4.6:-

Table No. 4.6: Marital Status of the Respondents

Married	*Un married*	*Total*
126	24	150
(84)	(16)	(100)

As the Table No. 4.6 shows, 84 percent respondents are married and 16 percent of the respondents are unmarried. Majority of the respondents are married who being the more responsible group can analyze the working and performance of the NGO and respond to the querries more objectively.

Income Status of the Respondents

Income is another consideration for selecting the respondents for the sample study. Those who need are naturally quite awakened to the benefits being distributed by various agencies. Those who do not need, they also believe that they do have the stake in the distributions as it is their money which is being distributed hence it should be used properly. So economic status makes the people responsible and they analyze the things in a proper perspective. Income- wise the respondents belong to the groups as shown in Table No. 4.7:-

Table No. 4.7: Income Status of the Respondents

Up to 1 Lakh p.a.	*2 Lakh p.a.*	*Above 2 Lakh p.a.*	*Total*
86	46	18	150
(57)	(31)	(12)	(100)

As the Table No. 4.7 shows, out of the total respondents, 57 percent have the annual income up to Rs. 1 lakh, 31 percent have their annual income up to Rs. 2 lakh and 12 percent of the respondents are in Rs. 2 lakh and above per annum income group. Income wise all the respondents belong to lower middle and middle class who are in a position to analyze the working of various organizations.

Awareness about the NGO-HPVHA

First and foremost thing for the office bearers, officials, beneficiaries and public in general is to know about the organization, its objectives and programmes, only then they can participate in the functioning and take benefit of various programmes of the organization. In order to know about popularity of the organization among the people the respondents were asked whether they know about the organization named HPVHA and the responses are as given in Table No. 4.8:-

Table No. 4.8: Awareness about the NGOs-HPVHA

To a Great Extent	*To Some Extent*	*Not at all*	*Total*
84	50	16	150
(56)	(33)	(11)	(100)

As the Table No. 4.8 shows, out of total respondents, 56 percent are aware about the NGO-HPVHA to a great extent, 33 percent are aware to some extent, whereas 11 percent are not at all aware about the NGO. This leads to the conclusion that majority of the respondents are well aware of the NGO, hence in a position to take benefit of its services.

Awareness about the Working of HPVHA

Knowledge about the working of an organization is a must to the beneficiaries only then they can derive benefits out of that. Are the people aware of the functioning of the HPVHA– this question was put to the respondents and the responses are as given in Table No. 4.9:-

Table No. 4.9: Awareness about the Working of HPVHA

To a Great Extent	*To Some Extent*	*Not at all*	*Total*
74	57	19	150
(50)	(38)	(12)	(100)

As the Table No. 4.9 indicates, 50 percent of the respondents know the functioning of HPVHA to a great extent, 38 percent know to some extent and 12 percent respondents are not at all aware of the functioning of HPVHA, which means that beneficiaries are well aware of the functioning of HPVHA, hence in a position to utilize the services of the NGO.

Services Being Provided

The beneficiaries should also be aware of the services being provided by the NGO so as to derive benefits out of them. In order to know about the awareness of services being provided by the HPVHA, the selected respondents were asked as to what services are being provided by HPVHA and the response are as given in Table No. 4.10:

Table No. 4.10: Services Being Provided by HPVHA

Running Health Awareness Campaigns	*Reproductive Health of Women*	*Healthy Highway Project, Control of STD/HIV/AIDS*	*Total*
67	51	32	150
(45)	(34)	(21)	(100)

As the Table No. 4.10 reveals regarding the services of HPVHA, 45 percent of the respondents believed that HPVHA is running awareness campaigns, 34 percent believed that HPVHA provides services in the reproductive health of women and 21 percent of the respondents replied that HPVHA is conducting Healthy Highway Project i. e. awareness, prevention and cure of STD/ HIV/AIDS etc., which shows that respondents are well aware of the services being provided by the NGO-HPVHA.

Benefit of the Services being Rendered by HPVHA

Services being rendered by the NGO, HPVHA can be termed as useful only if the people believe that they are being benefited, by way of awareness about health issues, programmers being run by the health institutions for the benefit of masses and the remedies, treatments available in various health problems. HPVHA otherwise also is focusing on the reproductive health of women, child health needs, and healthy highway project which include awareness, prevention and control of STD/HIV/AIDS like diseases. In order to know the role of HPVHA in this regard, the selected respondents were asked if they believe that people are being benefited with the services of HPVHA, and there is some change and reduction in the health problems of the people, their responses are as given in Table No. 4.11:-

Table No. 4.11 : Benefit of services being Rendering by HPVHA

To a Great Extent	*To Some Extent*	*Not at All*	*Total*
74	59	17	150
(50)	(39)	(11)	(100)

As the Table No. 4.11 shows, 50 percent of the respondents replied that they are being benefited to a great extent, 39 percent responded that they are being benefited to some extent, whereas 11 percent of the respondents said that they are not at all being benefited by the services being rendered by the HPVHA in their area, which means that majority of the people are utilizing and being benefited with the services being provided by the HPVHA. Only those who are not at all related with the health problems in which the services are being provided are not getting any direct benefit of the services of the organization hence they replied that they are not at all being benefited.

Through documentary sources and field investigations it is amply clear that HPVHA is a well-structured voluntary organization with clear objectives and goals. HPVHA is a State level Non-Governmental Organization, which was established in 1987, with an objective to improve the health of the people. Since then it is working for the community health and helps the grassroot level voluntary organizations to plan, implement and evaluate voluntary development programs especially in the field of the health sector. HPVHA liaison for the grass root organizations with the State government, National Government and International Agencies so as to promote social justice in the provision and distribution of health services in Himachal Pradesh.

The organization is registered under the Society's Registration Act of 1860 and Foreign Contribution Registration Act 1976. The membership of HPVHA is available to all the health and development non-profit making registered organizations. At present HPVHA is involved in health related projects such as Reproductive Health, Promotion of Low Cost Primary Health Care through alternative system of medicine, Prevention and Control of STD/HIV/AIDS, Child Health and Rights, Capacity Building of NGOs, Advocacy and Information Dissemination. It is with these projects that HPVHA is working to improve the health of the people of Himachal Pradesh.

From the available information through documents, such as annual reports and other literature of the organization and the field investigations, we come to the conclusion that HPVHA is a well-organized state level federation of voluntary organizations engaged in health and development activities. The organization is providing valuable services in community health and helping the grassroot level organizations to plan, implement and evaluate their programmers. It is an important liasioning organization with the state and national government and international agencies to ensure provisions and distribution of health services in Himachal Pradesh. HPVHA is focusing on the vulnerable, unreached and remote locations. It has undertaken projects on Reproductive Health, Alternative System of Medicine, Prevention and Control of STD/HIV/AIDS, Disability, Child Health and Rights, capacity building of NGOs and information disseminations. Filed investigations show that people are well aware of the organization and its activities and working. The organization is providing great services in health sector especially for the pregnant women, children and other vulnerable sections of the society. The initiatives and performance of the HPVHA has benefited the people and health problems of women, children and STD/HIV/AIDS related problems have been addressed to some extent.

Himachal Gyan Vigyan Samiti (HGVS)

The *Himachal Gyan Vigyan Samiti* (HGVS) is a mass based voluntary organization working in the entire State of Himachal Pradesh. It was registered in November, 1991 and formally inaugurated on 14 th June, 1992 to carry out a definite task to initiate a state wide churning in order to create a conducive environment and demand for literacy.[24] It is a unit of the *Bharat Gyan Vigyan Samiti* that has over 25 state units, 350 district units and nearly three lakh members and India People's Science network at the national level which is also referred to as people's science movement.[25]

The back ground of *Bharat Gyan Vigyan Samiti* goes back to the *Kerala Shastra Sahitya Parishad* whose objective was social transformation, through the application of science and technology. In the 1970's and 1980' s the *Kerala Shastra Sahitya Parishad* had grown into a mass organization and organized jathas (a socio-cultural caravan for development communicator) as a tool for mass mobilization on various issues. In 1987, other organizations came together with the *Kerala Shastra Sahitya Parishad* and organized the *Bharat Jan Vigyan Jatha* during the third anniversary of the Bhopal Gas Tragedy. In 1988 and 1989, the *Kerala Shastra Shitya Parishad* in collaboration with the district administration, undertook a campaign for literacy in Ernakulum district. The *Kala jathas* (cultural caravans) besides display of posters, banners and songs, created a climate for literacy. The campaign led to a substantial rise in literacy rates in the

Ernakulum district and this was followed by a campaign in Kottayam district and subsequently in all of Kerala in1989-1990.[26]

In 1989, the Ministry of Human Resource Development Government of India, decided to adopt the Ernakutam Model as a strategy for propagating literacy and facilitated the formation of the *Bharat Gyan Vigyan Samiti*, at the national level. The history of *Bharat Gyan Vigyan Samiti* has been classified by Denzil Saldanha into four distinct phases (i) the period from 1989 to 1993 that was characterized by mobilization for literacy, (ii) the period from 1994 to 1997 that was marked by a transition from literacy to other developments, initiatives, such as natural resource management, watershed development, health, basic education, formation of saving groups as a result of women's mobilization; (iii) the period from 1998 to 2001 that was marked by an attempt to consolidate the expansion and diversity of sectorial interventions through decentralized institutionalization; and (iv) the period from 2002 to the present that is characterized by advocacy with the central government for policies related to rights issue.[27]

Organizational Structure

The organizational structure of the *Himachal Pradesh Gyan Vigyan Samiti* (Constitution of the HGVS is enclosed as Annexure II) consists: [28]

- State level conference, which is the highest organ of the organization and it is held annually.
- After the membership campaign and renewal of membership, there is five stage structure of the organization i.e. *Panchayat* ward level conference; *Panchayat* conference; Block conference; District conference and State conference.
- Lowest level unit *is Gyan Vigyan Kendra* at *Panchayat* ward level with a minimum membership of 10 and membership is to be renewed every year.
- Higher level units are *Panchayat*, Block District and state. The office bearers of all these units are elected in annual conferences held at all the levels and current membership is about 35,000

From primary unit to state level units, the members of Council, Executive Committee, Core group and Delegates for the conference shall be given in Table No. 4.12, and various level core group constituted by the office bearers is shown in Table No. 4.13.[29]

Table No. 4.12: Primary unit to State level Committee of HGVS

Stage	*Council*	*Executive committee*	*Core Group*	*Delegate for conference*	*Lower unit structure*	*Minimum Member*
State	31 - 55	21 - 31	7 - 9	Bases of membership		
District	21 - 35	7 - 21	5 - 7	40	2 Block	500
Block	No	7 - 15	5 - 7	25	5 Panchayat	250
Panchyat	No	5 - 11	3 - 5	20	IGVK	50
Gyan Vigyan Kendra	No	3 - 5	3	All members		20

Table No. 4.13: Various Stage Level Core Group

State	*President*	*Vice President*	*Secretary*	*Treasure*	*Joint Sec.*
District	President	Vice President	Secretary	Treasure	Joint Sec.
Block	President	Vice President	Secretary	Treasure	Joint Sec.
Panchayat	President	Vice President	Secretary	Treasure	Joint Sec.
Gyan Vigyan	President	Vice President	Secretary	Treasure	Joint Sec.
Kendra	President	Vice President	Secretary	Treasure	Joint Sec.

Objectives of the HGVS

The birth of any voluntary movement is always with a dream, a vision. The *Himachal Gyan Vigyan Samiti* (HGVS) envisages a society capable of understanding its problems, finding solutions and creating processes and system for working out these solutions. A society that is participatory, democratic, scientific and free of gender, caste, class and religious bias. A society in which each individual has been empowered to act to the utmost of his/her capability to contribute for a dignified existence for herself/himself and for the common goal.[30]

The objectives of the *Himachal Gyan Vigyan Samiti* at the time of its formation were as under:

I. Working towards creation of a fully literate society, not just 3 R's but a tool for greater awareness and empowerment and contributions towards a higher quality of life.

II. To make people aware about the causes of their problems, enhancing their capabilities for tackling those problems, to increase their initiative and participation in development. To work for objective development where they are the subjects or recipients. To focus towards human resource development more than infrastructural development.

III. To generate voluntarism and a volunteer culture in society where an individual willingly contributes a part of his/her time, energy and capability towards the betterment of society.

IV. Providing an interface between experts in different fields and the common masses so as to liberate knowledge and information from the bondage of technical language and idiom. Also to make technical persons sensitive to the needs and experiences of the common people with greater respect for collective, traditional and folk knowledge.

V. Inculcating a scientific temper in the society and to take scientific methods and techniques to the people.

VI. To work towards empowerment of women as well as empowerment of all disadvantaged sections of the society.

VII. Working towards creation of a continuously learning society and a library movement.

VIII. Working towards preservation of a collective community solidarity and culture. To preserve the plurality and identity of the local culture under attack of consumerist and globalized culture. To preserve those values from traditions which are relevant in the present context and to reject obscurantist practices and beliefs?[31]

The above objectives call for a very massive, sustained and dedicated effort at all levels of the society and the organization is striving to move these by working in the following thrust areas;[32]

(1) Education

Himachal Gyan Vigyan Samiti works for education at three levels i.e. Literacy; as a voluntary mass movement; elementary education; universal enrolment, quality in formal education; more joyful, relevant and child friendly education to prevent failure and dropouts; continuing education targeted towards the whole of the society, providing lifelong, informal learning opportunities of people's choice e.g. income generation, livelihood and social issues.

(2) Development

Himachal Gyan Vigyan Samiti is trying to lessen the gap between the experts and users in various developmental sectors like horticulture, agriculture and animal husbandry etc. There is an effort that all their developmental programmes, extension services and schemes converge and reach the people in accordance with their needs and aspirations.

(3) Health

Himachal Gyan Vigyan Samiti strives to create a demand for health for all, placing health in people's hands by making them more aware about preventive health, hygiene and the importance of primary health care.

(4) Environment

It is spreading awareness about environment with a balance between ecological and human concern. Tapping natural resources in a scientific, sustainable and sensitive manner.

(5) Participatory Democracy

Himachal Gyan Vigyan Samiti works for the participatory planning at grassroot level, micro planning, sensitization, capability building of *Panchayat Raj* functionaries, *Panchayat* resource mapping etc.

(6) Gender

Raising women issues, working for capability building and empowerment of women through training, festivals, seminars and workshops.

(7) Library Movement

Making efforts towards establishment of a reading culture in society, encouragement to village libraries, people oriented literature in the language of the masses.

The *Himachal Gyan Vigyan Samiti* adopted the methodology to take through the following strategies.

(i) Training, orientation, workshops, seminars and conferences, group discussions, house to house surveys, observation of days etc.

(ii) Material preparation of three kinds:

- Environment building material: folders posters, publicity material, songs;
- Resource material for organizers, activists;
- Material for the common masses.

(iii) Mass mobilization through *Kala Jathas*, Village, Ward and *Panchayat level* meetings.

Himachal Gyan Vigan Samiti works at three levels:

(i) Intervention at policy level

(ii) Creating, facilitating and providing supportive role to community based organizations at grassroot level e.g. Mother-Teacher Associations, Self Help Groups, *Gyan Vigyan Kendra, Mahila Mandals, Yuva Mandals,* and Continuing Education Centers etc. for collective action.

(iii) Taking awareness or mass campaigns to people.[33]

Income and Expenditure of the HGVS, as shown in the Annual Reports are given in the Table No. 4.14:-

Table No. 4.14: Income and Expenditure Statement of HGVS

Year	*Income*	*Expenditure*	*Balance*
2002-03	5,52368	5,52368	Nil
2003-04	1,17,4036	1,174036	Nil
2004-05	9,121964	912964	Nil
2005-06	827521	827521	Nil
2006-07	10,65,297	10,65297	Nil

Programmes Undertaken

As *Himachal Gyan Vigyan Samiti* is the state unit of *Bharat Gyan Vigyan Samiti*, so all the programmes decided at the national level are also implemented at the state level. The initial years of the *Bharat Gyan Vigyan Samiti* interventions in the literacy campaigns were marked by major social mobilizations. The *Bharat Gyan Vigyan Jatha*[34] organized between 2nd October and 14th of November 1990 was one of most ambitious mass mobilizations and motivational exercise the country and perhaps the whole world had ever witnessed. It involved more than 5000 artists and several thousands of organizers apart from large number of village, block and districts *Samitis* that were formed. These *Jathas* succeeded in generating a new sense of optimism in the minds of thousands of social activists, intellectuals and administrators, apart from lakhs and lakhs of ordinary men and women. *Bharat Gyan Vigyan Jatha* was conducted in about 330 out of the total 450 district of India including all districts of Himachal Pradesh[35] with the perspective to initiate a mass action for national regeneration to liberate India from, illiteracy, ill health, ignorance and poverty.

The achievement of *Bharat Gyen Gyan Vigyan Jatha*– 90 were not uniform all over the country and were weak especially in the state of Uttar Pradesh, Bihar, Rajasthan, and hence fresh *Kalajatha* programme was conceived by the *Bharat Gyan Vigyan Samiti*. The *Bharat Gyen Gyan Vigyan Jatha*-92[36] consisted of two main components viz. *Kalajatha* and teacher exchange programme. *Kalajatha* progemmes were to be organized mainly in the states of Uttar Pradesh, Bihar, Madhya Pradesh, Rajasthan and Orissa whereas the teacher exchange programmes were planned to expose teacher and students to excitement of innovative teaching-learning experiences.

The objectives of *Bharat Gyen Gyan Vigyan Jatha*-92 was to develop informal machinery for rapid information transfer and mutual reinforcement among literacy workers at all level and to reach every village in 250 districts with a call to stamp out illiteracy[37]

In view of the persistent demand for a special emphasis to mobilize women and focus on issues relating to literacy and women's equality the programme named as *'Samata' Gyan Vigyan Jatha*[38] of women was organized for education, equality and peace. It was felt that there was clearly a need for women to develop their abilities and shape within the literacy movement to emerge as leaders with an eye to carve out a place for women's issues on the agenda of the literacy movement. An important objective of the *'Samata Jatha'* was to forge a linkage between women's movement and women in the literacy campaign.

All India People's Science Movement was engaged in one major communication and mobilization exercises called *Hamara Desh*[39] (our Country) in between 15th of August 1993 and 28th of February, 1994, with the programme focused on encouraging local capability building for self-reliance. This campaign was conducted through diverse activities like *Bal Melas* or children festivals that brought together children and teachers from different places and spheres to share their experiences while living in other's home and thousands of such festivals were organized in different parts of the country including Himachal Pradesh[40]

Another programme 'Joy of learning'[41] was a means of developing interest in children towards education in general and science in particular. Learn and get inspired by science and technology form every day phenomena around as fun and not as fatigue. The joy of learning campaign was organized at *Gram Panchyat* level, block, district level and national level. At every level the programme was conducted for two different age groups i.e. 6-11 years and 12-14 years. Separate set of programmes was organized for each group. Apart from school going children, others like dropouts and non-school going children were also invited as participants.

'Desh Ko Jano Desh Ko Badlo',[42] was an initative to assist common mass as well as activists to examine analytically and critically the processes and products of development during the years after India' s freedom. The programme had two major streams of activities– educational and developmental. The educational activities comprise of exchanges on many subjects, such as, development of local economy, access to natural resources, public finance, power, tele- communications and transport, employment opportunities, *Panchayati Raj* etc. In case of developmental plans the programmes focused on encouraging local area planning and resource mapping and carried the message of local capability building for self-reliance.

The National Literacy Mission was set up by the Government of India in recognition of the need for priority attention to literacy for speeding up the development process and was launched by the Prime Minister of India on 5th may, 1988 with the objective to impart functional literacy. Up to November 2002, 587 districts out of 600 in the country had already been covered under the total literacy campaign, including *Mandi* district of Himachal Pradesh, of which 202 districts had entered the post literacy phase and 187 in the continuing education phase[43]. The goal of the National Literacy Mission was to attain full literacy i.e. a sustainable threshold level of 75 percent by 2005. The mission sought to achieve this goal by imparting functional literacy to non-literates in the 15-35 age groups. This age group had been the focus of attention because they are in the productive and reproductive period of life; the basic objective was to create a generation which would ensure that their children are educated to realize the dream of 'Education for All'[44].

At the backdrop of overwhelming fragmentations and prevailing differences, *Bharat Gyan Vigyan Samiti* perceived that common people should come together to thump the forces of darkness though they were small in number but were able to bludgeon. It is to help this process of coming together that the people's science movement conceived the nation wide Jatha on Peace, Unity and Sovereignty[45] as a reassertion and public articulation of our convictions and education in health, in promotion of science and self-reliant development. It had all been premised in the credence of three pillars of peace, unity and sovereignty.

With the right to education bill on the anvil for introduction on the parliament, all *Bharat Gyan Vigyan Samiti* state units were involved in a nationwide *Shiksha Samvad* that was initiated with the national education assembly held in July 2005 in Calicut.[46] It was decided in this assembly that state wide conventions and meeting be held which shall focus on the 'Right to Education' Bill.

The 'Continuing education' in literacy is a social engineering process having multifaceted dimensions of continuing the educational processes having its components in literacy, skill training, awareness buildup, information dissemination, cultural wake up etc. It is a polyvalent programme of education, which can be implemented only with the participation of all type of social organizations and institutions including local self-governments and people's movements. It is a total societal education in which people of all walks of life can take active part and derive benefits but the neo-literates, socially and economically deprived classes and women being at the central part.[47]

Continuing education was understood in the limited sense of providing some additional education to those who have concluded formal education. In developing countries like India, it was further limited to the objective of providing certain useful skills to those who have completed their basic literacy course. It was used to impart new skills to equip people to face the challenges as it is important to acquire the skill and culture of learning tolerant which leads us to the concept of a learning society where support is provided to all members of the society for facilitating learning in all situations in life. The *Jan Vachan Andolan* and *Jeevan Shala* Programmes both addressed learning and literacy solutions at the village level.[48] So the HGVS has undertaken large number of activities and programmes aimed at the vulnerable sectors so as to create society capable of understanding its problems, finding solutions and creating processes and systems for working out these solutions.

In the context of all these activities and programmes undertaken by the HGVS, in Himachal Pradesh we tried to ascertain the ground realities of working and performance through the present study. For this purpose a survey was carried out in Mandi District of Himachal Pradesh where the HGVS is operating quite actively. For the purpose of investigating the working and role performance of the HGVS the researcher interviewed, 150 office bearer beneficiaries and general public in the operational area, whose socio – economic profile and the opinion on the working and performance of the NGO is being presented in the following pages.

Sex-wise Distribution of Respondents

In order to make the sample representative, due weightage has to be given to both the sexes in the society, as both reactivity participating and taking benefits of the working of various voluntary organizations in the society. The respondents for the present study are from both the sexes as shown in the Table No. 4.15:-

Table No. 4.15: Sex-wise Distribution of Selected Respondents

Male	*Female*	*Total*
42	108	150
(28)	(72)	(100)

As the Table No 4.15 shows, out of total 150 respondents, 42 respondents are male whereas 108 are females which constitute 28 percent and 72 percent of the sample respectively as women are quite active in the organization, hence their number is more than the male respondents.

Marital Status of the Respondents

Marital status of the respondents is also quite important in order to select responsible and responsive respondents. Married people, due to their status, needs and aspirations are more responsible and also vigilant to the things happing around and they always try to derive benefits out of the activities of various organizations beneficial to them. The marital status of the respondents for the present study is as shown in Table No. 4.16:-

Table No. 4.16: Marital Status of the Respondents

Married	*Unmarried*	*Total*
138	12	150
(92)	(8)	(100)

As the Table No. 4.16 shows, out of total 150 respondents 138 are married and only 12 are unmarried. As such sample is constituted by 92 percent married and only 8 percent unmarried respondents. Married respondents are in majority as being more vigilant, conscious about the happening around and are more responsive and responsible.

Age-wise Distribution of Respondents

Age is also important factor in the selection of respondents. People belonging to active age group i.e. between 18 to 55 years are more vigilant and active in participation in the various activities taking place in the society in comparison to aged people. Young, at the same time, mature respondents, can understand the purpose of investigations and respond objectively to the quorries of the researcher. The respondents in the present study belong to the age group as shown in Table No. 4.17:-

Table No. 4.17: Age-wise Distribution of Respondents

18-35 years	*36-55 years*	*56-75 years*	*Total*
55	67	28	150
(37)	(45)	(18)	(100)

The data of the Table No. 4.17, reflects that 37 percent of the respondents belong to the age- group of 18-35 years; 45 percent belong to the age- group of 36-55 years and 18 percent respondents belong to the age- group of 56-75 years. Which means that majority of the respondents belong to active age- group who are involved in activities of HGVS.

Education-wise Distribution of Respondents

Education is an asset of an individual and plays a great role not only in bringing awareness among the individuals but also to create a powerful society. Educated individual can understand the role of various agencies working for the society and take benefit out them. They are also in better position to know and analyze the working and performance of any organization. Education wise the sample is constituted as given in Table No. 4.18:-

Table No. 4.18: Education-wise Distribution of Respondents

Up to X	*Up to XII*	*Up to Graduate*	*Up to Post-Graduate*	*Total*
62	49	27	12	150
(41)	(33)	(18)	(8)	(100)

As the Table No. 4.18 shows, 41 percent of the respondents are educated up to 10th standard, 33 percent are educated up to 12th level, 18 percent of them are graduates and 8 percent of the respondents are post-graduates. Though all the respondents are literate, yet majority of them are not well qualified. The Researcher while interviewing, observed that respondents belonging to the weaker sections are less qualified. However, the targeted respondents are qualified enough to understand the role, working and performance of the organization working around them.

Income-Wise Distributions of Respondents

Income is also an important aspect to empower an individual and everyone in the society is struggling to earn more and more. Though majority seeks livelihood yet rich seek power. Income status of an individual makes him/her responsible citizen who is always vigilant to the things around. Income-wise the sample is constituted as shown in Table No. 4.19:-

Table No. 4.19: Income-wise Distributions of Respondents

Income upto1 Lakh p.a.	*Up to 2 Lakh p.a.*	*above 2 Lakh p.a.*
48	69	33
(32)	(46)	(22)

As the Table No. 4.19: shows, out of total respondents 32 percent of them belong to Rs. 1 lakh per annum income group, 46 percent of them belong to Rs. 2 lakh p.a. income group and 22 percent of the respondents belong to above Rs. 2 lakh p.a. income group which means the sample is constituted by the people having reasonable resources with them to meet their needs and are in a position to participate in the activities and working of other organizations serving their causes.

Awareness about the NGO–HGVS

First and foremost thing for the office-bearer, officials, beneficiaries and public in general is to know about the organization, its objectives, programmes etc. Only then they can participate in its functioning and take benefit of various programmes of the organization. In order to know about the awareness and popularity of the organization among the people the respondents were asked whether they know about the organization named *Himachal Gyan Vigyan Samiti* (HGVS) and the responses are as given in the Table No. 4.20:-

Table No. 4.20: Awareness about the NGO-HGVS

To a Great Extent	*To Some Extent*	*Not at all*	*Total*
71	50	29	150
(48)	(33)	(19)	(100)

As the data in the Table No. 4.20: shows, 48 percent of the respondents are aware about the *Himachal Gyan Vigyan Samiti* to a great extent, 33 percent respondents are aware of it to some extent and 19 percent are not at all aware about the NGO- HGVS, which leads to the conclusion that majority of the respondents are well aware of the NGO-HGVS. Certainly office bearers and beneficiaries are more aware in comparison to non-beneficiaries, who may not be utilizing the services of the NGO.

Awareness about the working of HGVS

Society should not only know about the NGO's around them but also should be aware of their programmes and working and people should participate in their activities so as to derive benefits from the working of NGO's. In order to know about this fact, respondents were asked whether they know about the working of NGO-HGVS and the response are as given in Table No. 4.21:-

Table No. 4.21: Awareness about the Working of HGVS

To a great extent	*To some extent*	*Not at all*	*Total*
70	47	33	150
(47)	(31)	(22)	(100)

As the Table No. 4.21 indicates 47 percent respondents are aware of the working of the NGO to a great extent, 31 percent are aware to some extent, whereas 22 percent are not at all aware about the working of the NGO-HGVS in their area, which leads to the conclusion that majority of the respondents are aware of the working of the NGO- HGVS and as such in a position to take benefits of the activities, programmes and services of the organization.

Services being provided by HGVS

The beneficiaries should also be aware of the services being rendered by the NGO, so as to derive benefits out of them and comment on the working and performance of the organization. In order to know about the awareness of services being provided, the respondants were asked as to what services are being provided by HGVS and the responses are as given in Table No. 4.22:-

Table No. 4.22: Services being provided by HGVS

Awareness/campaigning about Literacy	*Women Empowerment*	*Science Education Among children*	*Total*
63	52	35	150
(42)	(35)	(23)	(100)

As the Table No. 4.22 reveals, out of the total respondents, 42 percent explained that HGVS is conducting literacy awareness campaigns, 35 percent said that it is working for the empowerment of women whereas 23 percent believed that it is working to popularize science education amongst the children in the area, which leads to the conclusion that people are aware of the working programmes and services being rendered by the NGO.

Benefit of Services Being Provided by HGVS

Services being rendered, programmes being undertaken by an organization can be termed as useful only if the people believe that they are being benefited by them by way of knowledge, awareness, more participation or resource mobilizations. As such the selected respondent were asked if they believe that people are being benefited with the services of HGVS and believe that NGO is performing well, the responses are as given in Table No. 4.23:-

Table No. 4.23: Benefit of Services and Performance of the NGO- HGVS

To a Great Extent	*To Some Extent*	*Not at all*	*Total*
81	62	07	150
(54)	(41)	(5)	(100)

As the Table No. 4.23 shows, 54 percent of the respondents believed that activities being undertaken and services being provided by the NGO-HGVS are benefitting them and the NGO is performing well to a great extent, 41 percent believed to be benefitted to some extent whereas 5 percent of them responded that they are not at all being benefitted, may be that these people are not actively participating in the activities of the NGO, whereas majority of the respondents believed that they have been benefitted with the programmes undertaken by the NGOs – HGVS and it is performing well.

The available data through secondary sources i.e. annual reports and other literature of the NGO-HGVS shows that the organization is well established and quite systematic in its area of operation. It has got a democratically elected organizational structure, right from the *Panchayat* ward level to state level and all its office-bearers are duly elected at their respective levels. Organizational units of the NGO have clearly defined membership and office-bearers and the formation of conference, council, committee, core group etc. is being done accordingly. The NGO has got well defined objectives and working accordingly in the thrust areas such as literacy, women empowerment, and popularizing science and technology development, environmental protection, participatory democracy, gender issues and library movement. The NGO campaigned vigorously through its

Kala *Jathas* to sensitize the masses about various issues of the society. Its literacy programmes have been quite popular as well as successful and people have been benefited with them.

The field investigations about the working and role performance of HGVS lead to the conclusions that it is quite popular in its area of operation. People are conversant with the activities, working and programmes being undertaken by the NGO. The services provided by the HGVS have proved quite useful and the targeted population has been benefitted with the programme and services of the NGO to a great extent. People believe that the NGO-HGVS is performing its role and activity well.

Society for Participatory Research in Asia (PRIA)

In 1978 an informal network of adult education inspired by Paulo Ferries and Myles Horton, the two pioneers of education for social change, constituted a forum for promoting Participatory Research in Asia, along with four other colleagues- Dr Anita Dighe, Dr. Walter Fernandes, Prem Chadha and Ganesh Pandey. Dr Rajesh Tandon started the Society for Participatory Research in Asia in February 1982, to promote the practice of participatory research as a contribution to knowledge building and social transformation. Society for Participatory Research in Asia began to emerge as an epistemological intervention, generating Knowledge from Below.[49]

Vision and objectives

Society for Participatory Research in Asia's (PRIAs) vision is of a world where informed, empowered citizen participate in the process of deepening democracy with tolerance towards its large numbers and diversity. These include the marginalized especially women. Citizens rights and responsibilities are nurtured through a balance between authority and accountability. A harmony between economic and social development is sought in an eco- friendly manner where local priorities are not sacrificed to global demands. Individual freedom and autonomy is sustained with collective solidarity. Its vision of a desirable world is based on values of equity, justice, freedom, peace and solidarity with a philosophy taken forward in all its actions 'Knowledge is Power.'[50]

The vision is to work towards the promotion of policies, institutions and capacities that strengthen the voices against marginalization of community and increase the participation of the marginalized in society. The idea is to improve their socio-economic status through democratic governance. PRIA's mission is to reach out through such governance to everyone in society and to ease their participation in the governance process[51].

Objectives

The basic objective of PRIA in India was to empower the marginalized, the poor, the depressed, women, *Dalits* and *Trials*. PRIA, meaning "beloved" in Hindi, broadened its mandate to include democratic governance in addition to or as a counterfoil to citizen participation. As per new strategic framework of PRIA 'Governance Where People Matter' is an attempt to integrate and converge different interventions in a holistic manner. The overall objective is to improve the standard of living of the marginalized families through their active participation in the effective utilization of development services, direct intervention of PRIA to yield effective voice of new leadership; and transparent and accountable self-governing institutions.[52]

PRIA launched a visionary initiative ' Strengthening Citizen Leadership and Citizen Collectives' which intends to mobilize and facilitate informal community based network and citizen associations that are working towards development issues at local levels for collective action. The initiative aims to build a network of democratically governed sensitized institutions and groups promoting voluntary action at grassroot level, managed with collective leadership.[53]

Organizational Structure

PRIA as a NGO is constituted by a Chairman, President, Treasure and Members. At present its office bearers are:-

Ms. Sheila Patel– Chairperson PRIA and founder-director of Society of Promotion of Area Resource Centre (SPARC), a voluntary of origination based in Mumbai.

Shri K. Shiva Kumar– Treasurer is a Chartered Accountant and is the Director of V. K. Foundation Gandhi Gram, Tamil Nadu.

Dr Rajesh Tandon– President and co-founder of PRIA

Ms. Lalita Ramdas– Member, has been active in literacy, non-formal education and women's empowerment issues in India and internationally.

Dr H. N. Saiyed– Member, is presently Director of National Institute of Occupational Health (NIOH), Ahmadabad.

Dr N. C. Sexena– Member is former Secretary, Planning Commission.

Shri Joe Madiath– Member, is the Founder– Director of a Voluntary organization, GRAM VIKAS, Ganjam, Orissa

MS Rita Sarin- Member is the Country Director of the Hunger Project, New Delhi.[54]

Key Resource Providers

PRIA is funded by the following agencies.

- CORDAID, the Netherlands
- IIZ/ DVV,Germany
- Institute of Development Studies (IDS),UK
- Ministry of Rural Development Agency (SIDA), New Delhi, India
- Swiss Agency for Development and Cooperation (SDC),New Delhi, India
- The Ford Foundation, New Delhi India [55]

Income and Expenditure Statement of PRIA for the period 2002-2003 to 2006-07, as shown in the Annual Reports, is given in the Table No. 4.24:-

Table No 4.24: Income and Expenditure of PRIA

Year	*Income*	*Expenditure*	*Balance*
2002-03	75.82	62.23	13.59
2003-04	82.82	71.81	11.01
2004-05	92.54	83.30	9.24
2005-06	93,661	94,676	1007
2006-07	2, 14,639	2, 03,639	11000

Programmes, Working and Performance of the Organization

PRIA has evolved its programmatic focus while responding to changing context and anticipating emerging trends. To understand its dynamic growth, its history is divided into six phases. Each phase follows a common intervention strategy, with the overall aim to empower the marginalized– the poor, oppressed, women, *Dalits* and the *Tribals.*

In each phase, the marginalized are taught to participate in decision making and governance thereby empowering them. Their learning is consistently organized around the constituency they belong to and the sector they represent. Each phase has strengthened the emerging relationship between local and global issues, between micro and macro actions and contributed bridging the gap between learning and doing.

In the first phase, 1981-1985,[56] grassroots groups were encouraged to act on the knowledge they possessed, to help them on the way, voluntary development organizations were trained on participatory methodologies.

In the second phase, 1986-1989,[57] voluntary development organizations were briefed on topic such as organizational management and participatory planning and monitoring. They were assisted with institutional capacity building support. Women oriented activities and literacy - based activities were supported.

In the third phase, 1989-1993,[58] a number of support organizations in different states of the country were promoted to provide context-specific support to local groups. There were campaigns on dust-related lung diseases. The emergence of the Voluntary Action Network India was supported.

In the fourth phase, 1994-1998,[59] direct work was initiated on strengthening *Panchayati Raj* Instuitions Trade Union and Non-Governmental Organizations. Doctors were sensitized on issues of occupational and environmental health. Network of collaborating regional support organization was formalized as a vehicle for undertaking joint programmes.

In the fifth phase, 1999-2000,[60] as an active member of global forums like International Forum on Capacity Building, SAARC Forum of support organizations, NGOS, Working group on the World Bank, CIVICUS, and World Alliance for Citizen Participation, Development Research Centre etc., PRIA got a unique opportunity to bring the voices and perspectives of the grassroots to influence global policies.

In the sixth phase 2000 onwards[61] series of events have been generating opportunities for evaluation of society for Participatory Research in Asia interventions. A convention in Bhopal, on Citizenship, Participation and Democracy, in November 1999, enabled the sharing of experiences from all over the country. This built up to a series of workshops during the 20th anniversary of PRIA on the theme 'Governance Where People Matter', which provided an occasion to take stock of the past and envision the future. An external evaluation of Panchayati Raj Institution programmes in May, 2002 highlighted many achievements and some recommendations for the future. Five key strategic considerations emerged in 2007 that hold relevance for the future: promotion of accountable and transparent governance; assurance of greater voice and influence of ordinary citizens on governance issues; reform of governance institutions; seeking of sensitive and strategic interventions that build civil society platforms, coalitions and partnerships that promote democratic governance; and reform interventions of all public institution.[62]

The village communities have been in existence in India for over centuries and *Panchayats* have been part of these communities since then. During the time of the Rig Veda (1200 B.C.), evidence suggests that self-governing village bodies called *Sabhas* and *Samitis* existed. The passage of time saw these bodies evolve into *Panchayats* (council of five persons) and they were functional institutions of grassroots governance in almost every village. The village *Panchayat* or elected council had large powers both executive and judicial.[63]

It was during British rule that the autonomy of *Panchayats* disappeared gradually with the establishment of local civil and criminal courts, revenue and police organizations, the increase in communications, the growth of individualism and the operation of the *Ryotwari* (Landholder wise) systems against the *Mahalwari* (village tenure system)[64]

During the clamor for *Swaraj* or self-rule leaders of the freedom movement could not agree on the status and role to be assigned to the institutions of rural local self-government. Gandhi was in favor of village *Swaraj* and strengthening of the village Panchayat to the fullest extent. But B.R. Ambedkar believed that the villages represent a regressive India, a source of oppression. The model state had to be built with safeguards against such social oppression and the only way it could be done was through the adoption of the parliamentary model of politics. The drafting of the Constitution for Independent India saw *Panchayati Raj* Institutions placed in the non- justifiable part of the constitution, the Directive Principles of State Policy, as article 40 and it reads: "the state shall take steps to organize village *Panchayats* and endow them with such powers and authority as may be necessary to enable them to function as units of self- government"[65]. However, no worthwhile legislation was immediately enacted either at the national or state level to implement it.

In the past 40 years since the adoption of the Constitution, *Panchayati Raj* Institutions have traveled from the non-justifiable part of the Constitution to one where, through a separate amendment, a whole new status has been added to their history. This was the 73rd Amendment and its coming into existence was the result of increasing recognition that the institutional initiatives of the preceding decade had not delivered, that the extent of rural poverty was still much too large and thus the existing structure of government needed to be reformed.[66]

Society for Participatory Research in Asia pioneered strengthening *Panchayati Raj* Institutions programme in seven States of the country in early 1995, just after first ever democratic elections to constitutional *Panchayats* were held in most of the states. It campaigned for the proper conduct of *Gram Sabha* Meetings in 6865 *Panchayats* in 17 States of India. The campaign involved youth, women, *dalits* and *tribals* to participate in the deliberations and decision making in *Gram Sabha* in ways meaningful to everyone in the community. It also assisted in the preparation of micro plans at the *Panchayat* level in 685 villages around the country in an attempt to address and prioritise the real issue of local people.[67]

Since a large percentage of elected *Panchayat* representatives were entering public offices for the first time, PRIA pioneered many innovative approaches to their capacity building. Over this period, nearly 120,000 elected *Panchayat* representatives were trained by PRIA; of these, nearly half were, women *Panchayat* leaders and 17570 were *Dalit Panchayat* representatives. PRIA provided ongoing field support to representatives through *Panchayat* Resource Centers at the block level in 73 locations.[68]

PRIA under its current framework' Governance Where People Matter'[69] has been working towards qualitative improvement in rural governance by capacity building of elected representatives and enhancing people's participation. Bottlenecks like lack of devolution of finances to *Panchayats;* tied funds and reluctance towards internal resource generation have created constraints for *Panchayat Raj* Institutions to be agents of social and economic development. Non-implementation of *Gram Sabha* resolutions put a break on the initial enthusiasm among people to participate in this very important grassroot level democratic institution.

A series of multi stakeholder dialogues were initiated at district level in several States including Himachal Pradesh, which brought elected representatives, municipal officials, block and district level government functionaries within the administration and Para statal bodies together with other stakeholders like citizen forum, Central Statistical Organization Non-Governmental Organization, media and academician looking for solution to common problems. The district level interface meeting was followed by state level multi stakeholder dialogues on issue of urban governance. These were successful in bringing state level political leadership and bureaucracy on a common platform with civil society organization for the first time on issues of urban governance.[70]

A series of development fairs were organized in the people friendly *Mela* mode in Himachal Pradesh. The event aimed at providing space and platform for local people from various stakeholder groups to informally interact and exchange a range of information amongst each other, with a focus on issues related to *Panchayati Raj* Institutions. The themes touched upon during the event included *Gram-Sabha* mobilization, information on development programmes of the state government, encouraging participation of women, schedule caste and tribes and other governance related issues. The audience targeted at included women, schedule castes and tribes, youths, self-help groups, members of *Gram Sabha*.[71]

In order to operationalize this programme framework two broad categories of interventions were attempted; strengthening civil society is a bottom–up process for generating pressure from below and articulation of demands from the marginalized sections of society; reforming governance institutions is a process of sensitization, orientation and capacitating of elected representatives and government officials so that they can respond and supply resources towards the priorities and needs being articulated through such voices.[72]

PRIA's Area of Operation or Area of Intervention

PRIA's intervention is an attempt to build new linkages between these voices and governance institutions creating and sustaining interface between demand and supply, voice and response as shown below.[73]

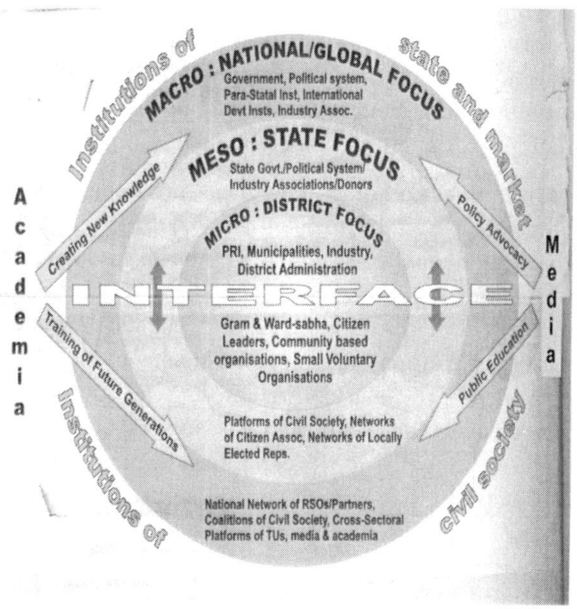

Programmes, Working and Performance of PRIA in Himachal Pradesh

In Himachal Pradesh PRIA's strategy was knowledge building, policy advocacy and capacity building. The efforts to work with state government and elected representatives to influence the 12th Finance commission were an important initiative. The 12th Finance Commission had been clearly mandated by Government of India not only to review progress of financial devolution to local bodies in light of the recommendations of 11th Finance commission but also to suggest principles for taxation and financial devolution in future.

The state resource centre in Shimla prepared a report based on the critical appraisal of recommendations and implementation of the two state finance commissions for local bodies. The process of preparation of the document involved state government; using its own data, local elected representatives of the three tiers of *Panchayati Raj* Institutions and other civil society groups. PRIA encouraged elected representatives particularly *Zila-Parishad* leaders to ask the 12th Finance Commission to have a dialogue with them as well, during its visit to the state. Since the Government of Himachal Pradesh was the host of 12th Finance Commission visit, PRIA had to undertake a balancing act of being included and yet not being seen as excluding those selected by the state government itself. The two elected representatives *(Pradhans)* from PRIA's micro field area, *Kangra* and *Hamirpur* Districts and other eight elected representatives, selected by government were briefed on the findings of the report prepared by PRIA. The meeting with 12th Finance Commission itself was a tame affair, though the Chairperson of 12th Finance Commission had both official report (which painted a rather positive picture of devolution) and the PRIA's report, (based on ground realities). The closing comment by the Chairperson and follow–up by state government since then, clearly endorsed the need for more effective financial devolution to local bodies in the state. Similar efforts are being made in several other state to ensure that the authentic voice of elected representatives and critical issues on the ground are effectively communicated to 12th Finance Commission[74].

Systematic and structured collaboration with academic institutions to promote teaching and research on participatory research, participatory development, civil society and democratic governance have been initiated by PRIA more than ten years ago. Inter professional Dialogues with schools of social work under the leadership of ASSWI were held during 1994-98. Five regional resource centers in the selected schools were setup during

2000 to further this effort. During the past three years, systematic seminars and joint collaborative efforts had been promoted in a number of universities and colleges across 18 states in India including Himachal Pradesh University Shimla.[75]

Reforming Governance requires learning about governance itself, governance institutions and how to engage with them, elected representatives of *Panchayats* and municipalities need to learn how to perform their new public roles, government officials need to learn how to work with the new governance framework; citizens need to learn how to participate in these opportunities; and intermediary civil society organizations need to learn how to intervene to make governance accountable.[76]

PRIA interventions supported learning on governance for these different stakeholders throughout this period. A large number of *Panchayat* representatives were provided orientation on their roles, importance of *Gram Sabha,* methods of micro planning and interfacing with government, officials-4337 *Sarpanchs* and ward *Panchs* were provided such learning opportunities in six states including Himachal Pradesh where 280 *Sarpanchs* and ward *Panchs* were oriented.[77]

Special efforts continued to be made to prepare women leaders to engage with governance institutions and processes more vigorously. More than 20,000 women leaders were provided such learning opportunities through structured events and exposure programmes nationwide in 12 states in India including Himachal Pradesh.[78]

In many locations of PRIA and partner's intervention area, the village/ ward level citizens collectives have been connected through the promotion of networks at the block or sub-block levels. The networks are gaining visibility by interfacing with higher tiers of governance institutions like *Panchayati Samities* and *Zila-Parshads.* Although most of these networks are in the nascent stage, they have made a modest beginning. A variety of interventions have been undertaken to nurture and strengthen these citizen networks. Regular meetings and structured workshops have been conducted to develop an understanding on the purpose of building large collectives and the management of networks. The citizen leaders found these networks working as mechanism for nurturing solidarity and for exchanging learning. In Himachal Pradesh in *Baijnath, Kangra, Rait* block of *Kangra* district and *Hamirpur* and *Bhoranj* block of *Hamirpur* district, the mobilization and informational process is spearheaded by the *Panchayat Mitras* who move from village to village conducting initial orientations with *Mahila*

Mandals and then facilitating this process by holding combined meetings of many Mahila Manuals at the block level or at any other preferred location. These block level meetings are generally facilitated by PRIA staff and or some invited block departmental official, where information regarding *Gram Sabha, Panchayats* micro-planning, need for citizen leadership and initiative, gender discrimination and other social stigmas are discussed. In this endeavor, interface and collaboration with the *Mukhya Sevika* and other block officials is sought and their services utilized. These efforts are bearing fruits as the citizen leaders, oriented and involved through this process are playing a key role through attending *Gram Sabhas* and initiating ward *Sabhas* and micro planning in their respective wards and *Panchayats*. A total of 236 grassroot networks in rural areas and 55 grassroot networks in urban areas have been promoted in 12 states including 95 rural and 10 urban networks in Himachal Pradesh.[79]

Dharamshala is one of the most visited tourist places in Himachal Pradesh, yet *Dharamshala* municipality is not a problem free area. Sanitation is one of the biggest problems in the town. The number of garbage disposal bins within the municipal limit were limited and the *Safai Karamcharis* seem to be accountable to no one. People living in this town believe that the numerous *Nalas* (drains) fllowing through the town form a natural garbage dump. What they don't consider is that the garbage eventually collects on the banks of these very *Nalas*. The efforts of mobilizing people in ward 2 of *Dharamshala* municipality area through a number of ward meetings finally proved to be successful when the residents got together and formed a rotating monitoring committee, which would stand guard near the *Nalas* every morning, the time most people throw garbage, and stop the defaulters. The problem has visibly reduced and at present they are planning to involve the municipality in dealing with the garbage disposal problem in their ward.[80]

In *Hamirpur* municipality in *Hamirpur* district, the participation of people in the municipal functioning is negligible. There is no formal interaction between the ward councilor and residents of the ward. People often do not participate in urban elections, as they have become apathetic to development and governance. In an effort to bring the residents of ward and their Ward-Councilor on the same platform, an interface between the councilor and the citizens was given the name *Seedhi Baat'. First "Seedhi Baat"* was organized in ward 5 of the Municipal Council. The success of first *"Seedhi Baat"* and good coverage given to it by media led to flooding of requests to facilitate similar processes in other wards as well. Candidate announced that after winning the election he would form *Mahilla Samities* to monitor the municipal functioning and make the system transparent and accountable. The candidate got a round of applause and appreciation from the citizens. Finally the battle was won by the candidate who had promised the involvement of people in the functioning of municipality.[81]

In terms of the objectives, programmes, working and role performance of the NGO- PRIA, field investigations had been carried out in two districts of Himachal Pradesh i.e. *Kangra* and *Hamirpur*. The selected respondents were asked various questions through structured Questionnaire-cum-Interview Schedule by the researcher and their responses are being presented in the following tables along with the analyses so as to analyse the working and role performance of the non- governmental organization. Total intervention of PRIA in 25 *Panchayats* of 5 blocks of two districts is as given below in Table No. 4.25:-

Table No. 4.25: PRIA's Area of Intervention

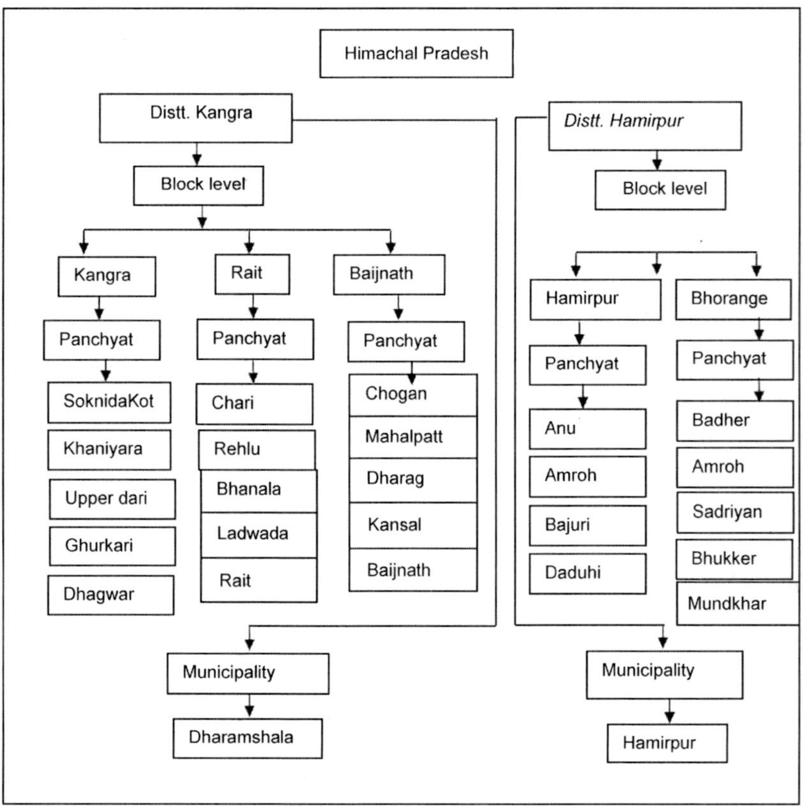

Field investigations provided a great role and responsibility to respondents as they are the primary source of data for the study. The respondents should be well aware of the working and performance of the organization and should know the purpose of investigations so that they could provide true and unbiased information. In the present study an effort has been made to seek the responses from the different sections of the society where the organization PRIA is working. The respondents selected for the present study are beneficiaries of the NGO PRIA from 3 different development blocks of *Kangra* district, 2 development blocks of *Hamirpur* district and municipal council of *Dharamshala* in *Kangra* district and municipal council of *Hamirpur town* from *Hamirpur* district. The socio-economic background of the respondents is as given in the following tables:

The respondents selected from the different *Gram Panchayats* and municipalities are distributed as given in Table No. 4.26:-

Table No. 4.26: District-wise distribution of respondents

Kangra	*Hamirpur*	*Total*
90	60	150
(60)	(40)	(100)

As shown in Table No 3.26: 90, selected respondents are from district *Kangra* which constitutes 60 percent of the respondents whereas 60 respondents are from *Hamirpur* district which constitutes 40 percent of the total respondent's as such due representation has been given to the district under study, keeping in view the size and the population of each district.

Age-wise Distributions of Selected Respondents

Age is an important factor of respondents as the participation in the various activities of the organizations is certainly affected by age factor. The selected respondents belong to the age group as shown in Table No. 4.27:-

Table No. 4.27: Age-wise Distributions of Selected Respondents

	18-35 years	*36-55 years*	*56-75 Years*	*Total*
Kangra Block	39 (52)	22 (29)	14 (19)	75 (100)
Hamirpur Block	22 (49)	18 (40)	5 (11)	45 (100)

(*Contd...*)

Dharamshala (M.C)	7 (47)	6 (40)	2 (13)	15 (100)
Hamirpur (M. C)	8 (53)	4 (27)	3 (20)	15 (100)
Total	76 (51)	50 (33)	24 (16)	150 (100)

As the Table no 4.27 shows, 51 percent of the respondents are from 18-35 years age- group, 33 percent from 36 -56 years age- group and 16 percent from 56-75 years age- group. Majority of the respondents are form 18-35 years age-group which is certainly a young and dynamic age- group and has the capacity to understand and know the role and working of any organization and urge to participate and derive benefits from various organizations working in the society.

Sex-Wise Distribution of Respondents

Sex is another important social factor in the society Traditionally India was a male-dominated society but now the female sex is also getting equal opportunities and they do understood the role and working of various organization and women themselves are actively participating in the activities of the NGOs. For the present study due representation has been given to both sexes and their distribution is as given in Table No. 4.28:-

Table No. 4.28: Sex-wise Distribution of Respondents

	Male	*Female*	*Total*
Kangra Block	34 (45)	41 (55)	75 (100)
Hamirpur Block	26 (58)	19 (42)	45 (100)
Dharamshala (M.C)	8 (54)	7 (46)	15 (100)
Hamirpur (M. C)	9 (60)	6 (40)	15 (100)
Total	77 (51)	73 (49)	150 (100)

As the Table No. 4.28 shows, among the total respondents 51 percent are male members and 49 percent are female members which clearly indicate that women are also active in the NGO and the present sample comprises both the sexes of the society equally.

Education-wise Distribution of Respondents

Education has an important role in the overall growth of individual's knowledge and understanding also plays very important role in understanding the various issues and problems of the society. Respondents should be educated enough to understand the issues and purpose of the investigation and should respond to the querries honestly with complete understanding and should provide necessary information without any prejudice and ill-will. Education certainly enables in this regard. Education-wise distribution of the respondents in the present study is, as given in Table No. 4.29:-

Table No. 4.29: Education-wise Distributions of Respondents

	Up to 10th	*up to12th*	*up to Graduate*	*PG and above*	*Total*
Kangra Block	16 (21)	30 (40)	24 (32)	5 (7)	75 (100)
Hamirpur Block	16 (36)	21 (47)	6 (13)	2 (4)	45 (100)
Dharamshala (M.C)	3 (20)	7 (47)	5 (33)	Nil	15 (100)
Hamirpur (M.C)	2 (13)	8 (53)	5 (34)	Nil	15 (100)
	37 (25)	66 (44)	40 (27)	7 (4)	150 (100)

As the Table No. 4.29 shows, 25 percent respondents are educated up to 10th standard, 44 percent are educated up to 12th level, 27 percent are graduates and 4 percent of the respondents are post graduates meaning thereby that majority of the respondents are educated enough to understood the purpose and issues of the study and they can respond to the querries of the present study.

Income-Wise Distributions of Respondents

Income of an individual is yet another factor influencing individual knowledge and understanding; the resourceful have access to various agencies and information portals whereas the resourceless may not be having access to various socio economic and political activities taking place in a given society. Those who are worried more about their two square meals are not being expected to take interest in the academic activities and may not like to respond. In order to know the economic background of the respondents, the study provides income wise distribution of respondents which is as given in Table No. 4.30:-

Table No. 4.30: Income-wise Distributions of Respondents

	Up to 1 lakh p.a.	*up to 2 lakh p.a.*	*above 2 lakh p.a.*	*Total*
Kangra Block	32 (43)	28 (37)	15 (20)	75 (100)
Hamirpur Block	21 (47)	13 (29)	11 (24)	45 (100)
Dharamshala (M.C)	5 (33)	8 (54)	2 (13)	15 (100)
Hamirpur (M. C)	6 (40)	7 (47)	2 (13)	15 (100)
	64 (43)	56 (37)	30 (20)	150 (100)

As the Table No. 4.30 shows, 43 percent of the respondents have their annual income up to Rs. 1 lakh, 37 percent up to Rs. 2 lakh whereas 20 percent respondents have their annual income above Rs. 2 lakh, which leads to the conclusion that respondents for the present study are from a reasonable financial background without worries about two square meals and can respond to the querries independently and impartially without any considerations.

Awareness about the NGO-PRIA

First and foremost thing for the office-bearers, officials, beneficiaries and public in general is to know about the organization, its objectives, programmes and working only then they can participate its activities and take benefit of various programmes of the organization. In order to know about the awareness of the respondents and popularity of the organization among the people the respondents were asked whether they know about the organization named PRIA, its objectives programme etc. and the responses are as given in Table No. 4.31:-

Table No. 4.31: Awareness about the NGO-PRIA

	To a great extent	*To some extent*	*Not at all*	*Total*
Kangra Block	39 (52)	24 (32)	12 (16)	75 (100)
Hamirpur Block	22 (49)	12 (27)	11 (24)	45 (100)
Dharamshala (M.C)	9 (60)	6 (40)	Nil	15 (100)
Hamirpur (M.C)	8 (53)	7 (47)	Nil	15 (100)
	78 (52)	49 (33)	23 (15)	150 (100)

As the Table No. 4.31 reveals, 52 percent of the respondents are well aware about the NGO, 33 percent are aware to some extent about the NGO whereas 15 percent are not at all aware about the NGOs which leads to the conclusion that majority of the respondents are aware of the NGO and they know about its organization, objectives and programmes.

Awareness about Working of PRIA

Knowledge about the working of an organization is must to the beneficiaries only then they can derive benefits out of that. Are they aware of the role and working of the NGO, PRIA, and this question was put to the respondents and the response is as given in Table No. 4.32:-

Table No. 4.32: Awareness about Working of PRIA

	To a great extent	*To some extent*	*Not at all*	*Total*
Kangra Block	30 (40)	28 (37)	17 (23)	75 (100)
Hamirpur Block	16 (36)	18 (40)	11 (24)	45 (100)
Dharamshala (M.C)	8 (53)	7 (47)	Nil	15 (100)
Hamirpur (M.C)	9 (60)	6 (40)	Nil	15 (100)
	63 (42)	59 (39)	28 (19)	150 (100)

As the Table No. 4.32 shows, 43 percent of the respondents are well aware of the role and working of PRIA whereas 39 percent are aware to some extent but 18 percent of the respondents are not at all aware of the role and working of PRIA which leads to the conclusion that majority of the respondent know as to what PRIA is and what for it is working.

Services Being Provided by PRIA

The beneficiaries should also be aware of the services being given by the NGO so as to derive benefits out of them and to assess the performance of the organizations. In order to know about the awareness of services being given by PRIA, the selected respondents were asked as to what services are being provided by PRIA and the responses are, as given in Table No. 4.33:-

Table No. 4.33: Services Being Provided by PRIA

	Awareness campaigns about local governance	*Capacity building of the masses*	*People- experts Interface*	*Total*
Kanga Block	34	23	18	75
	(45)	(31)	(24)	(100)
Hamirpur Block	23	17	5	45
	(51)	(38)	(11)	(100)
Dharamshala	8	5	2	15
(M.C)	(53)	(34)	(13)	(100)
Hamirpur (M. C)	6	7	2	15
	(40)	(47)	(13)	(100)
	71	52	27	150
	(47)	(35)	(18)	(100)

As the Table No. 4.33 reveals, 47 percent respondents believed that PRIA is conducting awareness campaigns for local governance, 35 percent responded that it is ensuring capacity building of the masses and 18 percent replied that PRIA is organizing people- expert interface services in the society. This leads to the conclusion that PRIA is rendering useful services for the benefit of the people so as to awaken them and empower them especially the marginalized section of the society. Awareness of the respondents also lead to the conclusion that they can analyze the performance of the NGO.

Benefit of the Services of PRIA

Services being rendered by an organization can be termed as useful only if the people believe that they are being benefitted by them by way of knowledge, awareness, participation, mobilization etc. and there is over all change in the lives of the people especially weaker sections usefulness of the services also prove the working and the performance of the organizations. In order to analyze the role of PRIA in this regard, the selected respondents were asked if they believe that people are being benefitted by the services being rendered by the NGO PRIA and the responses are as given in the Table No. 4.34:-

Table No. 4.34: Benefit of the Services of PRIA

	To a great extent	*To some extent*	*Not at all*	*Total*
Kangra Block	33 (44)	26 (35)	16 (21)	75 (100)
Hamirpur Block	25 (56)	13 (29)	7 (15)	45 (100)

(Contd...)

Dharamshala (M.C)	9 (60)	6 (40)	Nil	15 (100)
Hamirpur (M.C)	8 (53)	7 (47)	Nil	15 (100)
	75 (50)	52 (35)	23 (15)	150 (100)

As the Table No. 4.34 shows, 50 percent of the respondents believed that they have been benefited to a great extent with services being provided by PRIA, 35 percent believed this to some extent and 15 percent believed that they have not been benefited at all with the services being rendered by PRIA, which leads to the conclusion that PRIA is rendering useful services to the people so as to awaken them and empower them especially the marginalized sections and majority of the people are being benefited which show that the NGO is performing well by way of its activities, programmes and various services.

From the available document about the organization, objectives, and programmers of the NGO-PRIA, it comes out that it is a well established organization working in India and Himachal Pradesh and has also been covered fully by it. It has got well defined organizational structure right from national level to provincial level with clear objectives and people oriented programmes. PRIA is quite effective in *Kangra* and *Hamirpur* district of Himachal Pradesh and providing very useful services by way of training the newly elected *Panchayat* representatives especially the marginalized sections of the society so as to bring qualitative improvement in rural governance by capacity building of the elected representatives and enhancing people's participation. PRIA has made the voice of the representatives to be heard by the authorities and helped in creating accountable and transparent self-governing institutions.

The available documents and primary information from the office bearer and beneficiaries of PRIA leads to conclusion that it has got well defined organization from national level to block level and its objectives are to empower the marginalized sections, the poor, women *'dalits'* and *'tribals'*. Its mandate includes democratic governance through people participation. PRIA is working for improvement of standard of living of the marginalized section of the society through their active participations in the effective utilizations of development resources. Its direct intervention has led to the effective voice of the new leadership, transparent and accountable self- governing institutions, and democratically governed sensitized institutions and groups promoting voluntary action at the grass-root level managed with collective leadership.

PRIA took the initiative to train the newly elected *Panchayat* representatives, to strength *Panchayat Raj* Institutions, vigorous campaigning, awakened the masses to make effective use of *Gram Sabha.* It assisted in the preparation of micro plans at the *Panchayat* level and to prioritize the real issue. PRIA has also helped to sensitize the representative to raise resources locally and as such helped a lot to enhance the people participations and capacity building.

In Himachal Pradesh, PRIA initiated effectively in knowledge building, policy advocacy and capacity building especially in two important districts of State i.e. *Kangra* and *Hamirpur.* It got represented through PRIs representative the need for effective devaluation of financial resources in the state. PRIA collaborated with academic institutions especially Himachal Pradesh University to promote teaching and research in participatory development, civil society and democratic governance. PRAI took special initiative to prepare women leader to engage with governance institution and processes.

The analysis of programmers undertaken, working and performance of PRIA leads to conclusion that the organization is working actively and performing effective role in strengthening new *Panchayati Raj* Institutions by sensitizing people at grassroot level, people's representative, the officers and the officials dealing with these institutions. PRIA vigorously campaigned for proper conduct of *Gram Sabha* meetings, assisted in preparing micro planning at the *Panchayat* level, pioneered the innovative approaches for the capacity building of first time entrants of *Panchayati Raj* Institutions, provided ongoing field support to elected representatives of *Panchayati Raj* Institutions, worked for qualitative improvement in rural governance by capacity building of elected representative and enhancing peoples participation; spread awareness among the people over 'NREGA', Girl Child Education and Devolution of power to *Panchayati Raj* Institutions. Special programmes were implemented for girl child education in educationally backward areas. The organization worked with overall objective to improve the standard of living of the marginalized sections through their active participation in the effective utilizations of development resources. PRIA as such has a great impact in bringing out 'effective' voice of new leadership and transparent and accountable self-governance institutions.

The selected respondents from *Kangra* and *Hamirpur* district represent respective population proportionately and belong to young and dynamic age group and reasonably qualified to assess the role, working and performance of the NGO and are well a ware of the organization, objective and performance of the NGO PRIA.

They know everything about the NGO-PRIA and its working and believe that PRIA is providing very useful services to awaken the people in self- governance and their empowerment specially the marginalized section. PRIA is rendering useful services to bring qualitative change in rural governance and its intervention has helped the representative's voice hard and in the emergence and growth of accountable and transparent self-governing institutions.

Summative Remarks

In the present chapter organization, objectives, working and performance of the selected NGO' s-HPVHA, HGVS and PRIA have been detailed and analyzed with the available documentary sources and their working and performance have further been investigated through field investigations. All the three NGO's have a rich history and great experience in working with the people and have been working for them.

Himachal Pradesh Voluntary Health Association was established in 1987, as a registered non-profit making society under Societies Registration Act 1860, aimed at improving the health of the people. It is a State level federation of voluntary organization engaged in health and development activities. The HPVHA, liaisons for the grassroot non-profit organizations, with the State Government, National Government and International agencies, with commitment to promote social justice in the provision and distribution of health services in Himachal Pradesh. At present HPVHA is involved in health related projects such as reproductive health, promotion of low cost primary health care through alternative system of medicine, prevention and control of STD/HIV/AIDS, disability, child health and rights, capacity building of NGOs, advocacy and information dissemination.

HPVHA's organizational structure is broadly divided into two levels, the management team and the administrative staff. The policy decision is taken at the management level and at Executive Director and level and the some is implemented and conveyed down the line of command. HPVHA gets financial support from foreign as well as Indian agencies. Objectives of the HPVHA are: Justice in health care, optimum utilization of material or other available resources, buildup people's health movement to help in the evolution of low cost people-oriented health programmes with traditional skills of community, conduct research studies on primary health care, training and education to people to strengthen voluntary organizations for health and development etc.

HPVHA undertook the tasks of children health budget analysis of Himachal Pradesh Government for five year period, reproductive child health needs in unreserved and underserved areas, healthy highway project for prevention and control of STD/HIV/ AIDS.

The field investigations found that people know the NGO HPVHA and are well aware of its organization, objective, programmes undertaken and performance. HPVHA is providing commendable services in health awareness, reproductive health of women and prevention and control of STD/HIV/AIDS and people have been benefitted with the initiatives of the NGO. The role and performance of the organization has addressed the health related issues of the society to some extent and people believe that the organization is performing well in the social sector.

The second NGO under investigation in the present study is *Himachal Gyan Vigyan Samiti* (HGVS) which was registered in November 1991 and formally inaugurated on 14th June, 1992 to create conducive environment and demand for literacy. It is a unit of *Bharat Gyan Vigyan Samiti*. HGVS has got a well-structured organization with democratically elected office bearers. It has got five level structure of the organization i.e. *Panchayat* ward level conference, *Panchayat* conference, block conference, district conference and state conference.

Its objectives included creation of fully literate society, to focus toward human resource development, to generate voluntarism and volunteer culture, to inculcate scientific temper, empowerment of women and disadvantaged sections of the society, to preserve the plurality and identity of the local culture and to preserve relevant traditional values. The organization is working in the thrust areas such as: Educational Development, Health, Environment, Participatory Democracy, Gender Issues and Library Movement through methodology of Training, Orientation, Workshops, Seminars, Conferences, Participation and distribution of resource material and mass mobilization through Kala *Jathas*. HGVS works at three levels i.e. intervention at policy level, creating, facilitating and providing supportive role to community based organizations and taking awareness or mass campaigns to people.

The programmes undertaken by HGVS included *'Bharat Gyan Vigyan Jatha', 'Samta Gyan Vigyan Jatha'* focusing on literacy and women equality, 'Joy of learning' for developing interest in children towards education in general and science in particular, *'Desh Ko Jano Desh Ko Badlo',* Total literacy and continuing education campaign.

The NGO-HGVS is quite active and effective in Himachal Pradesh and people are well aware of the organization and its objectives, role and performance. Field investigations also found that HGVS is rendering great services in conducting awareness campaigns for literacy, women empowerment and science education. People have been benefited with the programmes and services being rendered by the NGO-HGVS and there is overall change in the society as the literacy and empowerment initiatives especially for the weaker sections have proved quite beneficial and as such the NGO's performance in social, political as well as economic sector is well accepted and recognized by the people of the region.

The third NGO included in the present study is Society for Participating Research in Asia (PRIA), which was started in India by Dr. Rajesh Tandon in 1982, to promote the practice of participatory research, a contribution of knowledge building and social transformation. Vision of the society is of a world where informed, empowered citizen participate in the process of deepening democracy with tolerance towards its large numbers and diversity.

The basic objective of PRIA in India was to empower the marginalized, the poor, the depressed, women, *Dalits* and *Tribals.* As per new strategic framework of PRIA 'Governance Where People Matter' is an attempt to integrate and converge different interventions in a holistic manner. PRIA's direct intervention is to give effective voice to new leadership and transparent and accountable self-governing institutions.

PRIA has got a national level organizational structure with its office bearers which include Chairperson, President, Treasurer and five members whereas State level or field level operations are carried out through established offices with required supporting staff. PRIA is financed by various international and national agencies.

PRIA has evolved programme focus while responding to changing context and anticipating emerging trends. The overall aim of the organization is to empower the marginalized, the poor, oppressed, women *Dalits* and *Tribals.* PRIA, through different phases conducted different programme such as encouraged grassroot groups to act on the knowledge they possessed, organizational management and participatory planning and monitoring, promoted context specific local groups, strengthened trade unions and NGOs, and conducted various workshops and conventions on citizenship, participation and democracy. PRIA pioneered strengthening *Panchayati Raj* Systems, it campaigned for proper conduct of *Gram Sabha* meetings, trained Panchayat representatives and under the current framework 'Governance Where People Matter' has been working towards qualitative improvement needed in governance by capacity building of elected representative and enhancing people's participation. PRIA also engaged in systematic and structured collaboration with academic institutions to promote teaching and research on participatory development, civil society and democratic governance. Its special efforts include preparing women leaders to engage with governance institutions. PRIA has organized its activities effectively in Himachal Pradesh and the present study substantiate the overall performance of the NGO carried out in *Kangra* and *Hamirpur* districts.

Field investigations revealed that PRIA is well known organization popular among the people and later are aware of its organization, objectives, working and role performance. People are well aware of PRIAs working and the services being provided by it . PRIA is providing useful services to awaken and empower the people especially marginalized sections. People have been benefitted with its services to a great extent and there is a change and improvement in the local governance, which is more transparent now and people's representatives have the say in local governance. Overall performance of the organization in the socio-political sector has proved quite useful for the society, especially the elected representative of the PRIs and proves that the NGO is performing its role as effectively as possible inspite of several limitations.

Notes

1. Mian Goverdhan Singh, *Himachal Pradesh:History, Culture and Economic,* Minerva Book House, Shimla. 1994 p. 1-2.
2. Op. cit., p. 221.
3. Op. cit. p. 222.
4. Op. cit., p. 223.
5. S. P. Punalekar; "Tree and the Bark: On Dialectics of Voluntary Organizations and Social Change in NGOs and Development, op. cit. p. 33.
6. Op. cit. pp-33-34
7. Government of India, *Seventh Five Year Plan, 1985 - 90*, New Delhi- Planning Commission, 1985 Vol. 2, pp. 98-70.
8. Komal Parmar, 'NGO' s in Globalization and sustainable level hood', in *NGO and Globalization,* ed. Asok Kumar Sarkar, Rawat Publication Jaipur, 2008, p. 33.
9. Swapan Garain 'Funding in NGO's sector in India' in *NGO's and Globalization (ed)* Asok Kumar Sarkar, Rawat Publications. Jaipur 2008 p. 220-21.
10. *HPVHA Annual Report 2002 - 03, B-* 37, sector 3, Main Road, New Shimla, Himachal Pradesh. p. 5.
11. *Ibid.*
12. *HPVHA Annual Report* 2003-04, pp. 6-7.
13. *HPVHA Annual Report* 2004-05, pp. 26.
14. *HPVHA Annual Report* 2008-09, p. 23.

15. *HPVHA Annual Report* 2004-05, p. 26.
16. *HPVHA Annual Report* 2002-03, op cit. pp. 9-10.
17. *HPVHA Vision* 2010, op.cit.
18. *HPVHA, Annual Report* 2003-04, op. cit. p. 6.
19. *HPVHA, Annual Report* 2003-04, op. cit. p. 7.
20. *HPVHA Annual Report* 2008-09, op. cit. p. 1-2.
21. *HPVHA Annual Report* 2004-05, op. cit. p. 10-11.
22. *HPVHA Annual Report* 2003-04, op. cit. p. 19-20.
23. *HPVHA Annual Report* 2005-06, p. 19.
24. Constitution, *Himachal Gyan Vigyan Samiti*, Tirath Niwas, Engine Ghar, Sanjauli Shimla.
25. Vinod Raina, 'From Universal Literacy to universal elementary education,' *Gyan Vigyan Varta*, New Delhi, p. 47.
26. Denzil Saldanha, *Civil Society Processes and the State; the Bharat Gyan Vijyan Samiti and the Literary Campaigns, Rawat* publications Jaipur 2010 pp. 45-55.
27. Op. cit p. 46.
28. Constitution, *Himachal Gyan Vigyan Samiti, op*. cit. p. 4.
29. *Ibid* p. 9.
30. Op.cit., p. 2.
31. Op.cit., pp. 2-3.
32. Himachal Gyan Vigyan Samiti: An introduction, Himachal Gyan Vigyan Samiti, op cit. pp. 4-5.
33. Op.cit., pp. 11-12.
34. *Gyan Vigyan Varta, Bharat Gyan Vigyan Samiti,* 4 Block, Avenue 21, Saket New Delhi p. 8.
35. *Annual Report- 1994 - 1995 Himachal Gyan Vigyan Samiti,* op. cit. pp. 11.
36. *Gyan Vigyan Varta, Bharat Gyan Vigyan Samiti,* op. cit. p. 10-11
37. *Ibid.*
38. Op. cit., p. 12.
39. Op. cit., p. 14.
40. *Annual report* 1994-95 *Himachal Gyan Vigyan Samiti, op. cit.* p. 13.
41. *Gyan Vigyan Varta, Bharat Vigyan Samiti,* op. cit. p. 15.
42. Op. cit., pp. 16-17.
43. Op. cit., p. 28.
44. Op. cit., p. 29.
45. *Gyan Vigyan Varta, Bharat Gyan Vigyan Samiti,* op. cit. p. 28.
46. *Gyan Vigyan Varta*, op. cit. p. 29.
47. *Ibid* p. 30.
48. *Ibid.*
49. *PRIA Annual Report* 1987-82, *op cit* p. 3.
50. *PRIA News*, op. cit. July-Sep. 2006

51. Op. cit., p. 7.
52. Op. cit., p. 8.
53. *PRIA Annual Report* 2002-03, 42, Tughlakabad Instuitional area, New Delhi, p. 15.
54. *PRIA, Annual Report,* 2008-09, op. cit. p. 30.
55. *Ibid.*
56. *PRIA, Annual Report* 1981-82, op. cit. p. 5.
57. *PRIA, Annual Report* 1986-87, op. cit. p. 4.
58. *PRIA Annual Report* 1989-90, op. cit. p. 4.
59. *PRIA Annual Report* 1994-95, op. cit. p. 5.
60. *PRIA Annual Report* 2005-2006, op. cit. p. 3.
61. *PRIA Annual Report* 2002-03, op. cit. p. 5.
62. *PRIA Annual Report,* 2006-07, op. cit. p. 5.
63. *PRIA News, opcit.* July-Sep. 2007.
64. *Ibid.*
65. D. D. Basu. Introduction to *The Constitution of India*. New Delhi: Prentice Hall of India Pvt. Ltd., 1998, p. 96.
66. *PRIA NEWS,* op cit., July–Sep. 2006.
67. *PRIA News*, op cit. oct- dec. 2006.
68. Ibid.
69. *PRIA Annual Report* 2002-03, op cit., p. 3.
70. *PRIA Annual Report* 2003-04, p.7.
71. Op. cit. p. 8.
72. *PRIA Annual Report* 2003-04, Op. cit., p. 11.
73. *PRIA Annual Report* 2003-04, Op. cit., p. 8.
74. *PRIA Annual Report* 2003-04, Op. cit., p. 22.
75. *PRIA Annual Report* 2003-04, Op. cit., p. 37.
76. *Ibid.*
77. Ibid. p. 38.
78. Ibid. p. 39.
79. Ibid. p. 41.
80. *PRIA Annual Report* 2003-04, op. cit., p. 33.
81. *PRIA Annual Report*, 2005-2006, op. cit., p. 31.

Chapter - 5

Contribution of NGOs in Socio-Political and Economic Development

In the current endeavour we have explored the contribution of the NGOs in socio-political and economic development of the people. The study is to assess the role of NGOs in bringing the socio-economic and political development in the area where these organizations are working. Since the study is an explorative one, a systematic approach has been used to measure the efforts of the NGOs. The source for analyzing the data was primary and documentary but most of the organizations have not at all documented their achievements. The interview schedule was helpful to get the details of activities, programmes and development that have taken place in the area.

NGOs have played a significant role in socio-political and economic development everywhere. One cannot imagine a society without voluntary action and a society without voluntary action is rather farce. The contribution of the voluntary organizations in the field of welfare of the children, women, distressed and helpless is noteworthy. The aged, widows, orphans, run-away etc. have often been helped by the NGOs. In the field of education, health, employment generation, political empowerment of masses and environment etc. the tremendous work has been done by the NGOs.

The state, in developing countries like India has the greatest responsibility to bring about planned socio- economic development and nation-building. The state is not an end in itself but a means to an end and that end is to promote all-round, balanced, integrated development of all citizens and the nation as a whole. As no state is self-sufficient or can live in isolation, it has to cooperate with other nations in order to promote international peace, justice and development of mankind. While the modern nation-state both in developed and developing countries should respect and recognize the functional autonomy of the structure and rights of civil society at the local, national and international level and subject to the existing legal-political order, the social institutions, on their part should conduct themselves in such a manner as to respect and protect the unity, territorial integrity and sovereignty of the nation-state.[1]

The civil society manifests itself through myriads of households, communities, associations, voluntary groups of different hues and kinds, social services workers, non-profit organizations, cooperatives, unions, women's development groups and environmental NGOs. Not only does it have its definite place in modern state but also performs vital functions for its members through the networks of these institutions. Both before and after the state came into being, the voluntary bodies have been rendering yeoman social service to the poor, needy, neglected, the old-aged, the sick and the downtrodden or relief work during natural calamities.[2]

The planners and policy makers in India who paid lip- service to citizen participation in development realized the importance of involving the voluntary sector in the country's decentralized development only since the sixth Five year plan (1980-85). Earlier the tendency of political decision makers and the development bureaucracy was to equate the work of voluntary agencies with only welfare activities and charity work[3] or the government sponsored cooperatives. The sixth five year plan identified 'new areas' in which NGOs as 'new actors' could participate in development. These areas included: optimal utilization and development of renewable source of energy, including forestry through the formation of renewable energy association at the local level; family welfare, health and nutrition, education and relevant community programmes in the field; health for all programmes; water management and soil conservation; social welfare programmes for weaker sections; minimum needs programme; disaster preparedness and management; promotion of ecology and tribal development and environmental protection and education.[4]

Today the NGO community is involved in virtually every aspect of development irrespective of a nation's resources or income. NGOs work as relief and welfare agencies, as public service agents for government and also a promoter of grass- root development, self-help and empowerment movements.[5]

In pre-independence India, in terms of scope of coverage in development activities, laissez-faireism occupied the top slot, voluntary action through philanthropy, associational works and individual actions stood next, while state intervention came last. Here, 'development' excludes the infrastructural activity like laying out of ports, railways and roads, setting up of communication networks or building up of essentials for capitalist development in banks, stock ex-change, insurance companies, etc. Rather, it includes instituting or extending facilities for agriculture, health and sanitation, education and allied human resource development or enrichment aspects. But after Independence, this hierarchical role was just reversed. Now state intervention claims the largest amount of development activity, because people who are in need of help, succour or assistance, expect it to come from the government through its plan outlays. So Frankenstein has taken the form of development planning in the country since 1950 and it has continued maintaining a tendency to envelope new areas and aspects of economic and social life and activity for obvious reasons: the unsatisfied wants and needs of the poor; the imbalances, conflict and incompatibilities occurring within the economic and social processes due to development itself; urgency to reduce concentration of wealth and income, hence to arrest monopolies; compulsions to catch up with the galloping scientific and technological progress in the world and to maintain national security; besides such other emergent reasons, as have tended to widen the ambit of planned development. All this fosters a centripetal tendency of the concentration of greater economic powers and political authority in the government, which means bureaucrats and political executives. All said and done they are normal human beings and prone to frailties and complexes to misuse the power and positions. Further, they seek to mould the pattern of development in the way of their own perception, practice and routine, oblivious of the expediency and relevance. Not surprisingly, stereotypes tend to stultify innovations in development context and modalities. Government is also to innovate because of its size which is compounded by the lack of requisite informality and initiative. So, dynamic and path breaking leadership in both political executives and bureaucracy is called for, to innovate in development. Voluntary organizations, groups and institutions can innovate and set new paths in schemes and projects and thus project comparative illustrations before the agent of development. The voluntary organizations can also modulate the details of programmes, schemes or projects to suit the requirements of particular localities or clientele groups underchanged circumstance.[6]

It is in the pathetic background that the role of NGOs which, Rajni Kothari prefers to call 'activists and non-party, non-state groups of organizations'[7], needs to be highlighted. Today, we have a whole spectrum of myriad voluntary and struggle-oriented radical groups in the country, who struggle on behalf of the poor,the landless, the *Dalits,* the *Harijans,* the *Adivasis,* the bonded labourers and many other socio-economic strata that were being discriminated against both by state policies and dominant elements in the social structure. They are the ones who try out new technologies to meet the needs of the needy and reach out to the poor in integrating them with the larger society and provide a safety valve in their tensions and ambitions generated by modern life. But service voluntary organizations like the Servant of India Society and the Servants of the People Society, conducting several development activities are umbrella agencies which are becoming rare, on account of the specializations involved in various development activities, the need to come close to the relevant clientele groups and reluctance in independent India of youth to take to life time social services for a pittance of honorarium inadequate for a quite decent standards of life.[8]

NGOs have expanded their network of activities into a variety of issues, particularly on the periphery of society and increasingly taking on new issues and problems as they crop-up and affect the masses, be it the problems of the ethnic or religious minorities, of the forest people affected by deforestations or the people in the north east. There are others who concentrate on important aspects of child labour, bonded labour, women labour and the labour of those who are forced to work below the subsistence level on waste land development, dairy development, biotechnology or water resources community health illiteracy, adult education, and child, youth and women's welfare[9].

In the beginning of the five year plan programme, while allocations were made for voluntary organizations, the state had admitted its limited scope in dealing with the social problems for which the state cannot provide a sufficient measure.[10] The seventh plan envisaged a more widened role for the NGOs. The document says:-[11]

- Supplementing government effort so as to offer the rural poor choice and alternative;
- Activating the delivery system and making it effective at the village level to responds to the felt needs of the poorest of the poor;
- Showing how village and indigenous resource could be used, how human resources, rural skill and local knowledge grossly under utilized at present, could be used for their own development.
- Training a cadre of grassroot workers who believe in professional voluntarism.
- Mobilizing financial resources from within the community with a view to making community to stand on their feet.

Non-Governmental Organizations, as such, have a great role in the developmental process of the country. Pressures of development have always brought the NGOs into the sharper focus, arousing new sets of high hopes and expectations. Their necessity is felt all the more strongly in emergency situations requiring people's involvement and cooperation on a massive scale. Official recognition of the role of voluntary organizations in the development process came in the Five Year Plan and since then it had been talked about in subsequent plans. NGOs have done good work. In the present liberalization of economy they have to play much more important role. To what extent they would be able to play the innovative role would depend upon the pattern of relationship between them and the Government. There is need to develop a relationship of mutual trust Government has to regard NGOs as equal partners in the process of development and NGOs have to operate within the constitutional and legal framework of the country.[12]

All this shows that the NGOs have become an inseparable part in the present day developmental efforts and they are not only supplementing government initiatives but also providing various services to the people. As such NGOs at the present juncture have turned out as the developmental outfits instead of charity associations and they are undertaking various self- planned and government sponsored development projects so as to improve upon the lives of the people, especially the marginalized sections.

NGOs in Himachal Pradesh are also undertaking various development activities for the people of the Pradesh. Various projects leading to the socio-economic and political development of the masses especially the under privileged sections are being undertaken by the NGOs. The NGOs under study i.e. HPVHA, HGVS and PRIA are also serving the cause of socio-economic and political development and contributing a lot in overall development of the people of this Pradesh.

Health is fundamental to national progress in any sphere. In terms of resources for economic development nothing can be considered of higher importance than the health of the people. For the efficiency of industry and of agricultural, the health of the workers is an essential consideration. Health is a positive state of well-being in which the harmonious development of physical and mental capacities of the individual lead to the enjoyment of a rich and full life.[13]

The growth of NGOs in health services predated structural adjustment programmes and up to the eighties, their role was seen essential as complementing the state in providing health services. From sixties the government offered subsidies and grant-in-aid to various NGOs to assist the state in the national health programmes. The most important of these was the family planning programme where the state activity solicited the assistance from NGOs to conduct sterilization, distribute and promote spacing methods and also impart health education. In addition to family planning, they were also involved with immunization and few disease control programmes like HIV/AIDS.[14]

Himachal Pradesh Voluntary Health Association (HPVHA) a State chapter of 'Voluntary Health Association of India' is one such voluntary organization which is working with such a social cause and the mission of the association is 'Making Health A Reality' for the people of Himachal Pradesh. It is network of 50 NGOs engaged in health and development activities all over the state and in district *Bilaspur* where the present investigation have been carried out. HPVHA is directly implementing two health related projects i.e. Family Planning and Prevention, Control and Cure of STD/HIV/AIDS.

In order to assess the contribution of the HPVHA in the social sector i. e. health related projects, a structured, Questionnaire-cum-Interview schedule was administrated to the selected 150 respondents i.e. office-bearers, officials, members, the beneficiaries and on the basis of their responses the contribution of HPVHA is being analyzed in the first part of this chapter.

Since HPVHA is working in the health sector hence to assess to contribution in this sector. The following issues were raised through the Questionnaire-cum-Interview schedule and the responses sought from the selected respondents.

Provider of Health Services

People's general health is an issue of immense social as well as economic importance because healthy people alone can contribute to build a healthy society and a nation. Health services in the yester years were in shambles and people were dependent upon the local *Vaids/ Hakeems* and faith healers. However, in the post- independence era network of health institutions have been established but their services are yet to reach the remote rural areas. What is the status of health services in the area of investigations, to investigate the issue the respondents were probed with the question as to who are the providers of health services in your area and the responses are as given in Table No. 5.1:-

Table No. 5.1: Provider of Health Services

Govt. Health Institutions	*Local Vaids/ Hakeem and other Practitioners*	*Faith Healer/ Exorcised*	*Total*
97	36	17	150
(65)	(24)	(11)	(100)

As the Table No. 5.1: shows, 65 percent people of the region are getting health services from the government institutions while 24 percent of the people are dependent upon the local *Vaids/ Hakeems* and other practitioners whereas 11 percent of the people still use the other modes of health cure i.e. faith healer and exorcist.

This leads to the conclusion that majority of the population is dependent upon the government health institutions but other traditional modes are also continuing as the whole population cannot reach the government institutions.

Working of NGOs in Health Sectors

Though systematic health services are certainly recommended by the regularly established health institutions yet the other organizations can supplement the efforts of the government institutions and in every region voluntary organizations are also working for the cause of people' s health. In order to know about the working and awareness of the people about the NGOs the selected respondents were asked whether any NGO is working in their areas, in the health sector and the responses are as given in Table No. 5.2:-

Table No. 5.2: NOGs in the Health Sector

Yes, To a Great Extent	*To Some Extent*	*Not atAll*	*Total*
76	47	27	150
(51)	(31)	(18)	(100)

As the Table No. 5.2: depicts, 51 percent of the respondents replied that NGO is working in the health sector to a great extent while 31 percent replied the entry of NGO in health sector to some extent whereas 18 percent find no role of any NGO in health sector in their areas.

This leads to the conclusion that NGO is certainly working in the health sector and people as such are aware of the activities of the NGO-HPVHA which is working in the health sector. Perhaps the people who are not utilizing the services of the NGO deny the existence and working of the NGO.

Activities of the NGO-HPVHA

People may take the benefit of the services being rendered by any organization only when they are aware of its working and activities. In order to assess the status of HPVHA in this regard the selected respondents were asked whether they are aware of the activities of the NGO-HPVHA and the responses are as given in Table No. 5.3:-

Table No. 5.3: Awareness of Activity of HPVHA

To a Great Extent	*To Some Extent*	*Not atAll*	*Total*
113	**26**	**11**	**150**
(75)	**(17)**	**(8)**	**(100)**

As the Table No 5.3 indicates, 75 percent of the respondents are aware of the activities of the NGO-HPVHA to a great extent, while 17 percent are aware of them to some extent, whereas 8 percent of the respondents do not know anything about the activities of the NGO-HPVHA.

This leads to the conclusion that majority of the people are certainty aware of the activities of the NGO hence can take the benefit of its services, however, the people unaware are those who have no health issues at the stake.

Health Related Activities/Services of the NGO

In order to further prove the awareness of the people and to analyze whether they are utilizing the services of the NGO- HPVHA, these selected respondents were asked as to which of the mentioned activities or services are being provided by the NGO-HPVHA and the responses are as given in Table No. 5.4:-

Table No. 5.4: Activities, Services of the HPVHA

Reproductive Health of Women	*Prevention control and Cure of STD/ HIV/ AIDS*	*Child Health Care*	*All of Above*	*Total*
27	31	12	80	150
(18)	(20)	(08)	(54)	(100)

As the Table No. 5.4: shows, 18 percent of the respondents believed that HPVHA is conducting activities, services for the reproductive health of women, 20 percent believed the activities and services for the prevention control and cure of STD/HIV/AIDS, while 08 percent of the respondents believed that HPVHA is working for the child health care, whereas majority of the respondents i. e. 54 percent replied that HPVHA is providing all the mentioned health related services.

It can be concluded that people are well aware of the activities being undertaken by the NGO-HPVHA and they know as to what services are being provided by the NGO yet some of the respondents are aware of only one aspect of the services, may be for the reason that they have experienced only that role of the NGO.

Health Check- up Camps by the NGOs

To ensure the benefit of various services to people, health check-up camps should be organized from time to time only then people can be benefitted. Regarding the frequency of the camps, the selected respondents were asked whether the NGO organizes regular health check-up camps and the responses are as given in Table No. 5.5:-

Table No. 5.5: Periodicity of Health Camps

Held Regularly	*Held Occasionally*	*Not Held at All*	*Total*
114	25	11	150
(76)	(17)	(7)	(100)

As the Table No. 5.5: shows, 76 percent of the respondents replied that NGO- HPVHA organizes camps regularly, while 17 percent replied that these are held occasionally, whereas only 07 percent of the respondents replied that they are not at all held.

We may conclude form the investigation that NGO is organizing health check-up camps from time to time and as such people are in a position to make use of the services of the NGO.

People's Participation in Health Check-up Camps and other Activities

People's participation is one of the necessary conditions for the working and success of an organization. Activities and services become redundant, if people do not make use of them. People should voluntarily come forward to become the part and parcel of the NGO's programme only then the development in the social, economic as well as political sector can be expected. Do the people voluntary participate in the camps and other activities to make use of the services of the NGO, this question was put to the selected respondents and the responses are as given in Table No. 5.6.

Table No. 5.6: People Participation in Camps and Other Activities

Yes, to a Great Extent	*To Some Extent*	*Not at All*	*Total*
113	26	11	150
(75)	(17)	(08)	(100)

As the Table No. 5.6: shows, 75 percent of the respondents replied that people participate in the camps and other activities of the NGO to make use of its services, to a great extent, 17 percent replied people's participation to some extent whereas 08 percent of the respondents believed that people do not takepart at all.

This leads to the conclusion that people are certainty utilizing the services of the NGO- HPVHA and taking benefit of them.

Activities of the Healthy Highway Project

The NGO, HPVHA is running two important health oriented projects in district *Bilaspur* i.e. Family Planning and Healthy Highway i.e. for Prevention, Control and Cure of STD/ HIV/AIDS especially among the vulnerable sections. In order to analyze the awareness of people about the activities/ services being provided under the project Healthy Highways the selected respondents were asked as to what activities are being organized under the project 'Healthy Highways' and the responses are as given in Table No. 5.7:-

Table No. 5.7: Activities under the Healthy Highways Projects

Aw areness about STD/ HIV/ AIDS	*To identify patients of STD HIV/ AIDS*	*Provision for prevention control and cure of STD/ HIV/ AIDS*	*Campaigning for use of contraceptives*	*All of above*	*Total*
21	20	18	15	76	150
(14)	(13)	(12)	(10)	(51)	(100)

As the Table No. 5.7: shows, 14 percent of the selected respondents replied that HPVHA under the healthy highways project is undertaking the activities of awareness about the sexually transmitted diseases STD/HIV/AIDS etc., 13 percent replied about the service to identify the patients for STD/HIV/AIDS, 12 percent replied that HPVHA is providing services for prevention, control and cure of STD/HIV/AIDS, 10 percent replied that HPVHA campaigns for the use of contraceptives, where as majority of the respondents i. e. 51 percent of them were of the view that all the above activities and services are being undertaken by the NGO-HPVHA.

This leads to the conclusion that HPVHA is providing great services in the health sector for the cause of family planning and prevention control and cure of STD/HIV/AIDS under the Healthy Highways Project.

Contribution in Prevention and cure of STD/HIV/ AIDs and Family Planning

In order to analyze the role of the NGO to prevent and control the STD/ HIV/AIDS and in family planning the selected respondents were asked whether they believe that the NGO- HPVHA has contributed to some extent in the prevention and cure of the STD/HIV/AIDS and family planning and the responses are as given in Table No. 5.8:-

Table No. 5.8: Contribution of the NGO in Health Sector

To a Great Extent	*To Some Extent*	*Not atall*	*Total*
105	34	11	150
(70)	(23)	(07)	(100)

As the Table No. 5.8 shows, 70 percent of the respondents believed that the NGO- HPVHA has contributed to a great extent to prevent control and cure the STD/HIV/AIDS and family planning, while 23 percent of the respondents believed the contribution of the NGO to some extent, whereas 07 percent of the respondents do not believe that the NGO has made any contribution for the prevention and cure of STD and issues of family planning.

From the investigation we may conclude that the NGO-HPVHA has contributed a lot in the prevention, control and cure of STD/HIV/AIDS and family planning under the two major projects undertaken by the NGO in the area of its operation.

Section of the Society Benefited

The NGO's role is to under take the activities and services for the welfare of the society, especially the weaker sections, who have little access to various services. In order to analyze the contribution of the NGO-HPVHA for the benefit of the different sections of the society, the selected respondents were asked as to which section of the society has been benefited the most with the activities and services of the NGO and the responses are as given in Table No. 5.9:-

Table No. 5.9: Benefit of the Services of the NGO

Children	*Women*	*Youth*	*Aged People*	*All of them*	*Total*
09 (06)	23 (15)	46 (31)	- -	72 (48)	150 (100)

As the Table No. 5.9: shows 6 percent of the respondents believed that the children have been benefited the most with the services and activities of the NGO, while 15 percent of the respondents believed the women as the most benefited section, while 31 percent of the respondents believed that youth and mature people have been benefited the most with the service of the NGO but the large section of the respondents i.e.48 percent of them believed that all the sections have been benefited with the activities and services of the NGO-HPVHA.

From the investigations we may conclude that all the sections of the society have been benefited with the health related activities and the services provided by the NGO-HPVHA.

Contribution of the NGOs in Social Development

NGOs'being the tools of the development are bringing about various social, economic and political changes in the society with their developmental initiatives. Is there any change and social development of the society with the initiatives of the NGO. With this objective the selected respondents were asked whether they agree that the contribution of the NGO-HPVHA for social welfare has helped in the social development in the area of its operation and the responses are as given in Table No. 5.10:-

Table No. 5.10: Contribution of the NGO in Social Development

Yes, to a Great Extent	*To some Extent*	*Not at all*	*Total*
87	54	09	150
(58)	(36)	(06)	(100)

As the Table No. 5.10: shows, 58 percent of the respondents believed that the NGO- HPVHA has contributed to a great extent with its activities and services in the social development of the area, while 36 percent believed the contribution to some extent but 06 percent of the respondents were also of the opinion that there is no contribution at all of the NGO in the social development of the region.

The investigations lead to the conclusion that the role, activities and the services which the NGO-HPVHA has provided to the people of the area has contributed a lot in the social development of the region of its operation.

Among the NGO' s working for the development of the people especially the marginalized sections of the society, Himachal Pradesh Voluntary Health Association (HVPHA), a state chapter of 'Voluntary Health Association of India' is one, which is working with an objective 'Making Health A Reality'. The NGO has undertaken various activities to provide health services to children, women and other vulnerable sections of the society through its various projects and programmes. In the present context the NGO is working with two important projects in district *Bilaspur* i.e. 'Family planning' and 'Healthy Highways'. In order to probe the contribution of the NGO in the social sector, the investigations carried out reveal that majority of the population is dependent upon the government health institutions for their medical needs and care but other traditional modes are also still continuing as the entire population cannot reach the government health institutions. The NGO-HPVHA is working in the health sector and the people are aware of its activities and taking benefits out of them. People are also aware of the services and the sections to which the NGO caters. Health check-up camps and other activities are being organized by the NGO regularly and people are utilizing the services of the NGO and taking benefit of its various activities and services. The NGO- HPVHA is providing great services under its projects in the health sector for family planning and prevention, control and cures of STD/HIV/ AIDS and as such contributing a lot in the health sector in its area of operation. All the sections of the society have been benefited with the activities and services of the NGO and the role, activities and services provided by the NGO has contributed a lot in the social development of the region.

Another non- governmental organization under investigation is, *Himachal Gyan Vigyan Samiti* (HGVS) which was registered in November 1991 and formally inaugurated on 14th of June 1992 to carry out a definite task, to initiate a statewide churning in order to create a conducive environment and demand for literacy.

If the education scenario in India is observed we find that there is drastic change in the field of education. The budgetary allocation of both Union and State Governments on education was 3.6 percent of GDP in 1992 which should have been minimum of 6 percent. In the year 2001-02, the same budget was reduced to 2.8 percent of GDP. The private consumption on education increased from Rs. 10,002 cores in1993-94 to Rs. 15,196 cores in 1998-99.[15] It is noticed that, when the government is reducing its expenditure on education, it is handing over the responsibility of elementary or primary education to imperialists or foreign institutions. For instance, among the foreign funded projects, the most popular District Primary Education Programme (DPEP) is funded by the World Bank, *Mahila Samkhya* by the Dutch government; *Shiksha Karmiand Lok Jumbish* are funded by SIDA. During the year 2000-01, the total amount of foreign funded projects was Rs. 1,076 cores. In higher education, 214 universities, 16 central universities, 28 deemed universities and thousands of colleges are being forced to mobilize a part of their funds from internal or private sources. The IITs and IIMs are being tied up with NRIs and TNCs.[16] The level research is being influenced by foreign funding, C.P. Bhambri is of the opinion that in the new phase of globalization, the western social sciences agenda has influenced the upper class academics of the Metropolitan Universities in India because of external funding in research.[17]

It is well known that government cannot do every thing and it does not have the professional wherewithal and competence to enter all vocations and make its mark. Besides, government does not have a universal outreach of the population and in particular in remote, interior and inaccessible pockets, who are in need of presence of government for getting some relief and succour out of the endless plight and predicament in which they are placed. While this is the inherent limitation of government there is another area where governments have little or no role to play even if it wishes to do so. This is the area of social mobilization for a particular cause, be it functional literacy etc. social mobilization is both a tool and instrument for arousing and awakening critical mass consciousness to do certain things which are of interest and relevance to the lives of the poor and deprived and not to do certain things which are not of such interest and relevance.[18]

In Himachal Pradesh also the governmental initiatives in the field of education are being supplemented by various other private and non-governmental or voluntary organizations and *Himachal Gyan Vigyan Samiti* is one of them. HGVS emerged with the primary purpose of placing literacy on the state agenda in a unique and a qualitatively, different manner. The HGVS brought within its umbrella a number of creative thinkers, academicians, activists, administrators and people from diverse back grounds. More than anything else millions of volunteers came together under the banner of HGVS, pledging solidarity and support of the total literacy campaign. The voluntary nature of the literacy movement was its distinguishing hallmark and strength. Fully literate society, capacity building of people, to increase peoples participation in development, human resource development, to generate volunteerism and voluntary culture, interface between experts and common people, inculcating scientific culture, empowerment of women, preserving collective community solidarity, plurality and identity of the local culture, relevant traditional values are other initiatives of the HGVS for the socio economic development of the society in Himachal Pradesh.

In order to find out the contribution of the HGVS for the socio economic development of the society various issues were discussed and probed with the information sought from the selected respondents for the NGO.

Awareness about the Activities of the NGO-HGVS

The first and foremost thing for the efficacy of an organization is its familiarity with the people for whom it is working. People should know the role, activities, programmes and the services being provided by the organization only then they can participate in its affairs and take benefit of the services. In order to probe this issue the selected respondents were asked whether they are aware of the activities being organized by the NGO-HGVS and the responses are as given in Table No. 4.11:-

Table No. 5.11: Awareness about the Activities

To a Great extent	*To Some Extent*	*Not atall*	*Total*
113	30	07	150
(75)	(20)	(05)	(100)

As the Table No. 5.11 shows, 75 percent of the respondents replied that they know about the activities of the NGO to a great extent, while 20 percent replied that they know about them to some extent, only 5 percent of the people are not at all aware of the activities of the NGO. Certainty office-bearers and beneficiaries are well aware of the activities whereas the respondents who are not directly related to the NGO in any way are not at all aware.

This leads to the conclusion that the NGO is familiar with the people and they know about the activities of the NGO in the socio-economic sector.

Programmes Undertaken by the NGO

In order to further probe the familiarity of the masses with the role, working, activities of the NGO- HGVS the selected respondents were asked as to what programmes are being undertaken by the NGO and the responses are as given in Table No. 5.12:-

Table No. 5.12: Programme of the NGO

Literacy campaigns	27 (18)
Human Resource Development	15 (10)
Interface between Experts and Masses	21 (14)
Women Empowerment	34 (23)
All ofabove	53 (35)
Total	150 (100)

As the Table No. 5.12: shows, 18 percent of the respondents believed that the NGO is campaigning for literacy, 10 percent know that it is working for human resource development, 14 percent know that HGVS has programme of organizing interface between experts and the masses, 23 percent of the respondents believed that the NGO has a sole objective of women empowerment whereas 35 percent of the respondents believed that the NGO- HGVS has all the above programmes in its field of activities.

This leads to the conclusion that most of the respondents have sectoral awareness i.e. programme in which they are interested or beneficiaries but a large number of the respondents are aware of the various programme under taken by the NGO which can ultimately be of great use to them.

People's Voluntary Participation in the Activities of the NGOs

Organization can succeed in its mission provided the people voluntarily participate in its activities. Ultimate beneficiaries of the programme and activities of the NGO are masses alone and if they show keen interest in the affairs of the organization and voluntarily participate in the activities, they can be benefited and society as a whole can go through a great change. Do the people voluntarily participate in the activities, of the NGO-HGVS, this question was put to the selected respondents and the responsesare as given in Table No. 5.13:-

Table No. 5.13: People's Participation

To a Great Extent	*To Some Extent*	*Not atAll*	*Total*
27	43	80	150
(18)	(29)	(53)	(100)

As the Table No. 5.13 indicates,18 percent of the respondents believed that people participate in the activities of the NGO to a great extent, while 29 percent believed the participation to some extent, whereas 53 percent of the respondents replied that people do not participate voluntarily in the activities of the NGO.

It can be concluded from the investigations that since various benefits accrue to the masses from the activities of the NGO hence should be keen to participate in the activities and programme of the NGO-HGVS but actually they are not enthusiastic of the activities of the NGO and do not volunteer themselves.

Impact of the Literacy Campaign of the NGOs

The NGO-HGVS initially started working in Himachal Pradesh towards creation of a fully literate society, not just 3R's but a tool for greater awareness and empowerment and contributions towards a higher quality of life. As such the literacy was the thrust area of NGOs working and what was its impact on the common masses to probe this issue, the selected respondents were asked whether the literacy campaign of the NGO has helped the common people and the responses are as given in Table No. 5.14:-

Table No. 5.14: Impact of the Literacy Campaign

To a Great Extent	*To Some Extent*	*Not at All*	*Total*
81	63	06	150
(54)	(42)	(04)	(100)

As the Table No. 5.14 depicts, 54 percent of the respondents believed that literacy campaign has helped the common people to a great extent, while 42 percent believed that it helped to some extent, where as 04 percent of the respondents believed that literacy campaign had not at all helped the masses. It was personally observed that population covered under the literacy mission was put to several tests and the success of the mission was verified by several agencies and there after post literacy mission was also carried out by the NGO.

This leads is the conclusion that literacy campaign of the NGO has helped the common people and ultimately improved upon their quality of life.

Creation of Self-Help Groups

Economic activities are essential part of a society and quality of life of the people depends upon its resources to meet their needs. Governmental agencies create various opportunities for the economic empowerment of the society yet it cannot reach every individual in every corner of the society. As such voluntary organizations can supplement the initiatives of the government by creating awareness about the various activities and organizing various groups to help themselves by organizing various activities for the benefits of its members. Self-help group as such can ensure the economic upliftment of the society and to probe whether the NGO has helped in this regard the selected respondents were asked whether the NGO has initiated the creation of self-help groups for the benefit of rural masses and the responses are as given in Table No. 5.15:-

Table No. 5.15: Creation of Self- Help Groups

To a Great Extent	*To Some Extent*	*Not at All*	*Total*
88	58	04	150
(59)	(38)	(03)	(100)

As the Table No. 4.15 indicates, 59 percent of the respondents replied that the NGO-HGVS has helped to a great extent to create or organize self-self- groups for the benefit of the rural masses, while 38 percent replied that the NGO helped the creation of self-help groups to some extent, whereas 03 percent of the respondents replied that the NGO has not at all helped in this regard.

This leads to the conclusion that the NGO-HGVS has also initiated a great step by creating and organizing self-help groups for undertaking various joint activities for the help and economic benefits of the masses especially the women.

Economic Activities of the Self-Help Groups

Through the joint efforts of the self-help groups various economic activities can be undertaken which can ultimately generate income to the members of the group. Government has also arranged various programmes such as easy loans, expert advice, training in various skills etc. for the effective working of the groups. But the biggest tragedy of rural masses is their little awareness about such activities and programmes and lack of initiatives in them. It is here that the NGO can help the masses especially the vulnerable sections of the society to create and organize self-help groups. The NGO- HGVS has helped to create the groups to a great extent but to probe whether these self-help groups have undertaken economic activities for the benefit of its members, this question was put to the selected respondents and the responses are as given in Table No. 5.16:-

Table No. 5.16: Economic Activities of the Self-Help Group

To a Great Extent	*To Some Extent*	*Not at All*	*Total*
37	89	24	150
(25)	(59)	(16)	(100)

As the Table No. 5.16: shows, 25 percent of the respondents replied that self-help groups have undertaken various economic activities for the benefit of its members to a great extent, while 59 percent of the respondents believed the role of self-help group in this regard to some extent, but 16 percent of the respondents do not believe at all in the economic efforts of the self-help groups. On further probe and observationsit was found the NGO has created many self-help groups who are being provided due support by the NGO and these groups especially constituted by women have also undertaken various economic activities such as preparing *pickles, jams, chutneys, Murabas* with the local material and other woolen products for the use of people and selling them in the market directly and these groups are earning good profits with their activities and as such generating income for the members, however, their number is not very large.

This leads to the conclusion that self- help groups have also helped in generating income to the members of the groups and as such helped in economic empowerment of the society but this role and activities are not very substantial.

Capacity Building of the Women

Women constitute half of the population of the Indian society and their upliftment helps not only their families alone but the entire society. However, Indian society being male dominated society did not provide enough space to them earlier but of late it has not only made the government alone to focus on women related issues but also the society itself has awakened to some extent to boost the initiatives of women. Women have been given special reservation in local self- government institutions, various training programmes are being conducted for their empowerment and women themselves are also coming forward and taking various initiatives. NGOs are also providing enough space in their activities for women and to probe the role of the HGVS in this regard, the selected respondents were asked whether the HGVS has organized training camps and other activities for the capacity building of the women, which is one of its objectives, the responses are as given in Table No. 5.17:-

Table No. 5.17: Capacity Building of Women

To a Great Extent	*To Some Extent*	*Not at All*	*Total*
97	26	27	150
(65)	(17)	(18)	(100)

As the Table No. 5.17: shows, 65 percent of the respondents replied that the NGO has organized various training programmes and other activities for the capacity building of women to a great extent, while 17 percent of the respondents believed the fact to some extent, but 18 percent the respondents replied that no such activities at all has been undertaken by the NGO. Majority of the members of the NGO- HGVS are women and may be that all of them have not got the due opportunities to take part in training programmes but it has been observed that their turn- out is quite impressive whenever the NGO organizes any protest or procession for them.

The investigations lead to the conclusion that the NGO has a great role in capacity building of the women and thereby empowering the women force of the society.

Raising Socio-Economic Problems of the People

Indian population especially rural women suffers from various socio economic problems and they have little say in decision making and lack of mechanism to address their grievances. Non-Governmental Organizations which were created with the objectives to address the various issues and problems of the masses and raises them at the appropriate platform to get them addressed, is a great source and mechanism to get the socio-economic problems of the people raised at the appropriate levels. Since interface between experts and common masses and raising the public issues at the appropriate platform is one of the objectives of the NGO-HGVS, to probe the role in this regard, the selected respondents were asked whether NGO raised various socio-economic problems of the people at various platforms and the responses are as given in Table No. 5.18.

Table No. 5.18: Raising Socio Economic Problem of the People

To a Great Extent	*To Some Extent*	*Not at All*	*Total*
98	44	08	150
(65)	(29)	(06)	(100)

As the Table No. 5.18 shows, 65 percent of the respondents replied that the NGO- HGVS has been raising the socio economic problems of the people at various level to a great extent, while 29 percent of the respondents believed so to some extent, but 06 percent of the respondents did not believe that the NGO is raising socio economic problems of the masses at an appropriate level. It was further observed that the NGO has been organizing various meetings, processions, protests to get the various problems of the farmers, producers of various products, women, and workers to get their problems addressed. NGO has also been conducting awareness campaign in the rural areas to organize them and create a platform for them where they can raise their voice over their issues.

All this leads to the conclusion that the NGO is playing a great role to get the socio economic problems of the people rose at the appropriate platforms and get them addressed.

Role in Environment Protection, Exploitation, and Preservation of Local Resources

Environmental protection and ecological balance at present is a big issue on which a great emphasis is being put by various international organizations, national agencies and local organizations. For the sustainable development it is essential that local resources are exploited very scientifically and also preserved for the future use and the ecological balance is maintained in the region so that the entire environment is protected. In this regard NGOs are doing a great job by sensitizing the masses and organizing them for protection of their environment which can help in the sustainable development and growth of the region. To probe the role of the HGVS in this regard, the selected respondents were asked whether the NGO has initiated activities for the protection of environment and proper exploitation and preservation of local resources and the responses are as given in Table No. 5.19:-

Table No. 5.19: Protection of Environment and Local Resources

To a Great Extent	*To Some Extent*	*Not at All*	*Total*
53	84	13	150
(35)	(56)	(09)	(100)

As the Table No. 5.19 shows, 35 percent of the respondents believed that the NGO- HGVS is performing the role of protection of environment and exploitation as well as preservation of local resources to a great extent, while 56 percent of the respondents believed so to some extent, but 9 percent of the respondents did not believe that the NGO is performing any such role.

All this leads to the conclusion that NGO do have a role in the protection and preservation of environment and local resources but they have nothing under their control except sensitizing people and raising the issue at appropriate levels. Sometimes destructive forces are more powerful and beyond the limit and control of NGOs, hence initiatives are also required at the governmental level and NGOs can cooperate and supplement governmental initiatives

Role of the NGO in Socio-Economic Development of the Region

NGOs have turned out as development outfits these days and performing a great role in the socio economic development of the region. The NGO-HGVS has also undertaken various programme such as fully literate society, capacity building, people participation in developmental activities, development of human resources, empowerment of women, to inculcate scientific temper etc. which ultimately can lead to the socio economic development of the society. What is the opinion of the selected respondents in this regard, to know this they were asked whether they agree that HGVS has helped in the socio economic development of the region and the responses are as given in Table No. 5.20:-

Table No. 5.20: Role of NGOs in Socio-Economic Development

To a Great Extent	*To Some Extent*	*Not at all*	*Total*
103	39	08	150
(69)	(26)	(05)	(100)

As the Table No. 5.20 shows, 69 percent of the selected respondents believed that the NGO-HGVS has helped to a great extent in the socio-economic development of the regions while 26 percent of the respondents believed that if has helped to some extent in the socio- economic development of the regions where as 05 percent of the respondents were of the opinion that NGO has no role in the socio-economic development of regions.

From the investigations we can conclude that the NGO has a great role in the socio-economic development of the regions as it has been raising issues developmental and other socio- economic at appropriate platforms, organizing the people for undertaking various activities leading to their empowerment.

The NGO-*Himachal Gyan Vigyan Samiti (HGVS)* registered in 1991 and formally inaugurated in June 1992 had a definite task to create a conducive environment and demand for literacy. As the government cannot meet the entire educational demands of the society so the private institutions, cooperatives and non-governmental organizations have a great role to supplement the government initiatives and the HGVS is one such organization. In addition to literacy the NGO has the objectives of human resources development, generate voluntarism and voluntary culture, providing interface between experts and masses, empowerment of women, health for all, protection of environment, capacity building of masses etc. HGVS as such is performing a great role and providing useful services in the area of its operation. From the investigations of various issues relating to the NGO, it comes out that NGO-HGVS is popular among the people and they know about the various socio-economic activities of the NGO. People are aware of the programmes being conducted by the NGO and people do participate in the activities and programmes of the NGO to some extent as they are beneficial to them. Literacy mission carried out by the NGO has helped the common people and improved upon their quality of life. NGO has also initiated a great step by creating and organizing self-help groups under taking various economic activities leading to economic benefit to the members and the initiative has helped to some extent in the economic empowerment of the society. Various training programmes and other activities organized by the NGO for women have helped in the capacity building of the women leading to their empowerment.

The NGO is playing a great role to raise the socio-economic issues of the masses and getting them addressed at the appropriate level. NGO has also a role in environment protection and proper exploitation and preservation of local resources. Various initiatives of the NGO have helped in the socio- economic development of the region and its people.

Third, Non-Governmental Organization under investigation in the present study is, 'Society for Participatory Research in Asia' (PRIA). The two pioneers of education for social change, Paulo Freire and Myles Horton constituted a forum for promoting 'Participatory Research in Asia in 1978. Dr. Rajesh Tandon along with four other started the Society for Participatory Research in Asia in February, 1982 to promote the practice of participatory research as a contribution to knowledge building and social transformation. PRIA evolved programmatic focus in responding to changing context and anticipating emerging trends. The overall objective of the organization is to empower the marginalized, the poor, the depressed; women, *dalits* and *tribal's* and they are taught to participate in decision making and governance there by empowering them. Through different phases the NGO encouraged the grassroot groups to act on the knowledge they possessed, briefed the voluntary development organizations on issues of organizational management and participatory planning and monitoring Support organizations were promoted to provide context-specific support to local groups, then direct work was initiated on strengthening *Panchayati Raj* Institution's, trade unions and NGOs. In 1999-2000 PRIA got a unique opportunity to bring the voices on perspectives of the grassroots to influence global policy. From 2000 onwards series of events have been organized that hold reference for future with the focus on promotion of accountable, transparent, democratic governance in which there is assurance of greater voice and influence of ordinary citizens on governance.

PRIA pioneered strengthening PRIs in seven states of the country in early 1995 and after 1995 *Panchayat* elections, it campaigned for proper conduct of *Gram Sabha* Meetings. It also assisted in the preparation of micro-plans at the *Panchayat* level. Since large percentage of elected representative were entering public offices for the first time, it initiated training programmes for them. The PRIA, under its current framework, "Governance Where People Matter' has been working towards qualitative improvements in rural governance by capacity building.

In Himachal Pradesh also PRIA initiated various programmes to improve upon the local governance by capacity building of the people and their local representatives. A large number of *Panchayat* representatives were provided orientation on their roles, importance of *Gram Sabha,* methods of micro- planning and inter-facing with government officials. Special efforts were to be made to prepare women leaders to engage with governance institutions and processes. PRIA as such is working actively and performing effective role strengthening *Panchayati Raj* system and empowering the people.

In order to analyze the contribution of PRIA the selected respondent were probed with different issues of its working and contribution and their opinion with observations are being presented in the following pages:-

Activities of PRIA

The vision of the 'Society for Participatory Research in Asia' (PRIA) is of a world where informed, empowered citizen participate in the process of deepening democracy with tolerance towards its large number and diversity. PRIA aims to improve the socio-economic status of people through democratic governance and as such political empowerment of the people is the thrust area of the organization. What did the people know about the organization and its activities,to probe this, the selected respondents were asked about the various activities being organized by the NGO-PRIA and their responses are as given in Table No. 5.21:-

Table No. 5.21: Activities of PRIA

Campaigning for peoples p articipati on in Governance	37 (25)
Campaigning for proper conduct of *Gram Sabha* Meetings	24 (16)
Training to elected r ep r es entati ves of PRIs	29 (19)
All the above	60 (40)
Total	150 (100)

As the Table No. 5.21 shows, 25 percent of the respondents replied that PRIA is campaigning for people's participation in governance, 16 percent replied that PRIA's main activity is campaigning for proper conduct of *Gram Sabha* meetings, 19 percent of the respondents opined that PRIA is providing training/ orientation to newly elected representatives of the PRIs, where as 40 percent of the respondents replied that PRIA is under taking all the above activities.

This leads to the conclusion that people are well aware of the activities being undertaken by the NGO and as such in a position to make use of its services.

Capacity Building of Marginalized Sections

Creating environment conducive for the people's participation in governances especially of the marginalized sections of the society is one of the major objectives of the NGO, PRIA. This is a work of utmost importance for the success of democracy because unless all the sections are in a position to participate in the decision making and governance, the democracy cannot succeed nor can people be empowered properly. Marginalized sections, the poor, deprived, *Dalits, Tribals,* women have not been provided equal opportunities since ancient past and unless these sections are empowered governance may not improve. In addition to other efforts NGOs have a great role to build the capacity of people for participation in governance. To probe this role of the NGO PRIA, the selected respondents were asked whether PRIA is working for the capacity building of the marginalized sections and the responses are as given in Table No. 5.22:-

Table No. 5.22: Capacity Building of Marginalized Sections

To a Great Extent	*To Some Extent*	*Not at all*	*Total*
76	65	09	150
(51)	(43)	(06)	(100)

As the Table No. 5.22 indicates, 51 percent of the respondents are of the opinion that PRIA has under taken the activities for the capacity building of the marginalized sections to a great extent, 43 percent believed this initiative to some extent, while 06 percent of the respondents did not believe so.

This leads to the conclusion that PRIA is engaged in the capacity building of the marginalized sections; the poor, the deprived, women, *dalits* and *tribals* so as to ensure their political empowerment.

Activities of PRIA for Strengthening PRIs

For political empowerment of the people it is essential that people are thoroughly oriented to participate in the local governance through PRIs so that they are oriented in the skills of democratic governance. What are the initiatives, of the NGO in this regard the respondents were asked as to what initiatives have been taken by PRIA to strengthen PRIs and the responses are as given below in Table No. 5.23:-

Table No. 5.23: Initiatives of PRIA for PRIs

Orientation of newly elected representatives	19	(13)
Campaigning for proper conduct of *GramSabha* Meetings	37	(25)
Assisting *Gram Panchayats* in Micro- Planning	45	(30)
All ofabove	49	(32)
Total	150	(100)

As the Table No. 5.23 indicates, 13 percent respondents believed that NGO- PRIA is providing orientation to newly elected representatives of the PRIs, 25 percent of the respondents believed that PRIA campaigns for the proper conduct of the *Gram Sabha* meetings, 30 percent of the respondents replied that PRIA is assisting Gram *Panchayats* in micro planning where as 32 percent of the respondents were of the opinion that PRIA is involved in all the above mentioned activities.

The investigation as such leads to the conclusion that the NGO is engaged in the activities which helps in the capacity building of the representatives of the PRIs and ultimately helps in the political empowerment of the people and strengthens democratic governance at the grassroot slevel.

Frequency of Camps/ Activities of PRIA

For the political empowerment of the masses especially the marginalized sections it is necessary that activities such as orientation programmes, training programmes and sensitizing programmes amongst the people are organized from time to time so as to keep up the momentum of the initiatives and prepare the people in the process of their political participation. In order to assess this role of the NGO-PRIA, the selected respondents were asked as to what is the frequency of camps and other activities organized by PRIA and the responses are as given in Table No. 5.24:-

Table No. 5.24: Frequency of Camps and Activities

Held Regularly	*Held Occasionally*	*No Activities at all*	*Total*
103	41	06	150
(69)	(27)	(04)	(100)

As the Table No. 5.24 depicts, 69 percent of the selected respondents replied that activities of the PRIA, camps etc. are held regularly, while 27 percent of the respondents believed that they are held occasionally, whereas 04 percent of the respondents were of the opinion that no activities or camps are not-held at all.

On the basis of the investigation and the available data we can safely conclude that PRIA is organizing various camps etc. from time to time to undertake necessary activities for the orientation and training of the people so to strengthen the political development of the rural society.

People's Participation in the Activities of the NGO

Initiatives of any organization can be fruitful provided people participate in the activities of the organization voluntarily and regularly. People participation help in their capacity building leading ultimately to their empowerment and development. Do the people participate voluntarily in the activities of PRIA, this question was put before the selected respondents and their responses are as given in Table No. 5.25:-

Table No. 5.25: People's Participation in the Activities of PRIA

To a Great Extent	*To Some Extent*	*Not atall*	*Total*
43	36	71	150
(29)	(24)	(47)	(100)

As the Table No. 5.25 shows, 29 percent of the respondents replied that people participate voluntarily in the activities of PRIA to a great extent, while 24 percent believed people's participation to some extent but majority of the respondents i.e. 47 percent replied that people do not at all participate voluntarily in the various activities and programmes of the NGO-PRIA.

From the responses it can be concluded that people's voluntary participation is not of a desirable level rather ensuring people's willing participation in the activities of NGO is a big problem itself.

Conduct of *Gram Sabha* Meetings and its Working

Gram Sabha is the grassroot level organization for participatory democracy in the *Panchayati Raj* System. However, its working shows that inspite of very important constitutional role given to this institution its meetings were not held properly nor the institution, was working effectively. In Himachal Pradesh four regular meetings of *Gram Sabha,* in addition to special meetings are organized every year but it was observed that members i.e. voters of the *Gram Sabha* area did not participate in the meetings resulting in the non-transaction of the business. However, the NGO-PRIA has campaigned vigorously for the proper conduct of meetings and participation of the members. Has the initiative brought out the desired change, to assess this aspect the selected respondents were asked whether the conduct of Gram Sabha meetings and its working has improved with the initiatives taken by the NGO- PRIA and the responses are as given in Table No. 5.26:-

Table No. 5.26: Gram Sabha Meetings and its Working

To a Great Extent	*To Some Extent*	*Not atall*	*Total*
43	103	04	150
(28)	(69)	(03)	(100)

As the Table No. 5.26 shows, 28 percent of the respondents believed that conduct of *Gram Sabha* meetings and its working has improved to a great extent with the initiatives taken by PRIA, while 69 percent i.e. majority of the respondents find the improvement to some extent but 03 percent of the respondents find no improvement at all.

The data as such leads to conclusion that the initiatives taken by the NGO has certainly improved the conduct of meetings and working of *Gram Sabha* yet the changes are not at all very substantial for various other seasons.

Participation of Marginalized Sections in PRIs

Panchayati Raj Institutions are the basic institutions established under the 73rd Constitutional Amendment Act, 1992, for the direct participation of the people at the grassroot level. Marginalized sections such as women, Scheduled Caste, Scheduled Tribes and other backward castes have been given special opportunities in these institutions by way of reservation of seats and offices for these sections. PRIA is specially working for the capacity building of the marginalized sections of the society to probe, whether its efforts have borne any fruits the selected respondents were asked whether the participation of marginalized sections has improved with the initiative taken by PRIA and the responses are as given in Table No. 5.27:-

Table No. 5.27: Participation of Marginalized Sections in PRI's

To a Great Extent	*To Some Extent*	*Not atAll*	*Total*
96	48	06	150
(64)	(32)	(04)	(100)

As the Table No. 5.27 shows, 64 percent of the respondents believed that initiatives taken by the NGO has improved in the participation of marginalized sections in the activities and working of the PRIs to a great extent, while 32 percent of the respondents believed the improvement in the participation level to some extent, whereas 04 percent of the respondents did not find any improvement at all.

This leads to the conclusion that participation in the activities and working of the PRIs in respect of marginalized sections has certainly improved but in addition to PRIA's intervention, reservation of seats and offices for these sections are also the other reasons for this improvement.

Growth of Women Leaders

Women who constitute half of the entire population of the country should also get their share of opportunities so as to really empower the society but the section has remained neglected for a long period. Now opportunities have come into their way and various NGOs are also initiating activities for the capacity building of women so that they can take up the leadership roles. Orientation and training as well as leadership development programmes are being conducted by NGOs for women folk which have resulted in the emergence and growth of women leadership. Opportunities created under various Acts and rules have also certainly offered leadership roles to women yet the NGOs are developing necessary skills and capacity in them. What is the role of PRIA in this regard to probe this aspect the selected respondents were asked whether they believe that initiative taken by PRIA has helped in the growth of women leaders in governance and the responses are as given in Table No. 5.28:-

Table No. 5.28: Growth of Women Leaders

To a Great Extent	*To Some Extent*	*Not atall*	*Total*
77	67	06	150
(51)	(45)	(04)	(100)

As the Table No. 5.28 depicts, majority of the respondents i.e. 51 percent replied that initiatives taken by the NGO-PRIA have helped in the growth of a women leadership to agreat extent, while 45 percent of the respondents believed the growth of women leaders to some extent, however, 04 percent of the respondents did not believe in the growth of women leaders.

From the available data it may be concluded that initiatives of the NGO has certainly helped in the development and growth and desired changes in their leadership qualities by its orientations and other activities, however, positions of leadership have come to women from other sources also.

Strengthening *Panchayati Raj System* and Empowerment of People

Grassroots level organizations provide direct opportunities to the people to participate in the governance and thereby empower the people. Democratic decentralization through *Panchayati Raj* Institutions under the constitutional provisions in India is a great step forward to empower the people. However, opportunities offered to them can bring out the change only when people are encouraged for their participation in governance and the NGO have a great role in this regard. The NGO PRIA specially works for strengthening PRIs and empowerment of the people especially the marginalized sections. Have the initiatives of PRIA strengthened the *Panchayati Raj* system and ultimately empowered the people, this question was put to the selected respondents and the responses are as given in Table No. 5.29:-

Table No. 5.29: Panchayati Raj System and the People

To a Great Extent	*To Some Extent*	*Not atall*	*Total*
49	93	08	150
(33)	(62)	(05)	(100)

As the Table No. 5.29 indicates, 33 percent of the respondents believed that PRIA's activities and programmes have helped to a great extent to strengthen PRIs and empower the people ultimately, however 62 percent of the respondents i.e. majority believed the change to some extent, but 05 percent of the respondents did not believe change in PRIs working and empowerment of people.

This leads to the conclusion that with the initiatives of PRIA to popularize the *Panchayati Raj* System and its working have considerably strengthened the system further and initiatives have also helped in the empowerment of the people.

Contribution in Political Development of the People

An opportunity for the people to participate in the governing process of the country itself is an object of their political development. Have the opportunities given to the people to participate in the governance and the initiatives taken by the NGO-PRIA contributed in the political development of the people and the region as a whole, the question was put to the selected respondents and the response are as given in Table No. 5.30:-

Table No. 5.30: Political Development of the People and the Region

Yes, to a GreatExtent	*To Some Extent*	*Not atAll*	*Total*
66	78	06	150
(44)	(52)	(04)	(100)

As the Table No. 5.30 shows, 44 percent of the selected respondents believed the contribution of the NGO-PRIA in the political development of the people and the region to a great extent where as 52 percent of them i.e. majority believed the contribution of the NGO to some extent, but 04 percent of the respondents did not believe any contribution of the NGO in the political development of the people and the region and this section of respondents are those who are not at all connected with the NGO in any manner but the common respondents.

As such we may conclude from the investigations that the NGO has certainly a great role in the political development of the people and the region. PRIA, the third NGO under investigation in the present study, which has a vision of a world where informed, empowered citizen participate in the process deepening democracy with tolerance towards its large number and diversity. The overall objective of the organizationis to empower the people especially the marginalized sections who are taught to participate in decision making and governance, leading ultimately to their political empowerment. PRIA pioneered in strengthening the *Panchayati Raj* system so as to build the capacity of the people especially the marginalized sections leading to their political empowerment.

Investigations reveal that PRIA undertook various activities for the empowerment of the people and people are well aware of them and in position to take benefits out of them. PRIA is actively engaged in the capacity building of the people and especially of the poor, the depressed, women, *dalits* and *tribal's* so as to ensure their political empowerment. PRIA is engaged in orientation and training of the elected representatives and as sisting PRIs in various acts which may ultimately strengthen democratic governance leading to empowerment of the people. PRIA is regularly organizing various activities and camps for the orientation and training of the people to ensure their political development. However, people's participation is below expectation and a big problem for the NGO. Initiatives of the NGO have improved upon the working of *Gram Sabha* and participation of marginalized sections has also improved considerably. Intervention of the NGO has helped in the development and growth of women leadership and its initiatives have helped in strengthening the *Panchayati Raj* System and empowerment of the people. The NGO has certainly played a good role in the political empowerment of the people and the region.

Summary of the Chapter

In the present chapter contribution of the three NGO s namely HPVHA, HGVS and PRIA in socio-economic and political development have been investigated and analyzed. NGO- HPVHA is one voluntary organization which is working with a social cause i.e. 'Making Health a Reality'. The NGO has undertaken various projects and programmes to provide health services to children, women and other sections of the society. Two important health projects of the NGO are 'Family Planning' and 'Healthy Highways carried out in district *Bilaspur* of Himachal Pradesh. Investigations reveal that majority of the population is dependent upon the government institutions for medical facilities and other alternative traditional modes such as *Vaids/ Hakeems* and faith healing are also continuing as the entire population cannot reach the government institutions. The role and activities of the NGO-HPVHA, which is working in the health sector, is well known to the people of the region and the organization organizes various health related activities from time to time. People are making use of the services of the NGOs and its initiatives in family planning and prevention, control and cure of STD/ HIV/AIDS have contributed a lot in the health sector of the region of its operation. All the sections of the population have been benefited with the activities and the services provided by the NGO and its contributions in the social sector are well accepted and recognized in the region.

Second, NGO under investigation is *Himachal Gyan Vigyan Samiti (HGVS)* which was formally inaugurated in June 1992 with a definite task to create a conducive environment and demand for literacy. In addition to literacy, the NGO's objectives included human resource development, generation of volunteerism and voluntary culture, providing interface between expert and the common masses, health for all, empowerment of women, protection of environment and capacity building of masses. Investigations reveal that the NGO is popular among the people and they are fully aware of the socio-economic activities of the NGO. People do participate to some extent in the various activities and the programmes being organized by the HGVS as they are benefited with them. Literacy mission of the NGO has helped the common people to improve upon their quality of life. By creating self-help groups the NGO has helped to involve the masses especially women in the economic activities and there by leading to their economic empowerment. The NGO-HGVS also organized various training programmes and other activities especially for women with an objective of capacity building of women leading to emergence and growth of women leadership and empowerment of women. The NGO also raised various socio- economic issues of the people at the appropriate level to get them addressed. HGVS has also taken initiative for the protection of environment, local resources, culture and traditions as per its objectives. Initiatives of the NGO-HGVS have certainly helped the socio-economic development of the region and its people.

The third, NGO under investigation is Society for Participatory Research in Asia (PRIA) with a vision of world where informed, empowered citizen participate in strengthening the democratic process with tolerance towards its large number and diversity. The overall objective of PRIA is to empower the people especially the marginalized sections- the poor, the depressed, women, *dalits* and *tribals,* who are taught to participate in decision making process and governance, thereby leading to their political empowerment. PRIA pioneered in strengthening the *Panchayati Raj* System by building capacity of the people leading to their empowerment.

Investigations in the present study reveal that PRIA organized various activities for capacity building of the people and they are well aware of the activities and programmes of the NGO. PRIA is engaged orientation and training of the elected representative of the PRIs and assisting these institutions in various activities so as to strengthen the democratic process at the grassroots level leading to empowerment of the people. PRIA regularly organizes orientation programmes, training camps for the elected representative as well as for sensitizing the masses but people's participation in them is below expectation and a big problem for the NGO. The initiatives of PRIA has improved the working of *Gram Sabha*, the grassroot level democratic institution and participation of marginalized sections, has also improved considerably. PRIA' s intervention has helped in the emergence and growth of women leaders and strengthening the *Panchayati Raj* system ultimately leading to the empowerment of the people. PRIA has certainly contributed in the political development of the region and its people.

Notes

1. Noorjahan Bavaed. *Non- Governmental Organizations in Development: Theory and Practice,* Kanishka Publisher, New Delhi, 2008. p. 6.
2. *Ibid.*
3. *Fourth Five year Plan,* 1967-74, Planning Commission, Government of India, 1970. pp. 420 & 421.
4. Noorjahan Bava, ed. Op. cit., p. 8.
5. Padma Seth, 'An Overview of Non-Governmental Agencies and Their Function', in Noorhajan Bava, op. cit. p. 77.
6. Dilip Kumar Parida, 'Voluntary Agencies in Development', in Noorjahan Bava, op. cite. pp. 210-11.
7. Rajni Kothari, 'Voluntary Organizations in Plural Society' in *Indian Journal of Public Administration,* op cit., p. 439.
8. Dilip Kumar Parida, Op. cit, p. 212.
9. Op. cit. p. 213.
10. Mangal Jai Deo, 'Voluntary Agencies viz-à-viz government', *Yojana*, Vol. 31, No. 4, p. 12.
11. Government of India, *Seventh Five Year Plan 1985-90*, Planning Commission, Governmen to India Press, 1985, Vol. II, p. 68.
12. T. N. Chaturvedi, 'Voluntary Organization and Development: Their Role and Functions' in Noorjahan Bava (ed.) op. cit., pp. 52-53
13. Government of India, *First Five Year Plan* 1952-57, Planning Commission, Government of India Press.
14. Rama V. Baru, 'Structural Adjustment and Health : The Changing Role of Non-Governmental Organizations in India', in AsokKumar Sarkar, *NGOs and Globalization,* Rawat Publications, Jaipur, 2008. p. 25.
15. http://www peoples march.com/publications/globalization/chapter 15. htm.
16. http://www. peoples march.com/publications/globalixation/chapter 15 htm.
17. Asok Kumar Sarkar, *NGOs and Globalization: Developmental and Organizational Facets,* Rawat Publications, Jaipur, 2008. p. 6.
18. Lakshmidhar Mishra, 'BGV Sin introspect and retrospect', *Gyan Vigyan Varta, Bharat Gyan Vigyan Samiti,* New Delhi, p. 56.

Chapter - 6

Problems Affecting the Performance of Non-Government Organizations

The Non-Governmental Organizations have become very important tools of socio-and economic development in India. Otherwise also, voluntary action has been a long tradition in India and occupies a pride place of especially in the field of welfare. The role of voluntary agencies is well recognized and the policy makers and administrators also recognize its contribution. With the launching of various development programmes after independence, voluntary effort has shifted its focus from welfare activities to the challenging field of rural development particularly in implementing the poverty alleviation programmes. They are engaged in various activities closely related to rural development. While some are directly working with poor, helping them to get the benefits of many anti-poverty schemes, some others train workers for organization engaged in rural transformation, still some more get development workers, specialists in various branches of knowledge and social workers together for seminars, conferences and workshops to exchange experience and learn from each other.[1]

The voluntary agencies have been involved in rural development, much before government's effort in this field was started. They were the early catalysts for new thrust in rural transformation and their role was that of pioneer, innovator, and scientists.[2]

The much increased stress on rural development in recent years has induced voluntary agencies to take up several development activities. From the once welfares and charity approach, the voluntary agencies are gradually changing and widening the outlook towards development. The role of voluntary agencies in rural development is assuming importance because of these special qualities like innovativeness, commitment among workers for effective implementation, flexibility in approach to suit local conditions, close contacts with local people, high level of motivation, minimum procedural practices, which are known to be missing among government functionaries. In general, the main goals of voluntary agencies in rural development are (i) to help the people to help themselves in their endeavours of progress; (ii) to stimulate and promote growth of inherent potentials among people for their development; (iii) to initiate a process of participatory development; (iv) to bring about social justice for disadvantaged group and create awareness about their rights and duties in our society and to (v) promote growth in social, political and economic aspects of life in rural areas.[3]

Since rendering service to poor is the main objective of the voluntary agencies, they are eminently suitable to undertake rural development works and also help in implementing government progrmmes. They have inherent capacity to organize rural poor and weaker sections for defending their rights. They are in a better position to organize rural masses for availing the collective benefits. Further, they can also make a positive contribution as watch-dogs of public interest close to the community.[4]

Though NGOs are certainly in a better position to undertake development programmes yet there have been high rate of failures of various developmental programmes due to a variety of reasons. There are many problems and hindrances which have been affecting the performance of Non- Governmental Organizations. Various studies conducted so far clearly indicate that Non-Governmental Organizations do have their share of problems affecting their organization, role and performance. Some of the socio- economic, administrative, political problems being faced by the Non-Governmental organizations are as under:-

One of the problems of voluntary agencies is to have a common forum with a mechanism of coordination among themselves as also between the national headquarters and their State and district branches. The linkages are needed both at functional and geographical levels. For this purpose, they need some minimal infrastructure for which it is very difficult to raise donations. Although, the government has accepted as a matter of policy providing financial assistance in the nature of administrative grants to these agencies but apart from the meager size of the grant and the various conditions attached thereto, this has not been able to help the voluntary agencies at the national level to perform their functions of coordination, leadership, guidance, innovation etc.[5] As such NGOs are facing a problem of common forum for coordination in the absence of adequate finances which affects the performance of NGOs.

For lack of proper policy, voluntary action in the field of social development has received a setback. Plan after plan, there has been increase in numerical growth of the voluntary agencies and their spread in different fields, like rural development, adult education, health, social welfare, child development etc. Yet in the absence of clear policy on: relationship of the government and the voluntary agencies, role of voluntary agencies in development and nature of community participation and public cooperation have created considerable problems, including absence of trained and qualified manpower of the voluntary agencies, competition among the voluntary agencies on the one hand, and between the government and voluntary agencies on the other[6]. So the NGOs have another problem facing them about the relationship with government.

Yet another problem being faced by NGOs is the erosion of old virtues. The organizations have been known in the past for their virtues and qualities more than the governmental institutions, that these are dedicated and impart human-touch, innovativeness with flexibility in their working and are nearer to the community having first hand knowledge of their problems and needs. Over the years these virtues have eroded, due to a variety of factors. Over anxiety to professionalize social welfare service and development coupled with disappearance of the dedicated workers of the past, the virtues of dedication and human touch among voluntary workers are now disappearing. Professionalism is one of the factors which makes inroads into the dedication and human-touch; however, it does not mean that all the professionals lack these qualities. With the introduction of grant- in-aid system, with rigorous rules and regulations and introduction of management concept in the voluntary agencies, they tend to become bureaucratic, some of them even copy work styles of the government, with the result that some of the voluntary agency have cost their quality of flexibility.[7] This also affects the performance of NGO.

The central social welfare board created a network of voluntary organizations with a fool-proof grants-in-aid system by starting from scratch in 1953, which today is the basis of financial assistance to voluntary organizations. However, it has now been realized that grant-in-aid system initiated by the central board which was followed by various state governments, had an adverse effect on voluntary action. The reason is that the voluntary agencies were given structured schemes prepared by the government, which they have to run as agents of the government. The grant-in- aid system of the government tied the hands of the voluntary agencies and when they were given free hand in preparing project proposals for innovative projects of community development and other projects they found it hard to work out-proposals for innovative projects. Today, voluntary agencies ask for schemes without realizing that the schemes are to be made by the voluntary agencies based on the felt needs of the community.[8] As such the loss of innovations is yet another problem affecting the overall performance of NGOs.

With the flow of funds from government sources, the voluntary organizations became increasingly dependent on their aids and assistance. In fact, in many cases their dependence on government aid increased considerably and they gradually abandoned their efforts to raise funds through public donations and contributions. Consequently, popular support for voluntary work declined considerably as also people's involvement and interests in their activities. As such the loss of public support and involvement in the activities of the NGOs is also a great setback to these organizations, which weakened their foundations and defeated the purpose of their existence.[9]

Government grants brought in an element of formalism and made it incumbent on the voluntary organizations to evolve and incorporate organizational rules and procedure for strict adherence. This, in turn, controlled and curved their spontaneity, informality and personal initiative. Further bureaucratization and formalization changed the basic character of the voluntary organizations and made them compulsive about organizational compliance and less responsive to the needs of the people.[10]

Bureaucratization brought in an element of hierarchy in the voluntary organization and changed the concept of peer group working for a common cause with devotion and commitment. Hierarchical arrangement of position brought in an element of unhealthy competition for capturing position of power. Also, collective and corporate decision-making became increasingly difficult in such hierarchical organizations. Thus, decision making tended to be more centralized in voluntary organization which, in turn, destroyed their corporate and collegiate nature.[11]

With power and patronage, voluntary organizations became highly politicized and tended to swing to the side of the power elite than to the people whom they were to serve. The politicians developed vested interests in voluntary organizations and used them for their political gains rather than helping them to freely accomplish their goal of serving the clientele group.[12]

As such the non-governmental organizations have lost the support and involvement of the people, have become bureaucratized and formalized, hierarchical arrangement has centralized decision making and vested interests have further politicized the NGOs.

In a short period, following independence, a sharp decline was witnessed in voluntary organizations supported and sustained by popular contributions. A society which had long tradition of building, organizing and running schools, colleges, libraries, reading rooms, hospitals and dispensaries, seems to have lost the urge to mobilize resources for such purposes. Resources are also not forthcoming for running and maintaining the existing ones. The schools, hospitals, which are being built by charitable trusts only carry label and cater to a certain clan of people who can really afford to pay their services. The charitable schools and hospitals charge high fees and are no longer within the reach of poor and the deprived. All this is in the name of voluntary sector, but surely not accessible to all, and most certainly not to the poor and the deprived[13]. As such the non-governmental organizations are facing the problem of sharp decline in voluntary spirit among people which has certainly affected the overall performance of the NGOs.

Village communities used to mobilize their own resources for building repair and maintenance of roads, public wells, temples, *dharamshalas* (Seraior inn). Trees were planted on the roadsides and arrangements were made for providing drinking water on the highways for travelling public. Social and cultural functions were organized round the year, all over the countryside with pubic donations and contributions. But this spirit of contributing for common and collective good seems of have become a matter of past.[14] As such it has become difficult to mobilize funds for meeting the increasing cost for public welfare activities. There is not only problem of resources in the countryside but also a change in the attitude of the people which ultimately affects the performance of NGOs.

NGOs are facing the problem of changed attitudes of the people due to variety of reasons which can be summarized as under[15]:-

First in order to contain the hope and aspirations of the people, aroused during the freedom struggle, the national government launched a variety of welfare, relief and development programmes. The government took direct initiative to provide education, health, welfare and recreational facilities in a big way. Furthermore it made public funds available to voluntary organizations for initiating and expanding services for children, women, old, handicapped, disabled, poor and the deprived. Voluntary Organizations also got lot of financial support from the government for extension and training work. Consequently, voluntary organizations tended to increasingly depend on the government. People withdraw as the grant support came in.

Secondly, increasing 'State Welfarism' changed the sensibility of the people. In the past, poor, deprived and the sick evoked lot of community sentiments and generous contributions were made for a meliorating their conditions. But this has become increasingly difficult now. Thus, the state support for welfare programmes in a way blurred and blunted the sensibility of the people and took away their urge and initiative to build and sustain their own institutions to cater to needs of various groups.

Thirdly, in the wake of electoral politics that followed independence, politicians developed vested interest in voluntary organizations and used them to consolidate and enhance their own influence base. Thus, voluntary organizations lost their wide community support base and became increasingly dependent on political support.

Fourthly, a lot of people who migrated from rural areas initially retained their root there. They had an inner urge and sense of obligation to extend help and assistance to their native village. They, therefore, mobilized resources to build institutions or assist needy individuals and families. In this process, a lot of money flowed from urban areas to villages for various social purposes. But slowly, as this generation of people lost their roots and settled down in cities, they stopped giving assistance for various activities which they supported earlier, consequently, a lot of urban funds which flowed to rural areas earlier declined considerably or stopped altogether.

The study clearly indicates the nature of socio-economic problems being faced by the Non-Governmental Organizations. The support base of NGOs has shrunk and they are totally dependent upon the government rather serving as agents of the governments and this has affected the overall performance of NGOs.

G. Narayana Ready[16] has observed some common irregularities among the voluntary agencies as follows: (i) Most of the agencies are headed by a strong and dominant personality without much devolution of power and autonomy to lower sections, thereby giving an impression that these are one man shows; (ii) Recruitment of personnel is generally done on the basis of caste, religion and other personal considerations, rather than judging the commitment and aptitude of the recruits; (iii) Exploitation of unemployed educated young men and women by paying meager salaries and by using them sometimes for anti- social activities; (iv) The programmes implemented are, by and large, "agency oriented" or "donor oriented", rather than "people oriented"; (v) Over–dependence on funding agencies and government rather than mobilizing local resources and funds; and (vi) A general tendency to blame other agencies and authorities, in case of failures, without attempting to recognize their approach and working methods.

Voluntary agencies also suffer from lack of professionalism. Most of the trained workers prefer to work in urban areas, rather than in rural areas. Thus these agencies do not have enough expertise and skills to complete various aspects of their work, like preparing projects. Proposals, statement of accounts, planning and implementation of schemes etc., further, they are heavily depending on dedication and sacrifice rather than competence and consistency.[17]

Finance is the most important support which the NGO's should get so as to continue with their activities. Though in the yester- years various welfare services were provided with the individual charity and collective efforts but the spirit of charity has gradually declined with the result that now voluntary agencies are dependent upon the government financial support. From time to time various agencies were created to finance the NGO'S for various government sponsored programmes, for poor and the deprived at the same time funds were also made available by foreign agencies to voluntary organizations for organizing relief and rehabilitation for draught and famine affected people.

But with extending financial help to voluntary organizations, there is talk of evolving a code of conduct to regulate their activities. There is lot of resentment about it and many activists have already expressed their apprehensions and are definitely opposed to the idea that has been mooted.[18] The voluntary organizations cannot escape the blame altogether for this state of affair. Most of them seem to have fallen for an easy option and have tended to lean heavily on the government or on foreign funding. In either case they start on shaky foundation with little or no financial support from the people or the community. In the absence of financial support from the people it would not be possible for voluntary organizations to maintain and assert their autonomy. The plea is not against the government or foreign funding but basically against what it entails for the voluntary organization in terms of their autonomy, internal organizational dynamics, relations with community and bureaucratic compulsions.[19] All these problems have repercussions on the overall performance of the voluntary organizations.

The single most formidable problem of voluntary organizations is perhaps one of assured funding. A majority of them, lacking in funds, as they do not have an independent source of income and depending on external financial support, are perennially haunted by paucity as well as their uncertainty of funds. Funding problem is so acute that many organizations are forced to drop midway even good ongoing programmes. Although it is the announced policy of government to give financial assistance to them, they get demoralized by the needlessly vexatious and delay-involving procedures of work, observed in the bureaucracy. Even when a particular grant has been sanctioned, its release is held up unnecessarily which has a paralyzing effect on voluntary action,[20] affecting the performance of the NGO.

Within the environment sector, the first problem that the voluntary groups face is that of lack of expertise and understanding. Ecological science is of a recent origin and there is an overall lacuna of scholarship and understanding. Thus notwithstanding the growth in the number of 'counter experts' and the conscious forgoing of links between the voluntary groups and universities and research institutions, lack of data and understanding end up diluting many of the arguments that the voluntary groups come up with. Given their limited budgets, most groups, individually or as part of a network, find it difficult to either retain expertise or carryout environmental impact analysis.[21]

There is long history and great diversity of charity and social service in India. Many voluntary bodies in the social and economic life of contemporary India draw their inspiration from spiritual and religious underpinnings (Hindu, Christian, Jain, Muslim or Parsee etc.). There are also secular organizations, some avowedly Marxist, which are impelled by universal human values and concern for social justice. All of them get support for the respect for compassion, self-denying sacrifice and service to the fellow beings which is part of the ancient and culture and value system in India's heritage. The great boost and inspiration for voluntarism must be traced to the advent and impact of Gandhiji in our national life. While leading a mass movement for political freedom, he drew on the religious value system and insisted that political liberation must go hand to hand with a sense of social responsibility and in banishing untouchability and regenerating the village economics. He anticipated the limitation and social distortions of macro- economic planning and rampant industrialization. Gandhiji is now looked upon not just as the prophet of decentralization and village level economic self- reliance, but the inspiration for meeting the ecological disaster and human degradation brought about by modern industrial civilization. The development professionals are not necessarily convinced of the Gandhian approach. But as social scientists in their search for alternative strategies for development with distributive justice, they too have come round to urge a grassroot upwards thrust. In this reoriented emphasis the developmental professional seems at times to be drawing inspiration from the effective activism of NGOs in affluent democracies. But the problems of voluntarism in a poor agricultural country are very different to those in the west. The Volga's here are necessarily weaker, more fragmented and specially dispersed. Moreover they cannot bank on adequate support of private philanthropy and are obliged to rely largely on institutional funding for their constructive programmes. Most Volga's, directly or indirectly, wholly or partially, are perforce obliged to seek government support. But when executing official programmes, they run-up against exacting bureaucratic procedures and accounting requirement and in the process their developmental thrust gets weakened.[22]

The more difficult problems for volunteering organizations is not in relation to government or donors, but internal to the organizations themselves. Voluntarism, which starts with individual motivation, predicates higher values and self-imposed discipline Volga's must function democratically in programming but they must not allow this attitude to overlook the imperative of public accountability. They must be vigilant against factionalism. The need for financial prudence and disciplined work ethics, which necessitates an organizational framework can also degenerate into individual or institutional authoritarianism.[23]

The ordinary run of supporting personnel in the voluntary sector is bound to be a mixed lot in quality and motivation. The lure of security and prestige associated with service with government and the envy of earnings in the corporate sector, siphons off much of the meritocracy away from grassroot organization. Not that those, who come forward to join the Volga's under economic pressures of unemployment, are necessarily incapable of adjusting to the ethos of Volga' s. But the voluntary organizations have to be reconciled to providing living wages and upgrade them to keep up with the creeping inflation. The more pernicious influence on the Volga's comes from the environment of consumerism, corruption, moral degeneration and the social ascendancy of the unprincipled.[24]

Another institutional problem for Volga's is to graft relevant technology, managerial, talent and professional skills to catalyze faster progress in the rural sector. Graduates in rural management or agricultural engineering are understandably reluctant to live and work for long years in the village. Motivated professionals are coming forward to make voluntary carriers in sector but when inducting qualified personnel, one has to be on guard that the emoluments of professionals do not lead to widening the alienating gulf from the village poor. There could also be friction with the typical grassroot worker who is less educated but a better communicator and catalyst for confidence building at the people level.[25] All these problems do have repercussions on the overall performance of the voluntary organizations.

Problems facing the non-governmental organization differ from organization to organization and place to place, however, there can be some common problems facing all the organizations. Some of the common problems enlisted by B.T Lawani are as under.[26]

Absence of Spirit of Volunteerism

The basic characteristic of voluntary organizations is volunteerism. Voluntary organizations worked as pioneers in early days but that enthusiasm seems to have faded these days. The extent of volunteerism is declining day by day and turning into professionalism. They hesitate to undertake new experiments voluntarily and are content with settling down in certain areas in grooves and are reluctant to move on, thus betraying the spirit of vigorous adventurism which should be hallmark of voluntary action.

Lack of Dedicated Leadership

Leadership qualities of the leaders in voluntary organizations determine the quality and condition of services by any voluntary organization. Especially dedicated leadership, 'Leadership for the sake of Leadership', is a most important governing factor in this regard. In the post-independence era, unfortunately, the voluntary organizations faced the crisis of leadership as the leaders who pioneered voluntary action and worked for it with spirit of devotion and dedication choose to enter politics to find berths in legislatures and parliament thus creating a vacuum for dedicated leadership in voluntary organizations.

Lack of Fund

Most of the voluntary organizations suffer from paucity of funds. Government does not give cent percent grants-in-aid for numerous programmes. Voluntary agencies have to make matching contributions which are sometimes unable to manage and are, therefore, unable to avail themselves of the grants. Most of the funds allocated to the various schemes are not revised for so many years which are rather most necessary to match the inhabiting rise in prices due to uncontrollable inflation, which further complicates their financial position, making them incapable of rendering services of quality. Voluntary organizations need to raise funds through various means and resources. The concept of charity is not so strong in the minds and hearts of the people as it was in the ancient society. Thus, the organizations languish for want of resources before the first year is out.

Inadequate Trained Personnel

It is believed that personnel working in the voluntary organizations may be of different kind. The main requirements of the personnel working in such organizations are a sense of dedication and commitment and interest in the social services. Voluntary organizations earlier were assumed to be served by unpaid social workers imbued with the spirit of service and did not require any special education or training. But the present trend of professionals in social services emphasizes proper education and training of personnel in the context of scientific and technological advancement impinging on the quality of services to be provided for various types of clientele. Adequate facilities for training of manpower do not exist, and wherever they exist as in National Institute of Public Corporation and Child Development and various institutes of health and family welfare rural development National Council for Educational Research and Training, Central Social Welfare Board etc. they are not availed by the voluntary agencies for lack of infrastructure and motivation and their location in the metropolitancities.

Lack of Coordination

The absence of coordination council of voluntary organization existing at local, state and national level has led to the common problems such as overlapping, duplication, non- coordination etc. The absence of such a common forum also incapacitates voluntary organizations to offer united stand against the government when it humiliates them by extraneous considerations at the behest of politicians and egoistic government officers. Coordinating organization like Association of Voluntary Association for Rural Development (AVARD), Coordination Council of Voluntary Association (CCVA) etc. are the few efforts in this direction. This state of affairs also does not facilitate exchange of information, data collection, research, training and publication and also does not create favourable conditions where common difficulties can be placed before the government.

Centralization in Urban Area

Voluntary Organizations are more developed in urban areas as compared to rural areas. The backwardness and ignorance of the rural people and lack of enthusiasm among social workers to work among them in the absence of availability of minimum comforts are the two important reasons for the backwardness of the voluntary organization in rural areas.

Deterioration in Quality of Services

Day by day the quality of service of the voluntary organizations is deteriorating. After independence India was declared to be a "welfare state" and a number of welfare schemes for the welfare of the downtrodden were introduced. The voluntary organizations, therefore, had to engage themselves in the social welfare services in many areas to meet the aspirations and hopes of the people and accept all available programmes whether they had the requisite resources in terms of money, men, material and technicalities. Comparatively, the numbers of voluntary organizations was less and the schemes declared by the government were more. The organization expanded their areas of services in which neither they had the professional competence nor the infrastructural development. With this sudden expansion of their activities without adequate preparation, the quality of their service was bound to deteriorate and to be below expected standards.

Misuse of Funds

It is a matter of fact that some unscrupulous elements have made fortunes by floating voluntary organization for their personal gains and managing grants from the government. It is a common experience that there have been serious charges of misuse and misappropriation of funds received as grants- in–aid from the government, foreign donors and raised through their own resources by the voluntary organizations, obliging the government to institute enquiries into these allegations by appointing commissions of enquiry and committees.

Lack of Public Participation

Voluntary organizations are meant to provide opportunities to the citizens for democratic participation but they have not been able to fulfill this obligation due to the method and manner in which they function, and failed to attract people, interested in constructive work and develop channels for people's enthusiastic participation. Some of the factors responsible for such a state of affairs are general backwardness of the people, absence of adequate number of dedicated persons, overemphasis on targets and time bound programmes, political interference and vested interests, easy availability of funds without proper planning and assessment of felt needs and safeguards for the community, distrust of agencies and workers who do not have a base in the community and are unable to with its support and lack of decentralization which could give a feeling of being partners in development rather than development being thrust from above.[27]

Monopolization of Leadership

It has been observed that there is growing tendency towards monopolization and interlocking of leadership at the top level of voluntary action groups and organization as is reflected in the same person being the President in one organization, Secretary in the other, Treasurer in the third and a member of the Executive in the fourth. Thus interlocking of leadership can be formulating, coordinated policies, programmes and activities, facilitating exchange of technical knowhow and experience and mobilizing people for common goal. But the greatest disadvantage of such leadership is that the fresh blood is not allowed to flow into the organization and leadership. Leaders in most of the groups would like to perpetuate themselves rather than allow the second rank leadership to grow. Instance of the position of importance of the same persons occupying for decades are numerous. The continuation of elected or nominated members for very long tenures in any group or agency makes them so powerful that they prove to be counter democratic.[28]

The success of voluntary agencies is limited by a number of major problems facing them. These include.[29]

(i) Inadequacy and lack of certainty of the flow of funds.

(ii) Ambivalent relation with the government and official agencies

(iii) Scarcity of competent and committed person to serve the voluntary agencies.

(iv) Inadequate and only symbolic participation of the beneficiaries in the management of voluntary agencies and their negative inclination towards self-help programmes sponsored by the voluntary agencies.

(v) Antagonism and occasional conflicts with local political interests.

There are certain perennial problems which voluntary agencies face in the process of seeking, getting and utilizing grants-in-aid, some of which are mentioned below:[30]

(i) Despite several years of working of the grants- in-aid system for various types of projects most of the voluntary organizations still have problem of formulation of proposal which are acceptable to grant giving bodies.

(ii) On the other hand, although voluntary agencies have accepted implementation of the schemes formulated by the grant giving bodies with financial assistance yet the structure and tailored schemes of grants-in-aid have placed limitation on their initiative and innovation based on community felt needs.

(iii) Newly established voluntary agencies find it difficult to get grants as according to the rules, normally agencies which have worked for less than three years, are unable to make a beginning of even well-conceived, well formulated projects based on the felt needs of the people because of non-eligibility for grant.

(iv) Preparation of the budget estimate to be submitted along with the project proposal and application for grants is yet another problem with the voluntary agencies as they are not used to working with budget estimate as they have neither the resources to budget nor staff to formulate budge estimate.

(v) Most of the voluntary agencies face the problem of attracting the really qualified and experienced professional staff for implementing their programme because of their small operations and meager financial resource. On the other hand, the grassroot level agencies do not have access to training resources at the local level where their untrained but experienced workers would be given training orientation, refreshers etc.

(vi) Since voluntary agencies were traditionally run and managed by the voluntary workers, there have been problem of adjustment and mutual appreciation of their roles and those of the paid staff.

(vii) The revision of the pay scales and allowance under the government consequent upon the implementation of recommendation of the pay commissions in the central and the state sectors has further aggravated the problem of staffing of the voluntary agencies as they cannot afford payment of salaries to the staff even to the extent of fiffty percent of what they get under the government including their perks.

(viii) Many of the voluntary organizations have the problem of space, particularly in the metropolitan areas not only for running the services but also for their office. On the one hand, there is dearth of land and exorbitant market rents and on the other, there is the absence of grants or local resources for constructing buildings.

(ix) Because of modernization, professionalization and introduction of management techniques, the voluntary organizations need certain minimum infrastructure and administrative expenses. Unfortunately grant-in-aid rules do not allow for such administrative expenditure except contingencies.

(x) Despite interaction between the donor and donee agencies, in the absence of attempt of giving rudimentary training in maintenance of accounts the major problems of the voluntary agencies have been the maintenance of proper books of accounts because of non-availability and financial affordability of accounts staff.

(xi) Audit is yet another difficulty with smaller organizations located in the rural and remote areas. Despite the fact that the central social welfare board accepts certificate of a local officer, like the block officer, yet most of the time they do not take responsibility of certifying free of charges the accounts of voluntary organization for which they have no official obligation. However, this facility, even if available is likely to be misused and three is likelihood of corruption entering voluntary agencies.

(xii) After independence, an element of professional training for social workers was introduced whereby more and more professionally trained social workers are not only engaged in the work of the voluntary agencies but some of them are also members of the boards and committees of voluntary agencies. However, there is lack of clarity on the respective roles and responsibility of lay voluntary workers and whole time paid professional social workers. This has created considerable irritants in the working of the voluntary agencies.

As analyzed in the previous chapters, the voluntary organizations in Himachal Pradesh are also well organized, with clearly defined objectives and undertaking various programmes for the development of masses, especially the deprived and the depressed classes. Non-Governmental Organizations are contributing a lot for the socio-economic and political development of the society.

Though the non-governmental organization under study, i.e. HPVHA, HGVS and PRIA are working in Himachal Pradesh with different programmes and providing different services to the people of the state in different districts yet they are also facing some socio-economic, administrative and political problems which are affecting the performance of the NGOs. Hence, the investigations to analyze the common problems affecting the performance of NGOs have been carried out, seeking information/opinions, from all the 450 selected respondents, in this study and the same are being presented in the following pages:-

Problems Facing the NGOs

In order to know about the main problems facing the non- governmental organizations the selected respondents were asked as to what are the main problems of the voluntary organizations in Himachal Pradesh and the responses are as given in Table No. 6.1.

Table No. 6.1: Main Problems Facing the NGOs in Himachal Pradesh

Lack of Adequate Financial Resources: 1
Lack of Democratic Organization Structure: 2
Lack of People's Participation: 3
No problem at all: 4

Selected Respondents From	*1*	*2*	*3*	*4*	*Total*
HPVHA	40 (27)	90 (60)	17 (11)	03 (2)	150 (100)
HGVS	91 (60)	13 (09)	38 (25)	08 (06)	150 (100)
PRIA	46 (31)	83 (55)	15 (10)	06 (04)	150 (100)
Total	177 (39)	186 (41)	70 (16)	17 (04)	450 (100)

As the Table No. 6.1 shows, 27 percent of the selected respondents form HPVHA believed the lack of adequate finances as the main problem while 60 percent believed the lack of democratic organizational structure as the main problem, whereas 11 percent believed lack of people's participation as the main problem, but 2 percent of the respondents find no problem at all.

Similarly 60 percent respondents from HGVS opined lack of adequate finances as the main problem while 9 percent believed lack of democratic organizational structure as the main problem, whereas 25 percent believed lack of people's participation as the main problem but 06 percent of the respondents see no problem at all in the organization.

31 percent selected respondents form PRIA believed lack of adequate financial resources as the main problem while 55 percent of them believed lack of democratic organizational structure as the major problem, whereas 10 percent opined that lack of people's participation is the main problem but 4 percent of the respondents see no problem at all in the organization.

In all 39 percent of the respondents believed inadequate financial resources as the main problem, while majority i. e. 41 percent believed as the lack of democratic organizational structure as the main problem, whereas 16 percent believe lack of people's participation in the activities of the NGOs as the main problem but 4 percent of the respondents find no problem at all with the NGOs. This leads to the conclusion that NGOs in Himachal Pradesh are certainly facing various problems and lack of democratic structure is the most prominent problem for them as organizational structure of HPVHA and PRIA are centralized one, followed by inadequacy of resources and lack of people' s participation.

Problems of Securing the Grants

In order to probe further the financial problems of securing grants, the selected respondents were asked as to what was the main problem in securing grants from the funding agencies; governmental as well as others and the responses are as given in Table No. 6.2.

Table No. 6.2: Problems of Securing Grants

Selected Respondents From	*Lack of Awareness for Preparing Proposals*	*Procedural Delays*	*Lack of Assured Finding*	*No Problem at all*	*Total*
HPVHA	38 (25)	49 (33)	61 (41)	02 (01)	150 (100)
HGVS	24 (16)	52 (35)	69 (46)	05 (03)	150 (100)
PRIA	15 (10)	46 (31)	83 (55)	06 (04)	150 (100)
Total	77 (17)	148 (33)	212 (47)	13 (03)	450 (100)

As the Table No. 6.2 indicates, 25 percent of the selected respondents from HPVHA believed that lack of knowledge and awareness about preparing proposals for securing grants from the funding agencies is the major problem, while 33 percent believed the procedural delays and paperwork as the big hurdle in securing the grants, whereas 41 percent believed lack of assured funding or financial assistance to NGOs as the major financial problem, but one percent of the respondents find no problem at all.

16 percent respondents from HGVS believed lack of awareness for preparing proposals for securing grants as the major problem, while 35 percent believed procedural delays as the main problem whereas 46 percent believed the lack of assured finances to NGO as the main problem in seeking grants from the funding agencies, 03 percent of them find no problem at all.

Similarly 10 percent of respondents from PRIA believed lack of knowledge and awareness to prepare proposals for securing grants as the main hurdle, while 31 percent find procedural delays, formalism as the main problem, whereas 55 percent of the respondents believed lack of assured funding to NGOs as the main financial problem but 4 percent of the respondents find no financial problem at all in their organization.

Majority of the respondents i.e. 47 percent believed lack of assured funding to NGOs as the main problem in securing grants from the funding agencies, while 33 percent believed procedure delays and paper work or formalities as the main hurdle, whereas 17 percent of the respondents believed lack of awareness and knowledge to prepare and submit proposal to funding agencies to secure financial assistance from them but 3 percent of the respondents find no problem at all.

The investigations lead to the conclusion that lack of assured funding is the biggest hurdle to secure grants from the funding agencies in the absence of which, there cannot be any pre-planning for undertaking the activities of the organization.

Procedural delays i.e. paper work, legal and normative formalities or bureaucratic interference is the second major problem followed by codal formalities for which NGOs, lack proper knowledge and awareness and all these financial problems are affecting the working and performance of Non- Governmental organizations.

Regular Audit of Accounts

In order to find out if the grants received by the NGOs are properly utilized and there are no misuses of funds the respondents were asked about the check on the grants i.e. whether the account of the organizations are being audited regularly and the responses are as given in Table No. 6.3:-

Table No. 6.3: Regular Audit of the Account

Respondents from	*Yes, being Audited Regularly*	*Audited Occasionally*	*Don't' know*	*Total*
HPVHA	45 (30)	59 (39)	46 (31)	150 (100)
HGVS	82 (55)	36 (24)	32 (21)	150 (100)
PRIA	37 (25)	54 (36)	59 (39)	150 (100)
Total	164 (36)	149 (33)	137 (31)	450 (100

As the Table No. 6.3 depicts, 30 percent selected respondents from HPVHA replied that audit of the organization is being undertaking regularly, while 39 percent believed it being undertaken occasionally, but 31 percent of there spondents are not at all aware of audit checks of the organization.

Similarly 55 percent respondents form HGVS replied that audit of the accounts of the organization is being undertaken regularly, whereas 24 percent replied that accounts are being audited occasionally, but 21 percent of the respondents have no knowledge about the audit of the organizational accounts.

25 percent respondents from the NGO-PRIA responded that audit of the accounts is being held regularly while 36 percent replied that it is being held occasionally, where as 39 percent of the respondents have no knowledge or information about the audit checks.

Majority of the respondents i.e. 36 percent respondents replied that audit of the accounts of the organization is being held regularly, while 33 percent believed it being held occasionally, whereas 31 percent are not at all aware of the audit process.

Investigations lead to the conclusion that though audit of the accounts is being held from time to time as most of the NGOs in Himachal Pradesh, are getting funds from the various governmental agencies but it is only the office-bearers and officials and active participants who are dealing with these matters and are aware of the process whereas majority of the respondents being beneficiaries are not at all well aware of the financial activities of their organizations. It was observed that HGVS which has a duly elected organizational structure do discuss these issues with the members whereas other two NGOs deal with these issues at the officials level hence general members or beneficiaries are not well aware of this process.

Financial Irregularities of the NGOs

In order to probe the financial dealings of the NGOs and to find the misuse of funds the selected respondents were asked whether any irregularity was reported in the audit reports of their organization and the responses are as given in Table No. 6.4.

Table No. 6.4: Financial Irregularities of the NGOs

Respondents from	*Yes, to some Extent*	*Not at all*	*Don't Know*	*Total*
HPVHA	46 (31)	60 (40)	44 (29)	150 (100)

(Contd...)

HGVS	77 (51)	23 (15)	50 (34)	150 (100)
PRIA	32 (21)	20 (13)	98 (66)	150 (100)
Total	155 (34)	103 (23)	192 (43)	450 (100)

As the Table No. 6.4 shows, 31 percent of the selected respondents from HPVHA replied the irregularities to some extent are being found in the accounts, while 40 percent believed that no irregularities are found in the financial transaction of the organization, but 29 percent of the respondents are not at all aware of financial irregularities of the organization.

Similarly 51 percent respondents from the NGO-HGVS replied that irregularities to some extent are being detected in the financial transactions of the organization, while 15 percent believed that there are no irregularities atall, whereas 66 percent of the respondents knew nothing about financial irregularities of the organization.

21 percent respondents from PRIA replied that irregularities to some extent are being found in the financial dealing of the organizations, whereas 13 percent believed that there are no irregularities while 66 percent of the respondents have no knowledge about the financial dealing and the irregularities found in the audit checks of the organization.

In all majority of the respondent i.e. 43 percent are not at all well aware of the financial dealings of the NGOs being the beneficiaries whereas 34 percent have found and know about the irregularities in the financial dealings of their organizations, where as 23 percent of the respondents believed that no irregularly was found in the financial dealings of the NGOs.

The field investigations lead to the conclusion that financial dealings of the NGO are not free from irregularities relating to misuse or misappropriation of funds but it is only office-bearers and the regular staff who are aware of this, whereas majority of the beneficiaries are not at all aware of this as they may not be informed about such issue. Only the members in HGVS discuss audit reports with the members in its annual conferences.

People's Contributions to NGOs

People's contributions in cash and kind can be one of the major sources of funding of NGOs and in earlier times voluntary organizations used to be run through charity. But, of late, especially in independent India welfare activities undertaken by the government through voluntary organizations opened the coffers of the state for financing the programmes sponsored by governments with the result that charity and voluntary donations from the people declined. But no organizations can solely run its entire activities with governmental grants which are most of the time project specific hence, people's contribution is of utmost importance for running any voluntary organization and to enquire about this fact from the selected respondents, they were asked whether you and other people contribute some funds to your organization and the responses are as given in Table No. 6.5:

Table No. 6.5: People's Contributions to NGOs

Respondents from	*To a Great Extent*	*To some Extent*	*Not atall*	*Total*
HPVHA	- (-)	31 (21)	119 (79)	150 (100)
HGVS	97 (65)	43 (29	10 (6)	150 (100)
PRIA	- (-)	21 (14)	129 (86)	150 (100)
Total	97 (21)	95 (21)	258 (58)	450 (100)

As the Table No. 6.5 indicates, only 21 percent of the selected respondents replied that the people do contribute financially to their organizations to some extent, whereas majority of them i.e. 79 percent replied that no financial contributions are being made to the NGO- HPVHA.

65 percent respondents from HGVS replied that financial contributions to the NGO are being made by them and other people to a great extent, where as 29 percent replied their contribution to some extent, only 6 percent of the respondents replied that they are not at all contributing and fund to the NGO.

Similarly only 14 percent of the selected respondents from PRIA replied that they are contributing financially to their NGO to some extent, whereas 86 percent of them did not contribute anything.

As such majority of the selected responds i.e. 58 percent replied that no contributions in terms of finances are being made to the NGOs by them or other people, whereas 21 percent believed their contributions to some extent, while only 21 percent believed the contributions to a great extent.

All this leads to the conclusion that the element of voluntary contributions from the members as well as people has declined to a great extent it is only in some organizations that finances are being secured from the beneficiaries or general masses in the form of membership fees or fees for some services. The charity component is almost missing in the present NGOs, who are being financed by various State/National governments and International agencies. If people do not contribute in the finances and initiatives of the NGOs they cannot expect good services and the overall performance is also affected with this problems.

Organizational Elections

In order to find out various political, administrative, organizational and social problems, the selected respondents from the selected NGOs were probed through the following questions. To know about the democratic structure and functioning of the NGO, the selected respondents were asked whether the office bearers of their respective organization are being elected regularly and the responses are as given in Table No. 6.6.

Table No. 6.6: Organizational Elections

Respondents from	*Yes, held Regularly*	*Yes, held Occasionally*	*Not atall*	*Total*
HPVHA	- (-)	11 (07)	139 (93)	150 (100)
HGVS	136 (91)	12 (08)	02 (01)	150 (100)
PRIA	- (-)	07 (05)	143 (95)	150 (100)
Total	136 (30)	30 (07)	84 (63)	450 (100)

As the Table No. 6.6 indicates, no respondent from HPVHA agreed that any organizational elections are held regularly; only 07 percent of them believed that elections are being held occasionally, whereas 93 percent of the respondents replied that no organizational elections are held in the NGO.

91 percent of the selected respondents from HGVS replied that elections to various positions in the organization are held regularly whereas 8 percent of them believed that elections are held occasionally, only one percent of the respondents believed that elections to various offices are not at all held.

No respondents from PRIA replied that any election of office-bearers in the organization is held; only 05 percent believed that elections are held occasionally, whereas 95 percent of them were of the opinion that there is no elected office in the organization.

It is only 30 percent of the total respondents who replied that elections to various offices of the organization are held, regularly, where as 07 percent believed that they are held occasionally but the majority i.e. 63 percent of the respondents replied that elections are never held in their NGOs. From the personal observation and queries as well as the organizational structure of the NGOs it was found that elections are held only in HGVS from the *Panchayat* level unit to state level conference whereas the organizational structure of the other two NGOs is centralized and based on National level office bearers.

This leads to the conclusion that element of democratic process is missing in most of the NGOs as they have neither democratic structure of the organization nor the democratic process of functioning. In the absence of democratic structure and procedure people's share of participation is bound to decline leading to affect the overall performance of the NGOs.

Monopolization of Leadership

With an objective to find out the leadership of the NGO whether it is cycled amongst the members or ascribed to some status holders the selected respondents were asked whether the same leaders or office-bearers occupy the various offices of the organization time and again and the leadership is monopolized, the responses areas given in Table No. 6.7.

Table No. 6.7: Monopolization of Leadership

Respondents from	*Leadership is Monopolized*	*Leadership and offices are Rotated*	*Don't Know*	*Total*
HPVHA	92	10	48	150
	(61)	(07)	(32)	(100)
HGVS	60	66	24	150
	(40)	(44)	(16)	(100)
PRIA	102	07	41	150
	(68)	(05)	(27)	(100)
Total	254	83	113	450
	(56)	(19)	(25)	(100)

As the Table No. 6.7 shows, 61 percent of the respondents from HPVHA replied that leadership in the organization is monopolized or the same leaders occupy the offices times and again, whereas 7 percent of the respondents believed that the leadership is being rotated amongst the different people but 32 percent of the respondents were not aware of the facts in this regard.

40 percent respondents from HGVS replied that leadership in the organization is in the hands of the same people, whereas 44 percent

responded that it is rotated between the different individuals while 16 percent of the respondents have no knowledge about this fact.

Similarly 68 percent respondents from PRIA believed that leadership in their organization is monopolized while 5 percent believed that it is held in rotation whereas 27 percent of them knew nothing about this issue.

In all, majority of the respondents i.e. 56 percent held that leadership in the NGOs is in the hands of the same individuals, whereas 19 percent believed that it is held by different individuals, while 25 percent of the respondents are unaware of the office-holders.

This leads to the conclusion that leadership in NGOs is monopolized and held by the same persons, may be, to some extent in rotation i.e. secretary of this year may be president for the next term and so on. So far as HPVHA and PRIA are concerned, they have a centralized organizational structure in which there are national executive committee whereas the field agencies are being run by the staff but in HGVS organizational elections are held periodically but the offices, though rotated yet held by the prominent individuals time and again, which ultimately leads to the conclusion that leadership in NGOs is more or less monopolized. Monopolization closes the doors for the young, dynamic and innovative leadership and the problem ultimately affects the overall performance of the NGOs.

Political Affiliations of the NGOs

With a view to investigate the political or ideological affiliation of the NGOs the selected respondents from all the NGOs were asked whether their organization practice any particular ideology or has got affiliation to some political party and the responses are as given in Table No. 6.8

Table No. 6.8: Political Affiliation of NGOs

Respondents from	*Yes, to Great Extent*	*Not atall*	*Don't Know*	*Total*
HPVHA	- (-)	92 (60)	58 (40)	150 (100)
HGVS	77 (51)	31 (21)	42 (28)	150 (100)
PRIA	- (-)	102 (68)	48 (32)	150 (100)
Total	77 (17)	225 (50)	148 (33)	450 (100)

As the Table No. 6.8 depicts, 60 percent respondents from the NGO-HPVHA believed that their organization is not at all affiliated to any particular political ideology or political party and 40 percent of them knew nothing about the political affiliations of their organization.

However, 51 percent respondents from the NGO-HGVS were of the firm opinion that their organization is linked to a particular political ideology or political party, but 21 percent of them replied that the NGO is affiliated to none, while 28 percent of the respondents were not at all sure of the political affiliations of their organization.

Sixty eight percent respondents from PRIA replied that their NGO is not at all affiliated to any particular political ideology or political party, but 32 percent of them knew nothing about the political affiliation of the organization.

In all 17 percent respondents believed that their NGO was affiliated to particular ideology or political party, whereas 50 percent of them believed that their NGO is not at all affiliated to any political ideology or party, while 33 percent of the respondents did know nothing about the political affiliations of their organization.

This leads to the conclusion that some of the NGOs are certainly affiliated to a particular political ideology but others do not believe in a particular political ideology or they aimed at public welfare in all political circumstances.

Trained and Skilled Workers

In the present scientific era, various scientific and technological innovations have revolutionized various services but to manage them, skilled and trained workers are required. NGOs are also deploying them so as to ensure better services to the people. In order to investigate this fact the selected respondents were asked whether trained and skilled workers are deployed in their organization and the responses are as given in Table No. 6.9.

Table No. 6.9: Trained and Skilled Workers

Respondent From	*Yes to a great extent*	*To some extent*	*Not at all*	*Total*
HPVHA	103 (69)	43 (29)	04 (02)	150 (100)
HGVS	93 (62)	49 (33)	08 (05)	150 (100)
PRIA	97 (65)	46 (30)	07 (05)	150 (100)
Total	293 (65)	138 (31)	19 (04)	450 (100)

As the Table No. 6.9 shows, 69 percent of the selected respondents from the NGO-HPVHA replied that skilled and trained workers are being deployed in their organization to a great extent to manage various technical services while, 29 percent of them believed the deployment to some extent, it is only two percent of the respondents who believed that no skilled or trained workers is there in the organization.

In the HGVS, 62 percent of the selected respondents believed that skilled and trained workers have been deployed in their organization to a great extent, while 33 percent of them believed the deployment to some extent, five percent of the respondents believed that no skilled and trained workers are there in the organization.

Similarly 65 percent of the respondents from PRIA replied that their NGO has deployed trained and skilled workers to a great extent, whereas 30 percent of them, believed this to some extent but 05 percent of the respondents did not believe that skilled or trained workers are there in the organization.

In all 65 percent of the respondents believed that trained and skilled workers are being deployed by the NGO to manage various technical services while 30 percent of the respondents supported this opinion to some extent, whereas 4 percent of them find no skilled workers at all.

On the basis of majority opinion, it can safely be concluded that at present various services being provided by the NGOs are being managed with the help of trained and skilled staff, however, the availability of the same may not be similar at all the places.

Use of Modern Techniques and Managerial Methods

In the present day working, the system has altogether changed as the modern techniques, skills and complete professional approach is being applied in undertaking various activities. For example, even in rural areas the roads are not being constructed manually but the latest machinery and trained staff is engaged for the purpose. NGOs, in order to provide better and expert services are supposed to use modern methods and machines. In order to investigate this fact in the working of NGOs in Himachal Pradesh, the respondents were asked whether modern techniques, managerial methods and professional approach is being adopted in their organization and the responses are as given in Table No. 6.10:-

Table No. 6.10: Use of Techniques and Managerial Methods

Respondent From	*To A Great Extent*	*To some Extent*	*Not atall*	*Total*
HPVHA	87 (58)	56 (37)	07 (05)	150 (100)
HGVS	43 (29)	67 (45)	40 (26)	150 (100)
PRIA	38 (25)	73 (49)	39 (26)	(150) 100
Total	168 (37)	196 (44)	86 (19)	450 (100)

As the Table No. 6.10 shows, 58 percent respondents from HPVHA replied that modern techniques, managerial skills and professional approach is being used to a great extent in the organization to provide various services to the people, whereas 37 percent replied the use to some extent but 5 percent of the respondents replied that the same are not being used. HPVHA is active in health sector, hence it is obvious that the organization cannot undertake its activities without using modern techniques and professionals.

Similarly 29 percent selected respondents from the NGO-HGVS responded the use of modern techniques and methods to a great extent, 45 percent believed itsuse to some extent, whereas 26 percent believed that no modern techniques or methods are being used. HGVS is undertaking activities relating to literacy, women empowerment and economic development of the marginalized sections of the society in which experts are required to advise, guide and awaken the masses more, than the modern machines.

25 percent respondents from PRIA believed the use of modern techniques and methods to a great extent, 49 percent believed its use to some extent, and 26 percent believed that no modern techniques and methods are being used in the organization. PRIA is working for empowerment of people through Panchayat Raj Institutions hence they also require experts and experienced professionals to train the people especially the elected representatives of the PRIs instead of modern machines and other professional skills.

In all 37 percent of the respondents believed the use of modern techniques, managerial methods and professionals in the NGOs to a great extent, whereas 44 percent of them believed its use to some extent and 19 percent respondents believed that no modern techniques or methods are being used.

This leads to the conclusion that though the NGOs are applying modern techniques, methods and managerial skills in their working yet the use is not so extensive, obviously for the reason that professionals using modern techniques and methods may not be available to the NGOs working in the rural areas. As such the performance of the NGOs is bound to be affected.

Information and Training about the Programmes to Beneficiaries Members

Any NGO can succeed in its objectives only when it works for the people and with the people. It should make the people aware of its programmes especially the beneficiaries and train its members in publicizing and conducting various programmes of the organization so that masses are benefitted. In order to assess this problem the respondents were asked whether their NGO provides information and training to its members and beneficiaries about the various programmes undertaken by the organization and the responses are as given in Table No. 6.11:-

Table No. 6.11: Information and Training to Beneficiaries Members

Respondents From	*To a great extent*	*To some extent*	*Not at all*	*Total*
HPVHA	42 (28)	67 (45)	41 (27)	150 (100)
HGVS	85 (57)	54 (36)	11 (7)	150 (100)
PRIA	52 (35)	67 (45)	31 (20)	150 (100)
Total	179 (40)	188 (42)	83 (18)	450 (100)

Table No. 6.11 indicates that 28 percent respondents from the NGO-HPVHA believed that information and training to the beneficiaries and members is being provided by the NGO to a great extent whereas 45 percent of them believed it so to some extent but 27 percent of the respondents believed that no information and training at all is being given.

From the NGO-HGVS 57 percent of the respondents believed that information and training is being imparted to a great extent, whereas 36 percent believed it so to some extent but 7 percent of them believed that no information and training at all is being given to the members and beneficiaries HGVS has a wide democratic network of organization hence its information and publicity and training network is quiteactive.

Thirty five percent of the selected respondents from PRIA believed that information and training to beneficiaries are being given to a great extent, whereas 45 percent of them believed it to some extent, but 20 percent of them replied in the negative.

Overall 40 percent of the respondents believed that information and training about the working and programmes of the NGOs is being provided to the beneficiaries and members to a great extent, 42 percent of them believed it so to some extent, but 18 percent of the respondents believed that no information and training at all is being provided.

The investigations lead to the conclusion that information relating to various programmes being undertaken by the NGOs and the training to undertake these programmes is being provided to the public especially to beneficiaries to some extent yet the network is neither very extensive nor much publicity based. NGO's having democratic structure and working has better level of dissemination of information than the centralized NGOs. Thus NGOs are also facing the problems of dissemination of information and training affecting their overall performance.

Coordination amongst Staff, Office-Bearers and Government Agencies

In order to conduct the activities of the voluntary organizations efficiently and effectively there should be proper coordination amongst the office bearers, staff, members, beneficiaries and government agencies at local, state and national level. Proper linkages and coordination with the governmental agencies can ensure more programmes, better exchange of information and financial assistance, better performance and fewer hurdles. But lack of proper coordination is one of the big problems of NGOs. In order to find out the ground realities among the NGOs under investigations, the selected respondents were asked whether there is problem of proper coordination among the office-bearers, staff members, of the NGO and the government agencies and the responses are as given in Table No. 6.12:-

Table No. 6.12: Coordination amongst office-bearer, Staff and Government Agencies

Respondent From	*To a great extent*	*To some extent*	*Not atall*	*Total*
HPVHA	77 (51)	42 (28)	31 (21)	150 (100)
HGVS	47 (31)	65 (43)	38 (26)	150 (100)
PRIA	36 (24)	67 (45)	47 (31)	150 (100)
Total	160 (36)	174 (38)	116 (26)	450 (100)

As the Table No. 6.12 depicts, 51 percent of the respondents from HPVHA believed that there is problem of proper coordination amongst the office-bearers, members of the staff and governmental agencies to a great extent, whereas 28 percent of them believed the existence of the problem to some extent but 21 percent of the respondents find no problem at all.

Similarly 31 percent of the respondents from HGVS, 31 percent believed the existence of the problem of coordination to a great extent, 43 percent believed it to some extent whereas 26 percent of them find no problem at all.

24 percent respondents from the NGO PRIA believed the existences of coordination problems to a great extent, 45 percent believed it to some extent whereas 31 percent believed that there was no problem of coordination at all. In all 36 percent of the respondents believed the existence of coordination problem to a great extent, 38 percent believed that to some extent but 26 percent of the respondents find no problem at all, so far as the coordination amongst offices-bearers staff and governmental agencies are concerned.

We can conclude from the investigations that problem of proper coordination amongst office-bearers, the staff members, beneficiaries of NGOs and the government agencies is prevailing which certainly affects the working and financing of NGOs and due services to the people and as such NGOs may not be in a position to perform well. Prevailing of the problem also leads to the conclusion that some effective mechanism are missing to maintain better level of coordination amongst the NGOs and governmental agencies and in this process ultimate sufferer are the people.

Quality of Services by NGOs

Since the time India was declared welfare state, a number of welfare schemes were introduced but the governmental agencies were not in a position to implement them all, hence the mechanism of voluntary organizations was engaged and used for the purpose. With the passage of time, finding lucrative offers from the government, number of NGOs increased to provide various services to the masses but the problem of maintenance of quality service cropped-up affecting the performance of NGOs and services to the people. Whether the problem of providing the quality service to the people is still existing or not, to probe this issue the selected respondents were asked whether their organizations is ensuring quality services to the masses and the responses are as given in Table No. 6.13.

Table No. 6.13: Quality of NGO's Service

Respondent From	*To a great extent*	*To some extent*	*Not atall*	*Total*
HPVHA	35 (23)	66 (44)	49 (33)	150 (100)
HGVS	47 (31)	68 (45)	35 (24)	150 (100)
PRIA	59 (39)	42 (28)	49 (33)	150 (100)
Total	141 (31)	176 (39)	133 (30)	450 (100)

As the Table No. 6.13 shows, 23 percent of the respondents from the NGO HPVHA believed that their organization is maintaining a level of quality services to the people to a great extent, whereas 44 percent of them believed it to be so to some extent, however, 33 percent of the responds believed that quality services are not at all being provided.

Similarly 31 percent respondents from HGVS believed that the organization is providing quality services to the people to a great extent whereas 45 percent of them believed it to be so to some extent, however, 24 percent of the respondents believed that quality services are not at all being provided.

So far as the NGO-PRIA is concerned, 39 percent of its respondents believed that quality of service is being maintained to a great extent whereas 28 percent believed the quality of service to some extent but 33 percent of the respondents believed that quality services are not at all being provided.

In aggregate, 31 percent of the respondents believed that NGOs are providing quality services to a great extent, 39 percent believed that quality of services being maintained by the NGOs to some extent, whereas 30 percent of all the respondents opined that quality of services is not at all being maintained.

From the investigators it can be inferred that in some organization quality of services may be of good standard but overall the quality of services being provided by the NGOs has deteriorated for the reasons that they lack skilled workers, dedicated leadership and the professional competence. As such the problem of maintenance of quality of services is certainly affecting the performance of NGOs.

Centralization of Decision Making Process

Decision making process itself has a great value for the organization. People-oriented, timely and unbiased decisions and decisions taken democratically have a great value for the organization as well as the beneficiaries or the public. However, undemocratic decision making process in which there is element of centralism and authoritarianism, itself is a great problem in the effective working and performance of a NGO. Whether the NGOs under study are facing this problem, to probe this, the selected respondents were asked, if there is centralization of decisions making process in their organization and the responses areas given in Table No. 6.14.

Table No. 6.14: Centralization of Decision Making Process

Respondents From	*To A Great Extent*	*To Some Extent*	*Not at All*	*Total*
HPVHA	114 (76)	32 (21)	04 (03)	150 (100)
HGVS	79 (53)	23 (15)	48 (32)	150 (100)
PRIA	106 (71)	42 (28)	02 (01)	150 (100)
Total	299 (66)	97 (22)	54 (12)	450 (100)

Table No. 6.14 indicates, that 76 percent of the selected respondents from HPVHA believed that there is centralization in the decision making process of the NGO to a great extent, while 21 percent believed the centralization to some extent, but three percent of the respondents find no centralization at all.

Similarly 51 percent respondents from the NGO-HGVS believed that there is centralization to a great extent, 15 percent believed it to some extent, and 32 percent find no centralization at all. HGVS has democratic structure hence they believed less centralization but ideologically the organization functions on the principle of democratic centralism.

71 percent respondents from the NGO-PRIA replied that there is centralization in decision making in the NGO to a great extent, while 28 percent believed the centralization to some extent whereas only one percent believed that there is no centralization at all.

In all 66 percent of the respondents believed that the decision making process of the NGOs is centralized to a great extent, whereas 22 percent believed the centralization to some extent, but 12 percent of the respondents find no centralization at all.

We may conclude from the investigations that decision making process of NGOs is highly centralized which can create further problem of acceptability and implementation of the decisions taken. Hence NGOs are still facing the problem of centralization of decision making process which affects the overall performance of the NGOs.

People Participation in the Activities of the NGOs

For the success of welfare and developmental programmes of NGOs and the NGO itself, it is essential that people voluntarily come forward to participate in the activities of the NGO. People's participation can ensure better performance and development initiatives, which may fulfill the objectives of the organization and the programmes undertaken. In order to find out whether people participate in the activities of the NGOs, the selected respondents were asked if peoples voluntarily participate in the activities of the NGOs and the response are as given in Table No. 6.15.

Table No. 6.15: People's Participation

Respondents From	*To A Great Extent*	*To Some Extent*	*Not at All*	*Total*
HPVHA	27 (18)	65 (43)	58 (39)	150 (100)
HGVS	43 (29)	72 (48)	35 (23)	150 (100)
PRIA	31 (21)	73 (49)	46 (30)	150 (100)
Total	101 (22)	210 (47)	139 (31)	450 (100)

As the Table No. 6.15 shows, only 18 percent of the respondents from HPVHA replied that people participate in the activities of the NGO voluntarily to a great extent, whereas 43 percent of the respondents believed voluntary participation to some extent but 39 percent of the respondents replied that people do not participate voluntarily in the activities of the NGO.

Similarly 29 percent respondents from the NGO-HGVS believed that people participate in the activities of the NGO voluntarily to a great extent, 48 percent believed participation to some extent whereas 23 percent of the respondents believed that people not at all participate voluntarily in the activities of the NGO.

21 percent respondents from the NGO-PRIA replied that people participation voluntarily in the activities of the NGO to a great extent, 49 percent believed the participation to some extent whereas 30 percent believed that people do not at all participate voluntarily in the activities of the organization.

In overall analysis, 22 percent of the respondents believed that people participation voluntarily in the activities of the NGOs to a great extent, 47 percent believed the participation to some extent, whereas 31 percent believed that people do not at all participate voluntarily in the activities of the NGOs.

This leads to the conclusion that people lack enthusiasm to be active participant in the affairs of the NGOs, rather they have to be motivated time and again to be the part of the NGO, which means that NGOs are still facing the a big problem of voluntary participation of the people, in spite of the fact that NGOs have emerged as the developmental outfits in the present circumstances. If people do not participate in the implementation of various programmes, it becomes difficult to undertake activities and the NGO also fails in its performance.

Spirit of Volunteerism among the People

Spirit of volunteerism is the hallmark of voluntary organizations. In earlier times it was the sole binding force to make the people to become the part of the charity organizations and now since more activities in place of charitable initiatives are being undertaken by the modern organizations hence the spirit of volunteerism must be all pervasive among the people. In order to assess the position at the ground level, the selected respondents were asked whether they believe that spirit of volunteerism is still prevailing among the masses or there is some decline in it and the responses are as given in Table No. 6.16.

Table No. 6.16: Spirit of Volunteerism

Respondent From	*Spirit of Volunteerism Prevails*	*There is Decline*	*There is Great Decline*	*Total*
HPVHA	32	77	41	150
	(21)	(52)	(27)	(100)
HGVS	46	67	37	150
	(30)	(45)	(25)	(100)
PRIA	39	69	42	150
	(26)	(46)	(28)	(100)
Total	117	213	120	450
	(26)	(47)	(27)	(100)

As the Table No. 6.16 shows, spirit of volunteerism among the people is still prevailing to some extent as 21 percent of the respondents from the NGO HPVHA believed the prevalence of it but 52 percent of the respondents believed that there is decline in it, where as 27 percent of them believed that there is a great decline in it.

Similarly 30 percent respondents from the NGO-HGVS believed that spirit of volunteerism is still prevailing, but 45 percent of them believed that there is decline in it . Whereas 25 percent of them believed that there is a great decline in the spirit of volunteerism among the people.

26 percent respondents from the NGO-PRIA believed that volunteerism is still prevailing among the people whereas 46 percent of them believed in its decline and 28 percent believed the decline to great a extent.

In all 26 percent of the respondents opined that spirit of volunteerism among the people is still prevailing whereas 47 percent of the respondents believed that it is declining and 27 percent of them believed that there is great decline in the spirit of volunteerism amongst the people.

We may conclude from the available responses that spirit of volunteerism which used to be hallmark of voluntary organization has declined to a great extent and the NGOs as such are facing the problem of absence of erstwhile spirit of volunteerism which is certainly affecting the overall working and performance of the NGOs.

Summary of the Chapter

Millions of Non-Governmental Organizations are engaged in various social sector activities helping the poor, deprived, disadvantaged and destitute. In the post- independence era flow of governmental funds to NGOs has helped a lot in their proliferation. Today NGOs have become great service provider in education, health, employment generation; self-employment, mother-child health care and several other sectors. In spite of the fact that they have become a very important tool of socio-economic development, the NGOs also have their share of problems. Various studies conducted so far reveal that NGOs are facing various socio-economic, political and administrative problems affecting their working and performance. There is problem of proper mechanism for coordination among them selves and with their district, state branches and national head quarters. Due to lack of proper policy NGOs are facing the problem of relationship with the government. There is yet another problem of erosion of old values of volunteerism facing the organizations. Due to governmental grant system NGOs are also facing the problem of innovations and have become solely dependent upon the government. In government grants also they have to face the difficulties of formalism and have become more obedient to government and less responsible to people. Centralization in the NGOs has eroded their corporate and collegiate nature and support and involvement of the people is missing from them. There is sharp decline in the voluntary spirit among the people and they hardly contribute anything to these organizations. Voluntary agencies also suffer from lack of professionalism and no skilled or trained worker is ready to work in the rural areas. Another problem facing NGOs is the use of relevant technology, managerial talent and professional skills. Professionals are not ready to work in villages. The studies reveal the overall problems of absence of volunteerism, lack of dedicated leadership, lack of assured funds, lack of trained personnel and lack of coordination. Centralization of NGOs in urban areas, deterioration in quality of services, misuse of funds, lack of public participation and monopolization of leadership as the major problems of the NGOs affecting the overall performance of the NGOs.

In the light of these studies, an attempt has been made to analyze the problems facing the selected NGOs in Himachal Pradesh which may be affecting the performance of their organizations. The investigations reveal that NGOs in Himachal Pradesh are also facing several financial, organizational administrative, political and social problems. Major problems of NGOs in Himachal Pradesh are; lack of democratic structure and working followed by inadequate resources and lack of people's participation. Lack of assured grants from funding agencies, paper work involved in securing the government grants, bureaucratic interference and lack of proper knowledge and awareness about finance and financial procedures are other financial problems facing NGOs in Himachal Pradesh. In order to check the misuse of funds and to find out irregularities in appropriating the grants received by the NGOs, audit of accounts is held from time to time but only office-bearers and staff members know about the process, whereas general members and beneficiaries are totally ignorant of the process. Financial dealings of the NGOs in Himachal Pradesh are not free from irregularities but only the office bearers and staff members know about them. Some of the NGOs do discuss these issues but only those which are based on democratic structure and functioning. Financial contributions from the public have declined to great extent. It is only the fees and other changes which are being collected by the NGOs for the membership or some professional services. The charily component of public contribution is almost missing in the NGOs, who are now totally dependent upon the government agencies for their financial needs.

The element of democratization is also missing in structure of most of the NGOs as they have neither democratic structure or democratically elected office bearers or the leadership nor process of functioning. Leadership in

NGOs in Himachal Pradesh is almost monopolized as no democratic process in electing the office bears is followed in most of the NGOs. NGOs in Himachal Pradesh do ascribe to a particular political ideology but majority of them are more particular about public welfare then the political affiliations. Though NGOs are using the services of trained and skilled manpower to some extent yet their availability everywhere is a problem affecting the delivery of services. NGOs in Himachal Pradesh are also applying modern technology, management methods and professionalism in their working to some extent but its use and availability in rural areas is a big problem itself. Information, training, publicity and network of the NGOs are also not so extensive, especially in the NGOs having centralized organizational structure. NGOs in Himachal Pradesh are also facing the problem of coordination among themselves, staff members, beneficiaries and government agencies which become a problem for effective functioning and performance, securing finances and to ensure due service to the beneficiaries. Though NGOs in Himachal Pradesh do emphasize quality of services, yet the same has certainly deteriorated for want of skilled and spirited workers, dedicated leadership and the professional competence. Hence the maintenance of quality of service is yet another problem facing NGOs in Himachal Pradesh, which is affecting the overall performance of the NGOs.

Non-Governmental Organization in Himachal Pradesh is also facing the problem of centralization of decision making process as the organizational structure in most of the NGOs is centralized. People do not participate voluntarily in the activities of the NGOs. Spirit of volunteerism is a hall mark of voluntary organizations but the investigations reveal that the same has declined to a great extent and the NGOs working in Himachal Pradesh are facing the problem of absence of volunteerism which is affecting their performance.

As such we conclude from the study that the NGOs in Himachal Pradesh do have their share of problems and are facing the problems of finances, lack of democratic organizational structure and working, monopolization of leadership, lack of trained and skilled as well as spirited workers, non-availability of modern technological support and professionalism, dissemination of information and training to beneficiaries and staff as well as members, lack of proper coordination, centralization in decision making process, people's non-participation and the declining spirit of volunteerism. All these problems are certainly affecting the performance of the Non-Governmental Organizations.

Notes

1. V. Krishnamurthi, 'Voluntary Action in Rural Dev: a survey'*Kurushetra* Vol. 34 (1) New Delhi Oct. 1985. pp. 33-36.
2. Sugata Dasgupta 'Voluntary Organizations in Rural development' *Voluntary Action*,Vol. 14 (1) January- February 1972, pp. 6-14.
3. G. Narayana Ready, 'Human Resources for Voluntar y Action'. *Khadi gramdoyog*, Vol. 33 (8) May 1987 pp. 331-335 as cited in I.U. Bhaskara Ready 'Role of Voluntary Agencies in Ruler Development' *The Indian Journal of Public Administration* , Op. cit. pp. 550.
4. Raj Krishna, 'TestingVoluntary Agencies: I t would be a futileexercise' *Yojna*, Vol. 28 (20 and 21) Nov. 1984, pp. 7-8.
5. D. Paul Chowdhary, 'Appraisal of Voluntary effort in Social welfare' *The Indian Journal of Public Administration* Op. cit. p. 497.
6. Op. cit. p. 498.
7. Op.citp. p. 499.
8. *Ibid.*
9. H. R. Chaturvedi, 'Role of Voluntary Organization in Rural Development', *Indian Journal of Public Administration,* Op cit. p. 537.
10. *Ibid.*
11. *Ibid.*
12. Op. cit p. 538.
13. *Ibid.*
14. Op. cit. p. 539.
15. Op. cit. p. 539-40.
16. G. Narayan Ready op. cit. pp. 555.
17. I .Uday Bhaskra Reddy op. cit. p. 556.
18. Lokayam No. 4 pp. 3-4 as quoted in HR. Chatruvedi, 'Role of voluntary Organizations in Rural India Development', *The Indian Journal* of *Public Administration* Op. cit. p. 543.
19. H. R. Chaturvedi-op. cit. p. 544.
20. Snriram Maheshwari, 'Voluntary Actionin Rural India' *The Indian Journal of Public Administration* , op. cit., p. 564-65.
21. Harsh Sethi, 'Environmentalism, Ecology and voluntary Action' *The Indian Journal of Public Administration*, op cit., p. 575.
22. J. S. Mehta, 'Challenges and Opportunities for Volunteerism', *The Indian Journal of Public Administration*, op. cit., p. 527.
23. Op cit pp. 528-29.
24. Op. cit. p. 529.
25. Op. cit p. 530.
26. B. T. Lawani, Op. cit. pp. 200-204.
27. K. D. Gangrade, *Developing Voluntary Action: Encyclopedia of Social Work*, Ministry of Welfare, Government of India, New Delhi, 1987, p. 227.

28. D. R. Sachdev, *Social Welfare Administrative in India,* Kitab Mahal Agency, Allahabad, 1992, p. 205.
29. I .S. Sundram, *Voluntary Agencies and Rural Development,* B. R. Publishing Corporation, Delhi, 1986, p. 201.
30. Paul D. Chaudhary, *Voluntary in Social Welfare and Development,* Sidharth Publishers, New Delhi, 1990, pp. 78-81.

Chapter - 7

Findings, Conclusion and Suggestions

Community or group life amongst the human beings is one of the earliest and the most enduring features of human existence on this earth. This natural inclination for living and working together with others, underlines the prevalence of various social groupings such as family clan, community, friendship, group organization etc. These groupings are composed of individuals who are interrelated and bound together in a network of relatively stable social relationship. Thus the human society is organizational, dominating every sphere of human activity in almost all the countries of the world. Organizations are not a modern invention but as old as human civilization, as we cannot live without them. Organization is a group of people constituted for a given purpose or for the attainment of a common purpose.

There are several types of organizations such as mutual benefit organizations, business concerns, service organizations and common wealth organizations in which public is the primary beneficiary group. Division of labour, power and communication are responsibilities deliberately planned to enhance the realization of specific goals, the presence of one or more power centre to control the concerted efforts of the organization and substitution of personnel i.e. removal of unsatisfied persons and assigning the task to others and transfer as well as promotion are some of the characteristics of an organization.

Since the present study deals with Non-Governmental Organizations or Voluntary Organization as such it is essential to know their meaning, characteristics and categories etc. Various definitions of experts lead to the conclusion that non- governmental organization or voluntary organization is an organization formed by persons to further common interest of its members with voluntary membership without the direct control of the state.

Simple charity, supplementing welfarism of the state, encouraging people's participation in implementing programmes for the benefit of the community, involving people in programme planning, raising resources, implementing activities, sharing fruits of development, conscience instilling and organizing people enabling them to demand and undertake planning and implementation of development programmes beneficial to them, are some of the strategies of the NGOs to meet their objectives.

Non-governmental organizations have been classified into seven categories i.e. charity, welfare, relief, rehabilitation, services, development of socio- economic environment and development of human beings.

Proper registration under the appropriate Act, administrative structure and duly constituted managing executive committee, definite aims, objectives and programmes in fulfillment of these and governance by its own members on democratic principles without any external control are some of the important characteristics of a non-governmental organization. Virtues of human touch, dedication, flexibility, self-reliance and nearness to the community are some of the other features of a NGO.

Volunteerism and voluntary organizations is not a new phenomenon but also existed in the ancient past and medieval India. It used to operate in the field of education, medicine, cultural promotion and succor in crises. The large scope of volunteerism in development during ancient and medieval India, however, did not mitigate the social inequalities of the rigid caste system, heaped on lower castes, especially the untouchables. The role of voluntarism in development in ancient and medieval India was not affected much by the inroads of the Muslims and their rule in different parts of the country.

India as such has a great tradition of voluntary services and in spite of rapid change; the urge to serve fellowmen is still strong and widespread. Right through the ages this tradition has been accepted as social obligation on the part of the individual towards his less fortunate brethren. Religion emphasized the virtue of *dan* i.e. free gift which encompassed different forms of social service.

There was a wave of social reform movements in the 19th and early 20th century which marked the emergence of new phase of social work in India Raja Ram Mohan Roy, Ishwar Chandra Vidyasagar, Keshab Chandrasen, Swami Dayanand Saraswati, Swami Vivekanand, Mahatama Phule, Sir Sayyad Ahmed Khan are the persons who brought about social change in India, during the 19th century, through voluntary agencies.

Volunteerism in development during the British rule received a boost in new religious, cultural and social surroundings, though traditional sources of volunteerism lost the leaven and intensity. The laissez-faire policy of the British government in economics, religious and social matters left another avenue of development open to the natives then to resort to self-help, another term of voluntarism. The Christian missionary educational institutions and hospitals and dispensaries set an example to the non-convert majorities both Hindus and Muslims to emulate. Schools and colleges were established by educational societies set up by English educated natives and different persons. Voluntary organizations proliferated and took part in various fields of social action during the British rule.

During the days of national movement, with the growth of volunteerism in social and welfare development, new movements were initiated in rural areas, including agricultural development in a few provinces. In the industrial sector, managing agency and other forms of legalized voluntary modes helped industrial and ancillary activities including banking and development. Gandhiji came on the Indian political scene in the beginning of 20th century and he contributed a lot in the development of voluntary organizations. To channelize the people's power at the grassroot level, he founded several voluntary organization and some of them are even working today in the 21st century.

After Independence voluntary action changed in its approach and structure and India was declared a welfare state and government undertook several welfare schemes under various plans and policies. It also encouraged voluntary organizations to undertake social welfare programems under the grant- in-aid programmes, with the passage of time voluntary organizations expanded their activities to cover practically every field of social welfare. They not only undertook programmes with their own resources but also organized projects sponsored by the state. Recognizing the importance of NGOs the government took concrete steps to assist voluntary agencies and greater scope and space in terms of action and finance was provided to them in every subsequent five year plans.

Thus the tradition of voluntarism in India is quite old which has undergone several changes with the passage of time. From charitable arena the focus has moved to developmental process and to-day NGOs have turned out as development outfits.

Several studies carried out by the academicians, scholars, researches at the national level and in other states reveal that the NGOs are performing very important role in the development process of the country. Though,

Voluntary organization or NGOs as they are called are occupying an important place in Himachal Pradesh also yet no substantial research work on the structure, working, contributions and problems affecting the performance of NGO's have been carried out in Himachal Pradesh, hence this study is an attempt in this direction.

Findings of the Study

The present study is based on the field investigations carried out on three state level Non-Governmental Organization i.e. Himachal Pradesh Voluntary Health Association (HPVHA), *Himachal Gyan Vigyan Samiti* (HGVS) and Society for Participatory Research in Asia (PRIA). The objectives of the study are to know and analyze the organizations, working, performance and contribution in the socio-political and economic development and to study and analyze the problems affecting the performance of NGOs in Himachal Pradesh.

Investigations carried out with the help of documentary sources and field survey into the organization, objectives, working and performance of the selected NGOs reveal that HPVHA which is working in the social sector was established in 1987 under Societies Registration Act, 1860 with an objective to improve the health of the community. It is a state level federation of voluntary organizations engaged in health and development activities. The HPVHA liaisons for the grassroot NGOs with the State Government, National Government and International Agencies to promote social justice and distribution of health services in Himachal Pradesh. At present HPVHA is engaged with health related projects such as Reproductive Health, Promotion of Low Cost Primary Health care through alternative system of Medicine, Prevention and Control of STD/HIV/AIDS, Disability, Child Health and Rights, Capacity Building of NGOs, Advocacy and Information Dissemination.

HPVHA's organizational structure is broadly divided into two levels i.e. Management Team and Administrative Staff. The policy decisions are taken at the management level and the Executive Director implements and convey the same down the line of command. HPVHA gets financial support from foreign as well as Indian agencies. Objectives of the HPVHA are: Justice in Health care, optimum utilization of material or available resource, build up people's health movement, to help in the evolution of low cost people oriented health programmes with traditional skills of community, conduct research studies on primary health care, training and education to people to strengthen voluntary organizations for health and development etc.

HPVHA undertook the children health budget analysis of Himachal Pradesh Government for a period of five years, reproductive child health needs in un-served and underserved areas and currently running two important projects for 'Family Planning' and 'Healthy Highways' for prevention and control of STD/HIV/AIDS. Field investigations reveal that people are familiar with the NGO-HPVHA and are well aware of its organization, objectives, programmes and performance. HPVHA is providing commendable service in health awareness, reproductive health of women and prevention and control of STD/HIV/AIDS and its 'Family Planning' and 'Healthy Highway' projects are performing well in the assigned sectors and people have been benefitted with the initiatives of the NGO. The role and performance of the organization has addressed the health related issues of the society to some extent and people believe that organization is performing well in this social sector.

Investigations carried out into the organizational structure, objectives, working and performance of the NGO-HGVS, which was formally inaugurated on 14th June 1992 reveal that it has got a well-structured organization with democratically elected office-bearers at all levels. It has got a five level structure of the organization i.e. Panchayat ward level Conference, Panchayat level Conference, Block Conference, District Conference and State Conference. Its objectives included creation of fully literate society, to focus towards human resource development, to generate voluntarism and volunteer culture, to inculcate scientific temper, empowerment of women and disadvantaged sections of the society, to preserve the plurality and identity of the local culture and to preserve traditional values. The NGO is working in the thrust areas such as; Education, Development, Health, Environment, Participatory Democracy, Gender Issues and Library movement through the methodology of training, orientation, workshops, seminars, conferences, participation and distribution of resource material and mass mobilization through *Kala Jathas*. HGVS works at three levels i.e. intervention at policy level, creating, facilitating and providing supportive role to community based organizations and taking awareness or campaigns to people. HGVS undertook various programmes such as *'Bharat Gyan Vigyan Jatha, Samta Gyan Vigyan Jatha* focusing on literacy and women equality, 'Joy of Learning' for developing interest in children towards education in general and science education in particular *'Desh Ko Jano Desh Ko Badlo'* was its total literacy and continuing education campaign.

The field investigations reveal that the NGO is quite active and effective in Himachal Pradesh and people are well aware of its organization, objectives, role and performance. The organization has rendered great services in literacy mission, women empowerment and science education. The programmes undertaken and the services rendered by the NGO has benefited the people of the region and people find a change in the society due to NGO's initiatives in literacy and empowerment. The people are satisfied with the performance of the NGO in the social, economic and political sectors.

The NGO–Society for Participatory Research in Asia (PRIA) started by Dr. Rajesh Tandon in India in 1982 is working with a vision of a world where informed, empowered citizens participate in the process of deepning democracy with tolerance towards its large number and diversity.

The basic objective of the PRIA in India was to empower marginalized; the poor, the depressed, women, the *Dalits* and the *tribals*. As per new strategic framework of PRIA 'Governance where People Matter' is an attempt to integrate and converge different interventions in a holistic manner. PRIA's direct intervention is to yield effective voice of new leadership and transparent and accountable self-governing institutions. PRIA has got a national level organizational structure with its office-bearers as Chairperson, President, Treasurer and five members, whereas state level or field level operations are carried out through established offices managed by the staff members. PRIA is supported financially by various international and national agencies. The overall aim of the organization is to empower the marginalized sections of the society and as such conducted programmes which encouraged grassroot groups to act on the knowledge they possessed, organizational management and participatory planning and monitoring. In order to strengthen PRIs, it campaigned for proper conduct of *Gram Sabha* meetings, trained elected representatives of PRIs and under the current framework 'Governance Where People Matter' has been working for the qualitative improvement in governance by capacity building of elected representatives and enhancing people's participation. PRIA also collaborated with academic institutions to promote teaching and research on participatory development, civil society and democratic governance. Its special efforts include preparing women leaders to engage with governance institutions and processes.

PRIA has organized its activities and conducted various programmes in Himachal Pradesh and the present study conducted in Kangra and Hamirpur districts of the Pradesh reveals that the NGO is familiar among the people and people are aware of its organization, objectives, working and performance. People are also aware of the services being provided by the NGO and believe that it is providing useful services to awaken and empower the people especially marginalized sections. People have been benefitted with the services of the NGO and believe that there is overall change and improvement in the local governance and people's representative have say in governance. People are satisfied with the performance of the NGO-PRIA which proved quite useful for the people and especially to the elected representatives of the PRIs.

Investigations into the contribution of the NGOs in the socio-political and economic sectors reveal that Non- Governmental Organizations have become inseparable part in the present day developmental efforts and they are not only supplementing governmental initiatives but providing various services to the people. NGOs at the present juncture have turned out as developmental out-fits in place of charity associations of yore and they are undertaking various self-planned and government sponsored developmental projects so as to improve upon the lives of the people in India especially the marginalized sections.

The NGOs under investigations i.e. HPVHA, HGVS and PRIA have under taken various developmental activities in Himachal Pradesh. Various projects leading to socio-political and economic development of the masses are being managed by the NGOs. Investigations into the contribution of the NGO-HPVHA reveal that it is working with a social cause 'Making Health A Reality'. The NGO has undertaken several programmes and projects to provide health services to Children, Women and other vulnerable section of the society. Two important projects of the NGO are, Family Planning' in which different initiatives to control the population have been taken by it and the 'Healthy Highways' which are operational in district *Bilaspur*. Investigations reveal that people are dependent upon the government institutions for their medical needs in the absence of which they have to rely on local *Vaids, Hakeems* and faith healers. People are familiar with the role and activities of the NGO-HPVHA in the health sector and the organization regularly organize health related activities and camps. People are making use of the services of the NGO and its initiatives in family planning and prevention and control of STD/HIV/AIDS have contributed a lot in the health sector of the region. All the sections of the society have been benefitted with the activities and services of the NGO and its contribution in the social sector is well recognized.

Investigations into the contributions of HGVS reveal that its initial objective was to create a conducive environment and demand for literacy, however, human resource development, generation of volunteerism and voluntary culture, interface between experts and common people, health for all, women empowerment, environmental protection and capacity building of the masses are other areas of interest for the NGO. The organization is popular among the people and they are well aware of its socio-economic activities and do participate in them. Literacy Mission of the NGO has helped the common people to improve upon their quality of life, creation of self-help groups, has helped in creating economic activities for the people especially the women who are earning through these groups by organizing various productive activities leading to their economic empowerment. Orientation and training programmes organized by the NGO for women have helped in the emergence and growth of women leadership leading to empowerment of women. The NGO has also helped in raising various socio- economic issues of the people at the appropriate level and getting them addressed from the authorities concerned. NGO has also taken initiative in environmental protection, preservation and exploitation of local resources, culture and tradition useful to the society. Activities and the programmes undertaken by the NGO have helped in the socio- economic development of the people and the region.

The NGO-PRIA which has an overall objective of empowerment of the people especially the marginalized sections, who are taught to participate in decision making process and governance, thereby leading to their political empowerment. PRIA pioneered in strengthening the *Panchayati Raj* system by building the capacity of the people leading to their empowerment. PRIA organizes various activities for the capacity building of the people and later are well aware of all those activities and programmes of the NGO. PRIA organizes orientation and training programmes for the elected representatives of the PRIs and assist these institutions through various activities so as to strengthen the democratic process at the grassroot level leading to political empowerment of the people. PRIA also organizes orientation and awareness campaigns for sensitizing the common masses over the issues of democratic governance but peoples' participation in these camps is very poor hence ensuring people's participation itself is a big problem for the organization. The initiatives of PRIA have improved the working of *Gram Sabha* and participation of marginalized sections has also improved considerably. PRIA's intervention has also helped in the emergence and growth of women leadership and the PRIs has also been strengthened considerably leading to people's empowerment. Initiatives of PRIA have certainly contributed in the political development of the region and its people.

Non-Governmental Organizations do have their share of problems which ultimately affects their overall performance. Though problems and deficiencies of NGOs differ from organization to organization and region to region, however, there are some common problems which affect the performance of all the voluntary organizations. Various studies reveal that availability of finances, funding agencies, financial support from people, proper utilization of funds, timely audit of funds, maintenance of quality services, availability of matching grants, enhancement of grants in terms of inflation are common financial problems facing NGOs. The concept of charity has almost declined and in the absence of desirable resources NGOs themselves are incapable of rendering various services to the people which ultimately affects the overall performance of the NGOs.

Lack of dedicated leadership, absence of support from the bureaucracy, excessive legalism and formalism, shifting of emphasis by the government from time to time, lack of professional and trained social workers, managerial talent and professional skill to catalyze faster progress in rural sector, lack of understanding between different groups, politicization of NGOs, controlling NGOs by the power hungry politicians or dominant persons, lack of coordination between NGOs and governmental agencies, centralization by NGOs tour ban areas are various other problems of administrative and technical nature affecting the performance of NGOs.

Absence of erstwhile spirit of volunteerism, dedicated youth volunteers, monopolization of leadership, lack of people's participation, lack of clarity of roles in the organization are some other recognized problems facing the NGOs.

Investigations into the deficiencies and problems of Non- Governmental Organization under study in Himachal Pradesh also reveal that these organizations working in this Pradesh are also facing several problems.

The investigations carried out relating to the problems affecting the performance of the non-governmental organizations in Himachal Pradesh reveal that here also NGOs are coming across several financial, organizational, administrative, political and social problems. Lack of assured funding, formalism and legalism involved in securing governmental grants, bureaucratic interference and lack of knowledge and awareness about financial procedures, irregularities in financial matters, absence of regular checks over the accounts, lack of transparency in financial dealings, absence of financial contribution from the people and total dependence of NGOs upon the government and other funding agencies are the major financial problems of NGOs in Himachal Pradesh affecting their performance.

NGOs in Himachal Pradesh are also facing several organizational, administrative and political problems, which are affecting the performance of NGOs. Findings reveal that some of the major problems in these categories facing NGOs are : lack of democratic structure and working of NGOs, monopolization of leadership, dominance of political ideology over some of the NGOs, non-availability of trained and skilled manpower, non-availability of professionals, modern technology and mangers in rural areas, lack of information and training network of NGOs, absence of coordination with the various governmental agencies and amongst themselves, to maintain quality in services in the absence of dedicated leadership and professional competence. Findings reveal that NGOs are also facing the problem of centralization of decision making process and the absence of spirit of volunteerism amongst the people which has also declined to a great extent.

Conclusion

Inclination for living and working together with other underlines the prevalence of various social organizations such as family, clan, community, friendship group and other such organizations. Organizations are as old as human society itself and it is a fact that we spend a good deal of our time in the various activities of different organizations existing in the society. Organizations of various nature have been dominating the human society and its activities in almost all the countries of the world and India is also no exception to such organizations. Organizations have been in existence since ancient past to fulfill a greater variety of social and personal needs and affected a large segment of people's lives, however in comparison to earlier organizations, modern organizations are more efficient than their ancient or medieval species because changed nature of society has made the social environment more congenial to organizations with the result that one or the other organization, governmental or non-governmental are dominating every sphere of human activity right from birth till death.

There are several types of organizations such as mutual benefit organizations, business organizations, service organizations and common wealth organization based on nature of activities and the individuals forming them. However, non- governmental organization or a voluntary organization is one, which is formed by persons to further some common interest of its members with voluntary membership and without any control of the State. Now-a-days non-governmental organization are registered under the appropriate Act, have their own managing or executive committees, definite aims, objectives and programmes and are governed democratically.

The tradition of voluntarism in India is quite old but with the passage of time it has undergone a tremendous change. From the tradition of charity the NGOs in modern India have turned out as developmental outfits. In the post-independence era the national planning process and implementation of various governmental programmes provided enough opportunities to NGOs, as the government was not in a position to carry out all the development activities itself. System of governmental grants supplemented the proliferation of NGOs. The policy of liberalization and privatization adopted in India after 1991 has further provided the scope for the proliferation of NGOs as the State is gradually withdrawing from the welfarism and NGOs are stepping in with the result that millions of them are working in India in every sphere of human activity.

Himachal Pradesh is also no exception to non-governmental organizations and hundreds of them are working in every nook and corner of the State. The investigations carried out relating to organization, objectives, programmes, working and performance of three State level NGOs in Himachal Pradesh lead to the conclusion that all the voluntary organizations are properly registered under the relevant Act and as such have their legal entity. All the NGOs have their specific aims and objectives and are conducting various programmes in fulfillment of those objectives.

All the NGOs have their organizational structure, but only one of them is organized on democratic principles e.g. HGVS, has democratically elected bodies right from the *Panchayat* level to State level but HPVHA and PRIA have centralized organizational structure. HPVHA is working in the health sector, HGVS aims at creation of fully literate society whereas overall aim of PRIA is empowerment of people especially of marginalized sections. Working and role performance of HPVHA proves that it is providing commendable health services leading to awareness among the people relating to health related issues. HGVS focused on literacy, women empowerment and developing interest in children towards science education with the result that there is overall change in the society. PRIA' s initiative to empower the people especially marginalized sections has brought out a change and improvement in the governance and now people and their representative have the say in local governance.

Non-governmental organizations have certain specific aims and objectives and adopt programmes which may help them to achieve their goals. NGOs in the yester years have the only objective to provide charitable services for the welfare of the society but today NGOs are supplementing the initiatives of the government leading to socio-political and economic development of the society. Investigations into the working of the selected NGOs in Himachal Pradesh lead to the conclusion that these organizations are providing various support services to the people and helping the people and the society as a whole in their development. Role of the HPVHA proves that their initiatives in health sector have brought out changes in the health consciousness of the people and contributing to the social development of the society. Activities undertaken by HGVS in the field of literacy, creating self-help groups and involving them in economic activities, initiatives for the capacity building of the masses especially the women have contributed in the emergence and growth of women leadership and as such the entire initiatives of the NGO have contributed in the socio-economic and political development of the society.

Investigations conducted into the working and contributions of the NGO-PRIA lead to the conclusion that in addition to other contributions it is providing a great deal of services in strengthening the *Panchayat Raj* System established after the 73rd amendment of the Constitution of India. Orientation and training programmes conducted by PRIA for the capacity building of the people, especially women and elected representatives of the PRIs have not only improved the working of PRIs but also led to the empowerment of the people. Various programmes undertaken by the NGO in different phases have certainly contributed to the political development of the people and the society as a whole.

Analyses of the role, working and performance of NGOs lead to the conclusion that these organizations are certainly a great help not only in supplementing the development initiatives of the State but also providing various services to the people and as such and contributing a lot in the socio-political and economic development of the society.

Studies conducted so far reveal that NGOs are facing several socio-political and economic problems which affect the performance of NGOs. The investigations into the working of NGOs in Himachal Pradesh also lead to the conclusion that situation here is also not very different. NGOs in Himachal Pradesh do have several financial, organizational, administrative, political and social problems which are affecting the overall performance of the NGOs. NGOs don't have adequate resources with them and there is no provision for assured financial assistance from the funding agencies. It is not easy to secure governmental grants as lot of formalities and procedures need to be adopted and NGOs are sometimes not well conversant with them. Misuse of funds cannot be ruled out and there is absence of complete transparency in the financial dealings of the NGOs, charity component in the finances of the NGOs is missing as the voluntary contributions from the people have declined. As such the NGOs are totally dependent for their financial needs on the governmental funding agencies with the result that they cannot meet out the entire demands of the people and in the absence of adequate finances their overall performance is affected.

Element of democratic governance is also missing in most of the NGOs and the same leadership is repeatedly occupying various offices of the voluntary organizations. In the absence of trained and skilled manpower, professionally competent managers and modern technology especially in the rural areas, timely availability of various services and quality of services are suffering. In the absence of proper coordination between the office-bearers, staff members, social workers, beneficiaries and various governmental agencies, general public at large is deprived of due services. Centralization in decision making process further affects people's participation and declining volunteerism is an evidence to this problem. As such various problems being faced by the NGOs are affecting the overall delivery of services and their performance.

In spite of the fact that non-governmental organizations in Himachal Pradesh are also facing many difficulties and problems their contribution in welfare and development cannot be denied. NGOs in Himachal Pradesh, accepting the challenges of development are carrying out various developmental responsibilities and supplementing the developmental initiatives of the various governmental agencies. The organizations at the grassroots level have certainly helped in bringing out socio- political and economic changes in the society, however, problems and difficulties being faced by the NGOs need to be addressed.

Suggestions

Based on investigations into the various aspects of the non-governmental organizations or the voluntary organization as they are addressed i.e. their organizational structure, aims, objectives, and programmes, resources, performance and socio- economic and political contributions as well as their share of problems, affecting their performance, few suggestions are being made which may help to strengthen these organizations in Himachal Pradesh. Available data, observations at the time of field investigations and discussions with the office bearers, staff members, social workers, beneficiaries of these NGOs and general public have certainly helped the researcher to understand and analyze the various aspects of the working of these organizations and to make some suggestions which may help to address their problems and strengthen these organizations:

(i) Provision of adequate financial resources is the basic and the most important need of the NGOs so as to undertake their activities but there is neither any proper policy nor provision for this purpose. There should be provision of assured finances from the funding agencies along with the increase in funds as per inflationary trends. Provision for unforeseen expenses as well as administrative expenses should also be there while sanctioning grants to a NGO.

(ii) At present most of the NGOs are undertaking the projects and programmes sponsored and financed by the governmental funding agencies and in the absence of local resources NGOs are not in a position to undertake need based programmes. Hence, it is required that efforts to generate the necessary resources locally or to raise the contributions from the people must be made, so as to meet the local needs of the people.

(iii) In the absence of regular check on the finances and accounts of the NGOs, misuse of funds and irregularities in them cannot be ruled out. Hence, it is suggested that there should be some competent agency to check the accounts as well as field work of the NGOs so as to ensure better utilization of resources and quality of work.

(iv) It has been found and observed that office-bearers, staff-members and social workers are not well conversant with various financial rules, regulations and procedures with the result that they have to face various administrative problems and also irregularities take place in the financial dealings of the organizations. It is, therefore, suggested that proper orientations, training and workshops over the financial rules, regulations and procedures should be organized from time to time.

(v) Charity was the most important financial resource of the voluntary organization in yester years and most of the services used to be provided with the donations from the public. The Charity component of public contribution and volunteerism is almost missing and the NGOs are totally dependent upon the governmental funding agencies for their financial needs. Hence, there is a need to take initiative to raise contributions from the public and to revive the spirit of volunteerism amongst the people.

(vi) Element of democracy, in structure and functioning in most of the organizations is missing with the result that there is centralization in decision making process. This has also affected people's participation and absence of the democratic process has helped in the monopolization of leadership resulting not only in decline of people's participation but also corruption and nepotism. Hence, there is need to encourage democracy in the NGOs and their organization as well as working should be based on democratic principles which can further encourage people's participation and transparency in the working of the organization. Democratization will further help in the emergence of innovative leadership worthy of taking new initiatives.

(vii) The present, study reveals that trained and skilled manpower to carryout various activities in a professional manner are not available especially in rural areas. This certainly affects the quality and pace of various services. This is a fact that trained and skilled people turn towards urban areas for their financial gains hence in these circumstances there is need to develop the local talent so that they could be retained in the rural areas. Proper training in the use of modern technology, skill development programmes and workshops need to be encouraged to prepare a team of skilled social workers locally. Staff members should also be thoroughly oriented and trained in social work.

(viii) There is absence of coordination amongst various NGOs, their staff members, social workers, beneficiaries and governmental agencies which ultimately affects the working of the NGOs and due services to the people. Hence it is suggested that co-ordination agencies at the district level, state level and national level should be established involving representatives of the beneficiaries, NGOs, experts and governmental agencies.

(ix) The basic objective of all the NGOs is to ensure the development and welfare and of the people especially the marginalized sections and government also accept this role of the NGOs. It is, therefore, necessary to create a proper infrastructure for the working of non-governmental organizations by providing them financial assistance for engaging professional staff and trained social workersas per need of the organizations for providing various services to the people.

(x) Quality of service is also a big causality in the working of NGOs as the services are neither provided by experts nor, there is any mechanism to maintain their quality. To maintain the quality of services, it is suggested that programmes should be assigned to NGOs after their proper assessment to carry out them and there should also be some agency, after the programme has been assigned, to keep watch on the quality of work and services.

(xi) During the investigations it was observed that programmes adopted by the NGOs are neither designed in consultation with the staff, beneficiaries and people nor designed on the bases of needs of the people rather most of the programmes are sponsored and assigned by funding agencies. It is suggested that to increase people's participation and to meet their developmental needs, NGOs should involve experts, staff members, beneficiaries and people in designing their programmes based on the needs of the society.

(xii) It was also observed that NGOs are based and engaged in various activities in urban areas or population around small towns whereas their services are needed more in rural areas, where the people are still suffering from backwardness, ignorance and lack of development. It is therefore, suggested that more NGOs may been encouraged to operate in villages and they may be given incentives in terms of financial grants.

(xiii) It is required that every non-governmental organization makes best use of its physical, financial resources and also generates the same as per their requirements, for this purpose, proper planning and policy, for generating resources and the proper use of available resources need to be formulated by involving office-bearers, experts, staff, beneficiaries and the people.

(xiv) No organization, however, beneficial it may be, can succeed in its mission without public education and relationship. Though voluntary organizations serve the cause of people yet to popularize them and to create a place for them in public action an extensive education programmes by way of seminars, workshops and community discussions should be promoted.

(xv) No amount of external initiatives can help until and unless people themselves are willing to participate, cooperate and volunteer themselves for the cause of development of the society. Therefore, people need to be sensitized and encouraged for their participation and active involvement in the activities of the non-governmental organizations.

To conclude, it is well-established that Non-Governmental Organizations are not a modern invention but an ancient tradition which has undergone a great change with the passage of time.

From the charity organizations of yesteryears, Non-Governmental Organizations today, have emerged as developmental outfits. They have acquired legal status and stature for themselves and carrying out number of programmes and projects supplementing the efforts of the government in the socio-economic and political development of the society. During the post- independence era system of grants-in-aid to NGOs under various five year plans provided a greater space for the functioning of voluntary organizations as the government itself was not in a position to carry out all the developmental activities at the grassroots level. Now the process of liberalization and privatization has further enlarged the scope for the proliferation of the Non-Governmental organizations, as they are now being called upon to provided 'delivery of services' that is, to implement local development programmes rather than supplement government programmes with the result that millions of them are working in different sectors in every nook and corner of India. Though NGOs do have their share of financial, organizational, administrative and social problems affecting their performance yet they are contributing a lot in the socio-economic and political development of the society.

Non–Governmental Organizations have a challenging role to play as catalysts of social change, harbingers of silent revolution, as educators, as conscientious, as sensitizers, as innovators, as experimentalist, as motivators, as awareness builders, as skill developers, as watchdogs of people's interests and in short, as 'friend, philosopher and guide". In the context of the new economic policy of liberalization in the country, they have to perform three specific functions viz., ensuring distributive justice, abolishing inequalities and judging every issue in terms of human rights.[1]

Non-Governmental Organizations as such have become part and parcel of the modern society and are here to stay for the cause of development and nation building. Government of the day has to appreciate accommodate and accept the NGOs as partners of delivering various development plans, projects and programmes effectively and strengthening participatory developmental process, on the other hand NGOs, while working in a transparent manner following certain ethics, should help the government in the socio-economic and political development of the people and strengthening the unity and integrity of the Nation. NGOs should always remember that they are there till the objective is achieved. They are not ends by themselves but means to achieve the ultimate end of socio-economic and political development of the society. Here the statement of former Prime Minister P.V. Narasimha Rao delivered while addressing the NGOs at *Vigyan Bhawan* on March 7, 1994 is worth mentioning. He said, "In all this we have to remember that the people must occupy the center- stage. At all times they should be the focus of all that we aim to do. Therefore, when I talk of a participatory approach to development, I have in mind approach where the people would be helped to help themselves. In other words, we should envisage a situation in our country where people would deal with their problems on their own in the not too distant a future, without having to depend upon outside agencies, In the ultimate analysis, the people should not merely change their masters; people should be their own masters. That is what people centered development is all about. Therefore, if a particular area is taken up by a Non-Government organization, it is not expected that it would function there for all time to come. A time should come when the people would have been fully mobilized and made aware of and empowered to deal with their own problems. In other words, the NGO should withdraw after the task is done and shift to other area where their services are needed.[2]

To conclude, the present study is a modest attempt to look into the various aspect of the NGOs in Himachal Pradesh and is very preliminary and inexhaustive in nature. This will certainly provide some feedback to governmental agencies, academicians and research scholars to reflect over the various issues involved in the organization and working of NGOs so that NGOs are in a better position to get realized the development dreams of millions of people who are still far away from the mainstream of developmental process.

Notes

1. V. R. Krishna Iyer, 'NGO's Role in Development Process', *The Hindu* (Madras), 26-6-95.
2. S. N. Mishra and M. S. Chaitalipal 'Non-Governmental Oranisations in Rural Development' as quoted in *Non- Governmental Organisations in Development,* Norjahan Bava (Ed) Kanishkai Publishers Distributors, N. Delhi-2008 Edition p. 153.

Bibliography

Books

Allipand, Terry, (1983), **Catalyst of Development Voluntary Agencies in India,** West Hartford, Kumarian

Altekar, A.S. (1958) **State and Government in Ancient India,** Delhi: Motilal Banarsidas.

Arora, N.D., (1983), **Theory of State: A Short Introduction,** New Delhi: Social Science Research Publications.

Avineri, Shlom, (1972), **Hegel's Theory of the Modern State,** Cambridge: Cambridge University Press.

Barnard, Chester I, (1950), The Functions of the Executive, Cambridge: Harvard University Press.

Basu, Ashok Rajan, (1985) **The Tribal Development Programmes and Administration of India,** New Delhi: National Book Organisation.

Bava, Noorjahan, (1981), **People's Participation in Development Administration in India: An Empirical Study of Tamil Nadu,** New Delhi: Uppal Book Publishers.

Beveridge, S.W.H., (1946) **Voluntary Action: A Report of Methods of Social Advances,** London.

Beveridge, William, (1979) **Voluntary Action in a Changing World,** London: Bedford Square Press.

Bose, Joel S.G.R. (2000) **NGO's and Rural Development: Theory and Practice.** Delhi: Concept.

Bourdellon, A.F.C. (Eds), (1967) **Voluntary Social Services: Their Role in Modern State,** London: Collier Macmillan.

Brown, David L. and David C. Korten, (1989) **Understanding Voluntary Organisation: Guilelines for Donors,** Washington D.C.: IBRD.

Chandhoka, Neera (1995) **State and Civil Society: Exploration in Political Theory,** New Delhi/California/London: Saga Publications.

Chandhoka, Neera and A. Ghosh. (Eds.), (1995) **Grassroots Movement and Social Change,** Delhi: Developing Countries Research Centre, University of Delhi Press.

Chandra, Snehlata, (2001) **Non-Governmental Organisations: Structure, Relevance and Function,** New Delhi: Kanishka Pubishers.

Chuudhary, D. Paul, (1991) **Profile of Voluntary Action in Social Welfare and Development,** New Delhi: Siddartha Publication.

Chaudhary, D. Paul, (1990) **Voluntary Efforts in Social Welfare and Development,** New Delhi: Siddartha Publication.

Clark, J., (1991) **Democratizing Development : The Role of Voluntry Oranisations,** London: Earthscan Publications.

Clayton, Andrew (Eds.), (1996) **NGO's' Civil Society and the Stte: Building Democracy in Transitional Societies,** Oxford: INTRAC.

Dantwala, M.L., Harish Sethi and Paravin Visasia (Eds.) (1998) **Social Change through Voluntary Action,** New Delhi: Sage Publications.

Dharmarjan, Shivani, (1998), **NGO Development Initiative and Public Policy,** New Delhi: Kanishka Publishers.

Dreze, Jean and Amartya Sen, (2005) **India Development and Participation,** New Delhi: OUP.

Dube, S.C., (1998) **Modernisation and Devleopment: The Search for Alternative Paradigms.** New Delhi: Vistaar Publications.

Eade, Deborah (ed.), (2005) **Development, NGOs and Civil Society,** New Delhi: Rawat.

Etzioni Amitai., (1975) **A Comparative Analysis of Complex Organisations,** New York: The Free Press.

Etzioni, Amitai, (1990) **Modern Organisations,** New Delhi: Prentice Hall of India Private Ltd.

Fernandes, Walter (Ed.), (1985) **Social Activists and People's Movement,** New Delhi: Indian Social Institute.

Fisher, Julie, (2003) **Non-Governments: NGOs and the Political Devleopment of the Third World,** New Delhi: Rawat Publications.

Franda, Marcus, (1983) **Voluntary Associations and Local Development in India,** New Delhi: Young Asia Publications.

Galbraith, John Keanth, (1969) **Economic Devleopment,** London: Harvard University Press.

Gandhi. M.K. (1939) **Hind Swaraj or Indian Home Rule,** Ahmadabad: Navajivan Publiching Reprint (1982).

Ganguli, H.C., (1964) **Structure and Processes of Organisation,** Bombay: Asia Publishing House.

Gangrade, K.D. (1987) **Encyclopedia of Social Work in India,** New Delhi: Ministry of Information and Broadcasting Government of India.

Geertz Clifford, (1971) **Old Societies and New States: The quest for Modernity in Asia and Africa,** New Delhi: Ameren Publishing.

Gross, Edward and Armitta, (1971) **Organisation in Society,** New Jersey: Prentice Hall Inc., Englewood Cliffs.

Gupta, R.K., (2006) **NGOs and Development,** New Delhi: Mahaveer and Sons.

Hall, Johan A. And G. John Ikenberry, (1997) The State, Delhi, World View.

Hall, John (Ed.), (1995) **Civil Society: Theory, History, Comparison,** Cambridge: Polity Press.

Hall Richard H., (1972) **Organisations Structure and Process,** New Jersey: Prentice Hall, Inc., Cliffs.

Harbison, Frederick, (1959) **Entrepreneurial, Organisation as a factor in Economic Development,** New Jersey: Princeton.

Heredia, Rudolf C., (1988) **Voluntary Action and Development: Towards a Prixis for Non-Governmental Agencies,** New Delhi: Concept.

Hicks, Herbert G., (1971) **The Management of Organisation,** Tokyo: McGraw till Book Company.

Hulme, Devid and Michael Edwards (Eds.) (1997) **NGOs, States and Donors: Too Close for Comport?** London: Macmillian Press Ltd.

Inamdar, N.R. (1956) **The Pattern of Public Administration in Kautilya's Arthasastra,** Orient through Nasik.

Jain Randhir B. (Ed.), 1985) NGOs in Development Perspective, New Delhi: Friedrich Ebert Slifung.

Jain, L.C., B. Krishnamarthy and P.M. Tripathi, (1985) **Grass without Roots,** New Delhi, Saga Publications.

Jain, Nabhi Kumar, (2006) **Hand Book for Non-Governmental Organisations: An Encyclopedia for NGO and Voluntary Organisation,** New Delhi: Nabhi's Publications.

Jain, R.B. (Ed.), (1995) **NGOs in Development Perspective,** Delhi: Vivek Prakashan.

James, P.J., (1995) **Non-Governmental Voluntary Organisations: The True Mission,** Kerala: Mass Line Publication.

Jessop, Bob. (1991) **State Theory: Putting the Capitalist State in its Place, Philadelphia:** Philadelphia State University Press.

Kainth G.S. and R.S. Bawa, (1986) **Economic Development and Structural Changes: An Empirical Investigation,** New Delhi: Inter-India Publication.

Kapoor, A.K. and D. Singh, (1997) **Rural Development through NGO's Jaipur:** Rawat Publications.

Karat, Prakash, (1988) **Foreign Funding and Philosophy of Voluntary Organisations,** New Delhi: National Book Centre.

Kaviraj, Sudipta And Sunil Khilnani (Eds.), (2001) **Civil Society: History and Possibilities, Cambridge: Cambridge:** Cambridge University Press.

Keane, John (Ed.), (1988) **Civil Society and the State: New European Perspectives,** London: Verso.

Korten, David C., (1989) **Getting in the 21st Century: Voluntary Action and the Global Agenda,** New Delhi: Oxford and IBH Publishing.

Kothari, Rajni, (1988), **Rethinking Development: In search of Human Alternatives,** New Delhi: Ajanta.

Kothari, S. and H. Sethi (Eds.) (1990) **The non-Party Political Process: Uncertain Alternatives,** London: Zed Books.

Kramer, R.M., (1981) **Voluntary Organisation in the Welfare State, Berkeley:** California University Press.

Kulkarni, P.D., (1984) **Voluntary Action-the Myth and Reality,** New Delhi: NIPCCD.

Kulkarni, K.M., (1969) **Voluntary Action in A Developing Society,** New Delhi: Indian Institute of Public Administration.

Lalitha, N,V., (1975) **Voluntary Action in India: A Study of Volunteers in Welfare Agencies,** New Delhi: National Institute of Public Cooperation and Child Development.

Laski, Harold J., (1984) **A Grammar of Politics, New Delhi;** S Chand and Company.

Lawani.B.L., (1999) **Non-Goverment Organisations in Development: Case Study of Solapur District,** New Delhi: Rawat Publications.

Lewis, David and N. Ravichandran, (2008) **NGOs and Social Welfare: New Research Approaches,** Jaipur: Rawat.

Lewis, David and Tina Wallace, (Ed.), (2003) **Development NGOs and the Challenge of Change: New Roles and Relevance,** Jaipur and New Delhi: Rawat Publications.

Lewis, Davis, (2003) **Development NGOs and the challenge of change: New Role and Relevance,** Jaipur: Rawat.

Lipset, Seymaur Martin, (1972) **Politics and the Social Sciences,** New Delhi: Anand R. Kundaji for wiley Eastern Pvt. Ltd.

Macdonald, Laura, (1997) **Supporting Civil Society: The Political Role of Non-Governmental Organisations in Central America,** London: Macmillion Press Ltd.

Maclver, R.M., (1964) **The Modern State,** London: Oxford University Press.

Majumdar, R.C., H.C., Raychaddhari and K.K. Dutta, (1984) **An Advanced History of India,** London: Macmillian.

Marlin, Seymour, (1972) **Upset, Politics and the Social Sciences,** New Delhi: Anand R. Kundaji for Wesley Eastern Pvt. Ltd.

Mashruwala, K.G. (1951) **Gandhi and Marx,** Ahamdabad: Navajivan Publishing House.

Metha, Ajay K., Anil K. Singh and Gert W. Knech (Eds.), (2003) **Society, Politics and the Voluntary Sector,** New Delhi: Konrad Adenauer Foundation centre for Public Affairs.

Mishra, R.P. (Ed.), (1983) **Local Level Planning and Development,** New Delhi: stering Publishers Pvt. Ltd.

Misra, dharmendra, (2005) **Participatory Governance through NGOs,** Jaipur: Aalekh.

Mooney, James D., (1939) **The Principles of Oranisation,** New York: Harper and Brother Publishers.

Morris, Marry, (1996) **Voluntary Work in the Welfare State,** London, Rsulledge and Kegan Paul.

Mukherjee, K.K., (994) **Emerging Social Changes and Voluntary Organisations: Challenges and Responses,** Ghaziabad: Gram Niyojan Kendra.

Muttalib, M.A. (ed.) (1985) **Voluntary Action in Education,** New Delhi: Sterling.

Narayana, E.A. (1990) **Voluntary Organisations and Rural Development in India,** Delhi: Uppal.

Narayana, E.V., (1990) **Voluntary Organisation and Rural Development in India,** New Delhi: Uppal Publishing.

Omvedt, G. (1993) Reinventing Revolution, and New York: ME Shape.

Oommen, T.K., (2004) Nation, **Civil Society and Social Movements: towards a Development Civil Society,** New Delhi: Macmillan India.

Panday, S.R., (1991) **Community Action for Social Justice: Grass Roots Organisation in India,** New Delhi: Sage Publications.

Patel, M.L., (1984) **Planning Strategy for Development,** New Delhi: Inter-India Publication.

Pathan, Shankar H., (1979) **Social Welfare, Health and Family Planning in India, New Delhi: Siddhartha Publications.**

Pawar, S.N., J.B., Amberkar, and D. Shirkant, (2004) **NGOs and Development: The Indian Scenario,** New Delhi: Rawat Publications.

Pruthi, R.K., (2008) NGOs, **Civil Society and Global Future** New Delhi: Raj publication.

Rudolph, Lloyd I., and John Kurt Jacobsen (Eds), (2006) **Experiencing the State,** New Delhi: Oxford University Press.

Sandram, I.S., (1986) **Voluntary Agencies and Rural Development,** Delhi: B.R. Publishing Corporation.

Sarkar, Ashok Kumar (Ed.), (2008) **NGOs and Globalisation: Developmental and Organisational Facets,** Jaipur: Rawat Publications.

Sayer, Jane, (1987) **Theory of State and Law,** Moscow: Progress Publishers.

Sen, A.C. (ed)., (1971) **Introducing Voluntary Agencies** in India, Delhi; Impex India.

Sethi, J.D., (1992) **Character of the Indian State: A Non-Marxist View,** Shimla Indian Institute of Advanced Study.

Shan Ghanshyam, (1990) **Social Movement in India: A Review of Literature,** New Delhi: Sage Publications.

Sharma, Soumitra, (1983) **Development, Strategy and the Developing Countries,** New Delhi: South Asian Publishers Pvt. Ltd.

Sills, David L. (Eds.) (1968) **International Encyclopedia of Social Science,** Vol. 16, New York: Machmillan Company and the Free Press London.

Singh, Mian Goverdhan (1984) **Himachal Pradesh: History Culture and Economy,** Shimla: Minerva Book House.

Singh, Ravi Shankar Kumar, (2003) **Role of NGOs in Devleoping Countries,** New Delhi: Deep and Deep.

Smith, C. and A. Freedman, (1972) **Voluntary Association: Perspective on the Literature,** Cambridge: Harvard University Press.

Sooryamoorthy, R. and K.D. Gangrade (2006) **NGOs in India: A Cross-Sectional Study,** Jaipur : Rawat.

Sourza, Aflredde. (Eds.), (1978) **The politics of Change and Leadership Development,** New Delhi: Manohar Publication.

Tagliere, Daniel A., (1993) **People, Power and Organisation,** New York: Amacom Publication.

Tandon, Rajesh and Ranjita Mohanty (Eds.), (2003) **Does Civil Society Matter? Governance in Contemporary India,** New Delhi: Saga Publications.

Tandon, Rajesh. (2003) **Voluntary Action, Civil Society and the State,** New Delhi: Mosaic Books.

Taylar, Richard, (1967) **The Encyclopedia of Philosophy,** New York: Macmillan Free Press, 1967.

Weiss, Robert S., (1956) **Processess of Organisation, an Arbor: Survey Research** Center University of Michigan.

Yeseskel, Hasenfeld, (1983) **Human Service Organisations,** Englewood Cleff B.J.: Prentice Hall.

Young, Pat, (1985) **Mastering Social Welfare,** London: Macmillan Education Ltd.

Articles

Alfred, Deamant, (1967), 'European Models of Bureaucracy and Development', **International Review of Administractive Sciences,** Vol. 8, No. 3.

Baviskar B.S., (2001) 'NGOs and Civil Society in India', **Sociological Bulletin,** Vol. 50, No. 1, March.

Baxi, Upendra, (1086) 'Activism at Crossroads with Signpost', **Social Action,** 36 : 4, Oct-Dec.

Beteille, Andre, (1999a) 'Citizenship State and Democracy' **Economic and Political Weekly,** Vol. XXXIV No. 36.

Beteille, Andre, (1999b) 'Civil Society, State and Democracy', **Economic Political Weekly,** 34 (49), 3471-72.

Bhambhri, C.P., (1987) 'The Modern State and Voluntary Societies', **The Journal of Public Administration,** Vol. XXXIII, No. 3, July-Sept.

Bhatt, Anil, (1995) 'Voluntary Action in India: Role Trends and Challenges' **Economic and Political Weekly,** Vol. XXX, No. 16, april 22-29.

Bhattacharya, mohit, (1987) **'Voluntary Associations, Development and the State',** The Indian Journal of Public Administration, Vol. XXXIII, No. 3, July, september.

Bhatterjee, Abhijit, (1985) 'Voluntary Agencies: identity crises', **Mainstream,** 23 (48), 27 July.

Biswas, N., (2006) 'On Funding and the NGOs Sector', **Economic and Political Weekly,** Vol. 39, No. 41 October 21-28

Chandhoke, Neera, (2003), 'Governance and the Pluralisation of State: Implications for Democratic Citizenship' Economic Political Weekly, Vol. XXXVIII, No. 28 July 12-18.

Chandhoke, Neera, (2005) 'Seeing the State in India', **Economic and Political Weekly,** Vol. XL, No. 12, March 12-18.

Choudhary, D. Paul, (1987) 'Critical Appraisal of Voluntary Effort in Social Welfare and Development since Independence', T**he Journal of Public Administration,** Vol. XXXIII, No. 3, July-September.

Duggal, R., (1998) 'NGOs, Government and Private Sector in Health', **Economic and Political Weekly,** Vol. 23, No. 13, March 19-25.

Gomes, Lawrence, (1989) 'Role of Voluntary and other Organization in Development', **Yojana,** 33 (22), 1 Dec.

Gopalan, C. (1985) 'The Mother and Child in India', **Economic and Political Weekly,** 20 (4), 26 January, pp. 159-166.

Hanumappa, H.G. and T.M. Sujatha, (1983) 'Mahila Mandals and the Rural Women' **Kurukshetra**, Vol. XXXI, No. 19, July.

Inandar, M.R. (1987) 'Role of Volunteerism in Development **The India Journal of Public Administration,** Vol. XXXIII, No. 3, July-September.

Iyengar, Sudarshan, (2000) 'Role of Non-Governmental Organisation in Development of Gujarat', **Economic and Political Weekly,** Vol. XXXV, No. 36 and 36 August 26-Sept. 2.

Jagannadham, V., (1987) 'Voluntary Action Agencies and Social Welfare', **The Journal of Public Administration,** Vol. XXXIII, No. 3, July September.

Jhunjhunwala, Bharat, (1986) 'Voluntary Work as Countervailing Power', **Economic Political Weekly,** 21 (14), 5 April.

Joshi, A., (1988) 'Bibliography on the Role of Voluntarism in Society', **Seminar,** 348, August.

Kapoor, Rakesh, (1996) 'Voluntary Action: Survival] Politics and Transformation', **Social Action,** Vol. 46, No. 1 Jan-March.

Karat, Prakash, (1984) 'Action Groups/Voluntary Organisations: A Factor in Imperialist Strategy', **The Marxist,** Vol. 2, April-June.

Kothari, Rajni, (1984) 'The Non-Party Political Process', **Economic and Political Weekely,** Vol. XIX, No. 5, Feb. 4-11.

Kothari, Rajni, (1986) 'NGOs, the State and World Capitalism', **Economic and Political Weekly,** Vol. XII, No. 50, Dec. 13-20.

Kothari Rajni, (1987) 'Voluntary Organisations in a Plural Society', The Journal of Public Administration, Vol. XXXIII. No. 3, July-September.

Mandedkar, V.G., (1987) 'Voluntary Associations: A Strategy in Development', **The Journal of Public Administration,** Vol. XXXIII, No. 3, July-September.

Mishra, Lakshmidhar, (2010) 'BGVS in introspect and retrospect' **Gyan Vigyan Varta,** Bharat Gyan Vigyan Samiti, New Delhi.

Muttalib, M.A., (1987) 'Voluntarism and Development-Theoretical Perspectives', **The Indian Journal of Public Administration,** Vol. XXXIII, No. 3, July-September.

Nandedkar, V.G., (1987) 'Voluntary Associations- A Strategy in Development', **The Journal of Public Administration,** Vol. XXXIII, No. 3 July-September.

Nuna, Sheel C., (1996) 'Centripetalvs Centrifugal Forces and the Role of NGOs' **Social Action,** No. 46 No. 1, Jan.- March.

Oommen, T.K., (1975) 'The Theory of Voluntary Associations in a cross-Cultural Perspective', Sociological Bulletin, 24.

Panda, Snehlata, (1987) 'The Journal of Public Administration, Vol. XXXIII, No. July-September.

Parkesh, Karat, (1988) 'Foreign Funding and the Philosophy of Voluntary Organisations', **The Marxist,** Vol. 3, July-Sept.

Renganathan, R., (2001) 'Role of Non-Governmental Organisations in Rural Reconstruction', **Third Concept,** Vol. 15, No. 74, August.

Roy, Bunker, (1987) 'Voluntary Agencies: twenty years from noun', **Mainstream,** 23 (28) 9 March.

Roy, Sanjit (Bunker), (1987) 'Voluntary Agencies in Development their Role, Policy and Programmes', **The Journal of Public Administration,** Vol. XXXIII No. 3, July-September.

Sarkar, Ashok, (2001) 'Development through non-governmental organisations in Break Valley: A Critical analysis', **Social Action,** Vol. 51, No. 1 January-March.

Seers, Dudley, (1972) 'What are we Trying to Measure', **The Journal of Development Studies,** April.

Sethi, Harsh, (2003) 'Difficult Times for NGOs', **Economic and Political Weekly,** Vol. XXXVIII, No. 46, Nov. 15-21.

Sharma, K.L., (1986) 'The Indian State and the NGO's: Some Reflections', **Social Action,** Vol. 46, No.1, Jan-March.

Srikanth, H., (1996) 'State, NGOs and Urban Community Development', **Social Action,** Vol. 46 No. 1, Jan-March.

Srivasatava, Jayati, (2005) 'NGOs and World Trade Organisation: The Democratic Dimensiton', **Economic and Political Weekly,** Vol. XL, No. 19, May, 7-23

Srivastava, Alka, (1999) 'Non-Governmental Organisation and Rural Development', **Social Action,** Vol. 49, No.1, Jan-March.

Srivastava S.P. (1999) 'Nature of Voluntary Action in India Total: A Critique', **Social Action,** Vol. 49, No.1, Jan-March.

Srivastava, S.S. and Rajesh Tandon, (2005) How Large is India's Non-Profit Sector?', **Economic and Political Weekly,** Vol. XL, No. 19, May 7-13.

Sunder, I, (2002) 'Environment Protection through Non-Governmental Organisations and Local Community Environment and People', **The Journal of Public Adminstration,** Vol. XXXIII No. 3, July-september.

Tondal, Rajesh, (1996) 'Changing Context and Challenges for Voluntary Action in India Today', Social Action, Vol. 46, No. 1 Jan-March .

Zahir, Sajjid, (2004) 'NGOs Sector in Bangladesh: An Review' **Economic and Political Weekly,** Vol. XXXIX, No. 36, Sept, 4-17.

Reports/Documents

Annual Report 2002-2003, Himachal Pradesh Voluntary Health Association, B-37, Sector II, Main Road, New Shimla, Himachal Pradesh.

Annual Report 2002-2003, Himachal Gyan Vigyan Samiti, Tirath Niwas, Engine Ghar, Sanjauli, Shimla.

Annual Report 2002-2003 PRIA, 42, Tughlakabad Institutional Area, New Delhi.

Annual Report 2003-2004, Himachal Pradesh Voluntary Health Association, B-37, Sector II, Main Road, New Shimla, Himachal Pradesh.

Annual Report 2003-2004 PRIA, 42, Tughlakabad Institutional Area, New Delhi.

Annual Report 2004-2005, Himachal Gyan Vigyan Samiti, Tirth Niwas, Engine Ghar, Sanjauli, Shimla.

Annual Report 2004-2005 PRIA, 42, Gughlakabad Institutional Area, New Delhi.

Annual Report 2005-2006, Himachal Pradesh Voluntary Health Association, B-37 Sector-II Main Road New Shimla, Himachal Pradesh.

Annual Report 2005-2006, Himachal Gyan Vigyan Samiti, Tirth Niwas, Engine Ghar, Sanjauli, Shimla.

Annual Report 2005-2006 PRIA, 42, Tughlakabad Institutional Area, New Delhi.

Annual Report 2006-2007, Himachal Pradesh Voluntary Health Association, B-37, Sector II Main Road New Shimla, Himachal Pradesh.

Annual Report 2006-2007, Himachal Gyan Vigyan Samiti, Tirth Niwas, Engine Ghar Sanjauli, Shimla.

Annual Report 2006-2007 PRIA, 42, Tughlakabad Institutional Area, New Delhi.

Vision 2010, HPVHA, B-37, Phase 1, Sector II, New Shimla, 2002.

Gyan Vigyan Varta: Journey of 20 Years, Bharat Gyan Vigyan Samiti, Basement of YWA Hostel. No. II, G-Block, Avenue 21, Saket, New Delhi.

NGO-Government Relations: A Source of Life or A Kiss of Death, Society for Participatory Research in Asia, 45, Sainik Farm, Khanpur, New Delhi.

The First Five-Year Plan 1952-1957 Planning Commission, Government of India, New Delhi.

The Third Five-Year Plan, Planning Commission, Government of India, New Delhi.

Fourth Five year Plan, 1967-74, Planning Commission, Government of India, New Delhi.

Seventh Five-Year Plan 1985-1990, Vol. II, Government of India, Planning Commission, New Delhi.

htt://www.peoplesmarhc.com/publications/globalisation/chapter15.15 html.

Newspapers

The Hindu

PRIA News

Annexure - I

Questionnaire Cum Interview Schedule (For HPVHA)

Section-A

1.	Name of the Respondent	....
2.	Age of the Respondent	18-15/36-55/56-75, years
3.	Sex of the Respondent	Male/female
4.	Educational Qualification of the Respondent	Illterate/Middle Std/Matric/ +2/Gr/PG
5.	Marital Status of the Respondent	Married/unmarried
6.	Income Status of the Respondent	upto 1 Lakh P.A./ 2 L.P.A./ Above L.P.A.
7.	Do you know about the NGO-HPVHA	To a great extent/to some extent/ not a all
8.	Are you aware of the functioning of the NGO-HPVHA	To a great/extent/to some extent/ not at all
9.	What are the services being provided by HPVHA?	Health awareness/reproductive healthy high way STD/HIV/ AIDS
10.	Do you believe that people are being beneficial with the services of HPVHA?	To a great extent/to some extent/ not at all

Section - B

11.	Who are the providers of the health services in your area?	Govt. Institutions/Vaids-Hakims/ local practioners, faith healers, exoricist
12.	Is there any NGO working in your region in the health sector?	Yes, To a great extent/to some extent/not at all.
13.	Are you aware of the activities of The NGO HPVHA?	Yes, To a great extent/to some not at all.
14.	Which of the following health related activities/services are being conducted by the NGO-HPVHA?	Reproductive health of women/ prevention control and cure of STD/HIV/AIDS Child health care/ all of above

15.	Are the health checkup camps being organised regularly by the NGO-HPVHA?	Yes regularly/held occasionally /not held at all
16.	Do the people voluntarily participate in the camps and activities to make use of the services of the NGO?	Yes, to a great extent/to some extent/not at all
17.	What are the activities being organised under the project healthy highways?	Awareness about STD/HIV/ AIDS to Identify cases of STD/HIV/AIDS/Compaign for use of contraceptives all of above.
18.	Do you believe that the NGO-HPVHA has contributed in the prevention and cure of STD/HIV AIDS and family planning?	Yes, to a great extent/ to some extent/not at all
19.	Which section of the society has been benefited the most with the service and activities of HPVHA?	Children/ youth and/aged people all of them
20.	Do you agree that the contribution of the HPVHA for social welfare has helped in the social development of the people and the area?	Yes, To a great extent/ to some extent/not at all.

Section - C

21.	What are the main problems of NGOs in Himachal Pradesh?	Lack of adequate finance Lack of democratic Organisation structure Lack of people's participation No problem at all
22.	What are the main problems in securing grants from the funding agencies?	Lack of awareness for preparing proposals/procedural delays/lack of assured funding/no problems at all.
23.	Are the accounts of your organisation audited regularly?	Yes regularly/audited occasionally/ don't know
24.	Was there any irregularly reported in the account audit report of your organisation?	Yes, to some extent/not at all./ don't know
25.	Do you and other people contribute some funds to you organisation?	Yes, To a great extent/to some extent/not at all.
26.	Are the office-bearer of your organisation elected regularly?	Yes regularly/Yes sometimes/ not at all
27.	Do the same leaders occupy the various offices in your organisation?	Yes leadership is monopolized/ leadership and offices are Rotated/ Don't know

28.	Does your organisation practice any particular political ideology or is affiliated to some political party?	Yes, to some extent/not at all./ don't know
29.	Are the trained and skilled workers deployed in your organisation?	Yes, To a great extent/to some extent/not at all.
30.	Does your organisation use modern technology managerial methods and adopt professionalism in its working?	Yes, To a great extent/to some extent/not at all.
31.	Are the members and beneficiaries of the organisation being provided information and training by your organisation?	Yes, To a great extent/to some extent/not at all.
32.	Is there any problem regarding proper coordination amongst the staff members, officer bearers of your NGO and the government agencies?	Yes, To a great extent/to some extent/not at all
33.	Is your NGO providing quality services to the people?	Yes, To a great extent/to some extent/not at all.
34.	Do you believe that there is centralisation in the decision making process of your organisation?	Yes, To a great extent/to some extent/not at all
35.	Do the people participate in the activities of your organisation voluntarily?	Yes, To a great extent/to some extent/not at all.
36.	Do you believe that the spirit of volunteerism still prevails among the people?	Yes, it prevails/there is decline/ there is great decline"

Annexure - I-A

Questionnaire Cum Interview Schedule
(For HGVS)

Section-A

1. Name of the Respondent	....
2. Sex of the Respondent	Male/female
3. Marital Status of the Respondent	Married/unmarried
4. Age of the Respondent	18-15/36-55/56-75, years
5. Educational Qualification of the Respondent	Upto XI-XII/Graduate/PG
6. Income Status of the Respondent	upto 1 Lakh P.A./ 2 L.P.A./ Above L.P.A.
7. Do you know about the NGO-HGVS?	To a great extent/to some extent/not a all
8. Do you know about the working of the NGO-HGVS?	To a great/extent/to some extent/not at all
9. What are the services being provided the NGO-HGVS?	Compaigning and awareness about literacy/women empowerment/science education among children
10. Do you believe that people are being beneficial with the services of the NGO-HGVS	To a great extent/to some extent/ not at all

Section-B

11. Are you aware of the Activities of the NGO-HGVS?	To a great extent/to some extent/ not at all
12. What are the Programmes being undertaken by the NGO-HGVS	Literacy compaigns/Human Resource/Development/ Interface between Experts and Masses/ Women Impowerment/all of above
13. Do the people Voluntarily Participate in the activities of the NGO	To a great extent/to some extent/not at all

14. Has the literacy campaign of the NGO helped the common people	To a great extent/to some extent/ not at all
15. Has the NGO initiated in the creation of Self-Help Group for the benefits of people?	To a great extent/to some extent/ not at all
16. Has the Self-Help Group undertaken economic activities for the benefit of its members?	To a great extent/to some extent/ not at all
17. Has the NGO-HGVS organised training camps and other activities for the capacity building of women?	To a great extent/to some extent/ not at all
18. Has the NGO-HGVS raised the various socio economic problems of the people at the appropriate platforms?	To a great extent/to some extent/ not at all
19. Has the NGO initiated activities for the protection of environment and proper exploitation and preservation of local resources?	To a great extent/to some extent/ not at all
20. Do you believe that the NGO HGVS has helped in the socio economic development of the region?	To a great extent/to some extent/ not at all

Section-C

21. What are the main problems of NGOs in Himachal Pradesh?	Lack of adequate finance Lack of democratic Organisation structure Lack of People's Participation/ No Proble at all
22. What are the main problems in securing grants from the funding agencies?	Lack of awareness for preparing proposals/procedural delays/lack of assured funding/no problem at all
23. Are the accounts of your organisation being audited regularly?	Yes regularly/audited occasionally/don't know
24. Was there any irregularly reported in the account audit report of your organisation?	Yes, to some extent/not at all/ don't know
25. Do you and other people contribute some funds to you organisation?	Yes, To a great extent/to some extent/not at all.
26. Are the office-bearer of your organisation being elected regularly?	Yes regularly/yes sometimes/ not at all
27. Do the same leaders occupy the various offices in your organisation?	Yes, leadership is monopolized /leadership and offices are rotated/ Don't know

28. Does your organisation practice any particular political ideology or is afiliated to some political party?	Yes, To a some extent/ not at all./ don't know
29. Are the trained and skilled workers depolyed in your organisation?	Yes, To a great extent/to some extent/not at all.
30. Does your organisation use modern technology managerial methods and adopt professionalism in its working?	Yes, To a great extent/to some extent/not at all.
31. Are the members and beneficiaries of the organisation being provided information and training by your organisation?	Yes, To a great extent/to some extent/not at all.
32. Is there any problem regarding proper coordination amongst the staff members, officer bearers of your NGO and the government agencies?	Yes, to a great extent/to some extent/not at all
33. Is your NGO providing quality services to the people?	Yes, To a great extent/to some extent/not at all.
34. Do you believe that there is centralisation in the decision making process of your organisation?	Yes, To a great extent/to some extent/not at all.
35. Do the people participate in the activities of your organisation voluntarily?	Yes, To a great extent/to some extent/not at all
36. Do you believe that the spirit of volunteerism still prevails among the people?	Yes, it prevails/there is decline/ there a is great decline

Annexure - I-B

Questionnaire Cum Interview Schedule
(For PRIA)

Section-A

1. Name of the Respondent	....
2. District to which he/she belongs	Kangra/Hamirpur
3. Age of the Respondent	18-15/36-55/56-75, years
4. Sex of the Respondent	Male/female
5. Educational Qualification of the Respondent	Upto XI-XII/Graduate/PG
6. Income Status of the Respondent	upto 1 Lakh P.A./ 2 L.P.A./Above L.P.A.
7. Do you know about the NGO-PRIA?	To a great extent/to some extent/ not a all
8. Are you aware of the role and working of the NGO-PRIA?	To a great/extent/to some extent/not at all
9. What are the services being provided the NGO-PRIA?	Awareness Compaign for local governance/capacity building of the masses/people experts interface
10. Do you believe that people are being beneficial with the services of the NGO-HGVS	To a great extent/to some extent/ not at all

Section-B

11. Are you aware of the Activities of the NGO-PRIA?	Compaign for people participation in governance/compaigning for proper conduct of Gram Sabha meeging/training elected respresentives of PRIs/ all of above
12. Is the NGO-PRIA working for the capacity building of marginalized sections?	To a great extent/to some extent/not at all

13. What are the initiatives taken by PRIA to strength PRIs?	Orientation of newly elected respondents of PRIs/ campaigning for proper conduct of gram sabha meetings/assisting gram Panchayat in micro planning/all of above
14. What is the frequency of comps and other activities organised by The NGO-PRIA?	Held regularly/held occasionally/ no activities at all
15. Do the people participate voluntarily in the activities of the NGO-PRIA?	To a great extent/to some extent/ no at all
16. Has the working and conduct of meeting of Gram Sabha improved with the initiative of PRIA?	To a great extent/to some extent/ no at all
17. Has the participation of marginalised sections improved with the initatives of PRIA?	To a great extent/to some extent/ no at all
18. Has the initiative taken by PRIA helped in the growth of women leaders?	To a great extent/to some extent/ no at all
19. Has the initiatives taken by PRIA strengthened the PR system and empowered the people?	To a great extent/to some extent/ no at all
20. Has the initiatives taken by PRIA contributed in the political develop ment of the people and the region a or whole?	To a great extent/to some extent/ no at all

Section-C

21. What are the main problems of NGOs in Himachal Pradesh? Organisation structure	Lack of adequate finance Lack of democratic Lack of people's Participation/ No problem at all
22. What are the main problems in securing grants from the funding agencies?	Lack of awareness for preparing proposals/procedural delays/lack of assured funding/no problem at all.
23. Are the accounts of your audited regularly?	Yes, regularly/audited organisation occasionally/don't known
24. Was there any irregularly reported in the accounts audit report of your organisation?	Yes, to some extent/not at all./ don't know
25. Do you and other people contribute some funds to your organisation?	Yes, To a great extent/to some extent/not at all

26. Are the office-bearer of your organisation elected regularly?	Yes, regularly/yes sometimes/ not at all
27. Do the same leaders occupy the various offices in your organisation?	Yes, leadership is monopolized /leadership and offices are rotated/ Don't know
28. Does your organisation practice any particular political ideology or is affiliated to some political party?	Yes, to some extent/not at all./ don't know
29. Are the trained and skilled workers deployed in your organisation?	Yes, To a great extent/to some extent/not at all
30. Does your organisation use modern technology managerial methods and adopt professionalism in its working?	Yes, To a great extent/to some extent/not at all
31. Are the members and beneficiaries of the organisation being provided information and training by your organisation?	Yes, To a great extent/to some extent/not at all
32. Is there any problem regarding proper coordination amongst the staff members, officer bearers of your NGO and the government agencies?	Yes, To a great extent/to some extent/not at all
33. Is your NGO providing quality services to the people?	Yes, to a great extent/to some extent/not to all.
34. Do you believe that there is centralisation in the decision making process of your organisation?	Yes, To a great extent/to some extent/not at all
35. Do the people participate in the activities of your organisaiton voluntarily?	Yes, To a great extent/to some extent/not at all
36. Do you believe that the spirit of volunteerism still prevails among the people?	Yes, it prevails/there is decline/ there is great decline

Annexue-II

हिमाचल ज्ञान विज्ञान समिति का संविधान

धारा 1. नाम

संगठन का नाम हिमाचल ज्ञान विज्ञान समिति (HGVS) है। यह समिति सभायें पंजीकरण अधिनियम (Societies Registration Act) 1860 के अंतगर्त पंजीकरण सं0 208/91 के रूप में पंजीकृत है। इसका पंजीकरण दिनांक 1 नवम्बर, 1991 को हुआ है।

धारा 2. मुख्यालय

समिति का मुख्यालय, तीर्थ निवास, इंजनघर, संजौली, शिमला–171006 है।

धारा 3. लक्ष्य एवं उद्देश्य

- क्रियात्मक साक्षरता।
- वैज्ञानिक दृष्टिकोण का प्रचार एवं प्रसार करना।
- बुनियादी शिक्षा का लोकव्यापीकरण, महिला सशक्तिकरण, सांस्कृतिक व स्वास्थ्य संबंधी जन आंदोलनों को मजबूत करना।
- विज्ञान और प्राद्यौगिकी संस्थानों तथा संगठनों का लोकतांत्रिकरण तथा विज्ञान और प्राद्यौगिकी नीतियों के समाज पर पड़ने वाले प्रभाव के बारे में लोगों को जागरूक करना।
- विज्ञान, वैज्ञानिक शोध और विज्ञान नीति को लोक हितकारी बनाने के लिए प्रयास करना।

- राज्य, देश और विदेश के दूसरे संगठनों के साथ तालमेल रखना जिनके लक्ष्य और उद्देश्य समिति के लक्ष्य और उद्देश्यों से मेल खाते हों।
- पर्यावरण संरक्षण एवं संतुलित तथा स्थाई विकास की दिशा में कार्य करना।
- जन हितकारी वैकल्पिक नीतियों को तैयार करना तथा उनका प्रसार करना।
- उपरोक्त विषयों पर शोध और प्रकाशन का काम करना।

धारा 4. सदस्यताः

4.1 सदस्यता की प्रक्रिया

- 12 वर्ष की आयु से ऊपर कोई भी व्यक्ति किसी भी जाति, धर्म, क्षेत्र, भाषा, लिंग आदि से संबंधित जो समिति के लक्ष्यों व उद्देश्यों तथा संविधान को स्वीकार करता/करती हो, समिति का सदस्य बन सकता/सकती है।
- सदस्यता का कार्यकाल केवल एक वर्ष तक होगा अगले वर्ष के लिए नवीनीकरण करना होगा।
- संगठन की सदस्यता जन सदस्यता के आधार पर क्षेत्र व संस्थाओं में की जाएगी।
- सदस्यता का नवीनीकरण प्रत्येक वर्ष के जनवरी माह में किया जायेगा तथा नए सस्स्यों को पूरे वर्ष शामिल किया जाएगा।
- सदस्यता को इकाईयों में संगठित किया जाएगा तथा राज्य सम्मेलन के बाद होने वाली सदस्यता को अगले सांगठिनिक वर्ष में शामिल किया जाएगा। सांगठनिक वर्ष से अभिप्राय एक राज्य सम्मेलन से दूसरे राज्य सम्मेलन तक की अवधि से है।

4.2 सदस्यता शुल्क

समिति के सदस्य को 5 रूपये प्रति वर्ष सदस्यता तथा नवीनीकरण शुल्क करना होगा।

4.3 सदस्यता से इस्तीफा

जो सदस्य संगठन से अपना इस्तीफा देना चाहे वह अपने इस्तीफे को संगंधित इकाई के पास लिखित रूप से भेजेगा/भेजेगी जिसमें संगठन छोड़ने के कारणों का विवरण दर्ज हो। संबंधित इकाई इस बारे बैठक में इस्तीफे के लिखित कारणों पर चर्चा एवं छानबीन करके इस्तीफे मंजूर करती है तो उसकी सूचना एवं स्वीकृति अपने से उच्चतर इकाई को देकर सहमति प्राप्त करेगी।

धारा 5. संगठन का ढांचाः

5.1 सम्मेलन

- राज्य स्तरीय सम्मेलन सर्वोच्च संस्था होगी।
- संगठन का सम्मेलन प्रत्येक वर्ष किया जाएगा।
- सदस्यता अभियान व नवीनीकरण के बाद संगठन के पांच स्तरीय ढांचे में सम्मेलन इस प्रकार से होंगेः

प्राथमिक इकाई (ज्ञान विज्ञान केंद्र)
पंचायत सम्मेलन
खण्ड सम्मेलन
जिला सम्मेलन
राज्य सम्मेलन

- संगठन की सभी इकाइयां अपने से उच्चतर सम्मेलन के लिए प्रतिनिधियों का चुनाव करेगी।
- विभिन्न स्तरों पर आयोजित सम्मेलनों में वर्तमान में कार्य कर रहे परिषद/कार्यकारिणी सदस्य सम्मेलनों में पदेन सदस्यों (Ex Officio Member) के रुप में भाग लेंगे।
- विभिन्न स्तरों पर सम्मेलनों में भाग लेने वाले प्रतिनिधियों के लिए परिषद/कार्यकारिणी प्रतिनिधि शुल्क (Delegation Fee) तथा प्रतिनिधियों की संख्या निर्धारित करेगी।

- सम्मेलन की विषयवस्तु के संबंध में परिषद ही अंतिम निर्णय लेगी और सम्मेलन के संचालन के लिए विभिन्न कमेटियों का गठन करेगी।
- सम्मेलन में पिछले वर्ष के कार्यों की समीक्षा और भविष्य के कार्यों का निर्धारण किया जाएगा।
- सम्मेलन में सांगठनिक वर्ष की वित्त रिपोर्ट प्रस्तुत करनी अनिवार्य होगी।
- सम्मेलन नई परिषद/कार्यकारिणी/कोर ग्रुप का निर्धारित सदस्य संख्या के आधार पर पिछली परिषद/कार्यकारिणी द्वारा प्रस्तुत प्रस्ताव के आधार पर चुनाव करेगा।
- सम्मेलन में नई परिषद का गठन सर्वसम्मति से किया जाएगा परंतु किसी कारणवश सर्वसम्मति न बन पाए तो गुप्त मतदान की व्यवस्था की जा सकती है तथा बहुमत का फैसला लागू किया जाएगा।
- विशेष परिस्थितियों में सम्मेलनों की अवधि में परिवर्तन करने का अधिकार राज्य परिषद को होगा।

5.2 परिचय

सम्मेलन द्वारा तय किए गए कार्यों को क्रियान्वित करने के लिए परिषद संगठन की निर्णायक इकाई होगी। केवल राज्य एवं जिला स्तर पर ही परिषद का गठन किया जाएगा। कार्यक्रमों एवं गतिविधियों के क्रियान्वयन, संचालन तथा मॉनिटरिंग के लिए परिषद अपने में से कार्यकारिणी तथा कोर ग्रुप का गठन करेगी, जिसकी संख्या विभिन्न स्तरों पर दी गई है। दैनिक कार्यों के क्रियान्वयन के लिए परिषद/कार्यकारिणी, राज्य परिषद समय–समय पर बैठकों के माध्यम से निर्णय, समीक्षा तथा वार्षिक कार्यों का लेखा जोखा सम्मेलन में प्रस्तुत करेगी। परिषद की एक वर्ष में न्यूनतम दो बैठकें होंगी।

5.3 कार्यकारिणी समिति

परिषद द्वारा तय किए गए कार्यों को परिषद की दो बैठकों के बीच की समयावधि में क्रियान्वयन के लिए कार्यकारिणी समिति जिम्मेवार होगी। परिषद की बैठकों के बीच की समयावधि में विभिन्न कार्यक्रमों को संचालित करने का अधिकार भी कार्यकारिणी के पास होगा बशर्ते कोई ऐसा कार्य न हो जिसमें संगठन के अंदर विवाद की स्थिति अपने की संभावना हो अथवा संगठन के हित में न हो। ऐसी स्थिति में परिषद की आपात बैठक बुलाकर ही निर्णय को अंतिम रूप दिया जाएगा। कार्यकारिणी की एक वर्ष में न्यूनतम तीन बैठकें होंगी।

5.4 कोर ग्रुप

कोर ग्रुप का अभिप्राय कार्यकारिणी समिति द्वारा चयनित पदाधिकारियों से है, जो कार्यकारिणी की दो बैठकों के बीच की समयावधि में लिए गए निर्णय लागू करेगा। कोर ग्रुप दैनिक कार्यों तथा विशेष परिस्थितियों में निर्णय लेने के लिए भी अधिकृत होगा जिसकी सहमति/अनुमोदन अगली कार्यकारिणी/परिषद बैठक में लेनी होगी। कोर ग्रुप की एक वर्ष में न्यूनतम छः बैठकें होंगी।

5.5 कार्यकारी केंद्र (Centre)

राज्य, जिला या खण्ड, स्तर पर कार्यकारी केंद्र से अभिप्राय संबंधित मुख्यालय में मौजूद पदाधिकारियों, कार्यकारिणी समिति सदस्यों तथा पार्षदों से है जो परिषद/कार्यकारिणी द्वारा लिए गये निर्णयों को लागू करने का ही कार्य करेगा।

5.6 उपसमितियां

सम्मेलन में निर्धारित विभिन्न प्राथमिकताओं/कार्यक्रमों के अनुरुप उपसमितियों का गठन किया जाएगा। इन उपसमितियों के संचालन की जिम्मेवादी मुख्यतः परिषद सदस्यों की रहेगी। परंतु विभिन्न विषयों/क्षेत्रों से संबंधित जानकारी रखने वाले विशेषज्ञ, साहित्यकारों/शिक्षाविदों, वैज्ञानिकों

आदि को इन उप–समितियों में विशेष आमन्त्रित सदस्यों के रूप में शामिल किया जा सकता है। इनकी सेवाओं का यथा अवसर किया जाएगा। उप समितियों की बैठकों की संख्या कार्यक्रम/गतिविधियों के अनुसार तय की जायेगी।

5.7 विभिन्न स्तरों पर संगठन की इकाईयां तथा आकार

5.7.1 राज्य इकाई

- राज्य स्तर पर सम्मेलन द्वारा लिए गए निर्णयों तथा तय किए गए कार्यों को लागू करने के लिए राज्य परिषद संगठन की सर्वोच्च इकाई होगी। कार्यक्रमों के आधार पर उस विशेष कार्यक्रम के संचालन हेतु विभिन्न उपसमितियों का गठन किया जा सकता है।
- राज्य परिषद को जिला संगठन की स्थिति के अनुसार किसी भी जिले, खण्ड/क्षेत्र में तदर्थ संगठन स्थापित करने का अधिकार होगा।
- राज्य परिषद संगठन द्वारा तैयार की जा रही लिखित सामग्री तथा मुखपत्र के लिए सम्पादक मण्डल गठित करेगी। संगठन के नाम से प्रकाशित होने वाली प्रत्येक सामग्री के लिए राज्य कोर ग्रुप की सहमति लेना आवश्यक होगा।
- राज्य परिषद, राज्य सम्मेलन का आयोजन करेगी तथा नई राज्य परिषद, कार्यकारिणी तथा कोर ग्रुप का चुनाव करेगी जो इस प्रकार से होगा

परिषद	31 – 55
कार्यकारिणी	21 – 31
कोर ग्रुप	7 – 9

- प्रदेश में अखिल भारतीय जन विज्ञान नेटवर्क से जुड़े अन्य संगठनों के अध्यक्ष/सचिव राज्य परिषद/कार्यकारिणी के स्थाई आमंत्रित सदस्य होंगे।

5.7.2 जिला इकाई

- राज्य के अनुरूप जिला स्तर पर जिला सम्मेलन सर्वोच्च संस्था तथा जिला परिषद सर्वोच्च इकाई होगी।
- जिला परिषद निचली इकाईयों के कार्यों का आकलन एवं मार्गदर्शन करेगी।
- जिला परिषद सम्मेलन का आयोजन करेगी।
- जिला परिषद स्वयं अपने फैसले पर या कुल सदस्यों में से कम से कम एक तिहाई सदस्यों द्वारा भाग किये जाने पर जिला सम्मेलन बुला सकती है, लेकिन इसके लिए राज्य परिषद/कार्यकारिणी समिति से पूर्वानुमति लेना जरूरी होगा।
- नियमित जिला सम्मेलन में ब्लाक सम्मेलनों द्वारा चुने हुए प्रतिनिधि भाग लेंगे।
- जिला सम्मेलन के लिए प्रतिनिधित्व का आधार जिला परिषद निर्धारित करेगी।
- जिला सम्मेलन, जिला परिषद की रिर्पोट पर विचार विमर्श तथा कार्य करेगा।
- जिला सम्मेलन, राज्य सम्मेलन के लिए प्रतिनिधियों का चुनाव करेगा।
- जिला इकाई के सचिव, राज्य कार्यकारिणी के तथा अध्यक्ष, राज्य, परिषद के पदेन सदस्य होंगे।
- जिला सम्मेलन, जिला परिषद, कार्यकारिणी तथा कोर ग्रुप का चुनाव करेगा

सम्मेलन के लिए प्रतिनिधियों की न्यूनतम संख्या	40 सदस्य
खण्ड इकाईयां	2 (खण्डों में)
ज्ञान विज्ञान केंद्रों की संख्या	10
सदस्यता	500
पंचायत इकाईयां	10
परिषद में सदस्यों की संख्या	21–35 सदस्य
कार्यकारिणी की संख्या	7–21 सदस्य

5.7.3 खण्ड इकाई

- खण्ड इकाई का सर्वोच्च संगठन, खण्ड सम्मेलन होगा, जिसमें पंचायत इकाईयों से चुने हुए प्रतिनिधि शामिल होंगे।
- खण्ड का सम्मेलन, जिला सम्मेलन के लिए प्रतिनिधि चुनेगा।
- खण्ड कार्यकारिणी संबंधित क्षेत्र के काम को चलाने और इकाई के कार्यों में तालमेल बैठाने की जिम्मेदारी निभाएगी।
- खण्ड स्तर पर सचिव, जिला कार्यकारिणी के अध्यक्ष, जिला परिषद के पदेन सदस्य होंगे।

  खण्ड स्तर पर परिषद के स्थान पर कार्यकारिणी को गठित किया जाएगा तथा कार्यकारिणी अपने में से कोर ग्रुप का इस प्रकार से गठन करेगी

सम्मेलन में प्रतिनिधि (न्यूनतम)	25 सदस्य
कार्यकारिणी	7–15 सदस्य
कोर ग्रुप	5 – 7 सदस्य
पंचायत इकाईयां	5 पंचायतों में
सदस्यता	250
ज्ञान विज्ञान केंद्र	5

5.7.4 नगर/शहरी इकाई

- संगठन की नगर इकाई शहरी क्षेत्र में नगर निगम (Municipal Corporation) के अधीन क्षेत्रों में गठित की जाएगी।
- नगर इकाई को खण्ड इकाई के समकक्ष माना जाएगा तथा इसके कार्य, ढांचा व अधिकार खण्ड इकाई के समान ही होंगे।

5.7.5 पंचायत/नगर पंचायत इकाई

- पंचायत इकाई का सर्वोच्च संगठन, पंचायत सम्मेलन होगा। इसमें ज्ञान विज्ञान केंद्र से चुने हुए प्रतिनिधि शामिल होंगे।
- पंचायत सम्मेलन, कार्यकारिणी समिति व कोर ग्रुप का चुनाव करेगा जो इस प्रकार होगा

सम्मेलन में प्रतिनिधि (न्यूनतम)	20 सदस्य
कार्यकारिणी	5–11 सदस्य
कोर ग्रुप	3–5 सदस्य
ज्ञान विज्ञान केंद्रों की संख्या	एक
सदस्यता (न्यूनतम)	50

5.7.6 ज्ञान विज्ञान केंद्र

- ज्ञान विज्ञान केंद्र संगठन की प्राथमिक इकाई होगा।
- ज्ञान विज्ञान केंद्र को गठित करने के लिए न्यूनतम सदस्य संख्या 20 होगी तथा ये केंद्र वार्ड/गांव स्तर पर गठित किया जाएगा।
- संस्थानों में ज्ञान विज्ञान केंद्रों के लिए न्यूनतम सदस्य संख्या 10 होगी।
- सालाना नवीनीकरण के तुरंत बाद ज्ञान विज्ञान केंद्रों के सम्मेलन आयोजित किए जायेंगे जिसमें

प्रतिनिधि	सभी सदस्य
कोर ग्रुप	3
कार्यकारिणी	3–5 सदस्य

संगठन की इकाइयों के आकार

प्राथमिक इकाई से लेकर राज्य स्तर तक की विभिन्न समितियों का आकार जिला/खण्ड/पंचायत की परिस्थितियों के आधार पर होगा। विभिन्न स्तरों पर प्रतिनिधियों तथा कमेटियों की संख्या निम्नलिखित प्रकार से होगी तथा इकाइयों के गठन हेतु न्यूनतम संख्या इस प्रकार होगी:

नोटः किन्नौर, लाहुलस्पीति, पांगी एवं डोडरा क्वार आदि दुर्गम क्षेत्रों की भौगोलिक परिस्थिति को ध्यान में रखते हुए उपरोक्त ढांचे को लागू करते समय छूट दी जा सकती है।

5.8 कोर ग्रुप के कार्यभार

अध्यक्षः

समिति की सभी संगठनात्मक बैठकों की अध्यक्षता करना।

- समिति की सभी संगठनात्मक बैठकों की अध्यक्षता करना।
- सचिव द्वारा तैयार बैठकों की कार्यवाही और निर्णयों आदि को प्रतिहस्ताक्षरित करना।
- समिति की ओर से प्रेस विज्ञप्ति जारी करना।
- समिति के वित्तीय प्रपत्रों को हस्ताक्षरित करना।
- समिति के बैंक खाते का संचालन करना।

उपाध्यक्षः

- अध्यक्ष की अनुपस्थिति में वित्त संबंधी प्रपत्रों को हस्ताक्षरित करने के साथ–साथ उनके सभी कार्यभारों का निर्वहन करेगा।

सचिवः

- परिषद / कार्यकारिणी / कोर ग्रुप के निर्णयों को लागू करना।
- परिषद, कार्यकारिणी व कोर ग्रुप की बैठक बुलाना, कार्यवाही लिखना और उसे सदस्यों तक पहुंचाना।
- वित्तीय नियमों की अनुपालना करना।
- समिति के बैंक खाते का संचालन करना।
- प्रेस कांफ्रेंस बुलाना तथा अध्यक्ष की अनुमति एवं सहमति से प्रेस विज्ञप्ति जारी करना।
- परिषद / कार्यकारिणी द्वारा अधिकृत किये जाने पर निचली इकाइयों की कार्यप्रणाली को व्यवस्थित करना।
- निचली इकाइयों को परिषद / कार्यकारिणी / कोर ग्रुप के निर्णयों की सूचना देना उनके क्रियान्वयन के लिए प्रयत्न करना।
- निचली इकाइयों की बैठकों में उपस्थित हो कर मार्गदर्शन करना।

सह–सचिवः

- सचिव के कार्यभाव निर्वहन में सहयोग देना।
- निचली इकाइयों की बैठकों व गतिविधियों में भाग लेकर मार्गदर्शन करना।
- संगठन की गतिविधियों का मूल्यांकन और उनके बारे परिषद/कार्यकारिणी/कोर ग्रुप को सूचित करना।
- परिषद/कार्यकारिणी द्वारा सौंपे गए उत्तरदायित्वों को निभाना।

कोषाध्यक्ष

- संगठन के कोष का नियमानुसार संचालन करना।
- संगठन के आय व्यय का ब्यौरा रखना।
- लेखा–परीक्षक की नियुक्ति के लिए कोर ग्रुप को संस्तुति भेजना
- चार्टेड एकाउंटेंट से संगठन का लेखा परीक्षा करवाना।
- वार्षिक सम्मेलन के लिए वित्तीय रिपोर्ट तैयार करना।
- संगठन द्वारा निर्धारित बैंकों से तालमेल।
- समिति के बैंक खाते का संचालन करना।

धारा 6. सामान्य नियम

- आमतौर पर संगठन में एक व्यक्ति एक पद्वति के सिद्वान्त के रूप में कार्य किया जाएगा लेकिन इसे परिस्थितियों/विकल्प को ध्यान में रखते हुए ही अमल में लाया जाएगा।
- एक पदाधिकारी को एक पद पर लगातार दो अवधियों तक ही जिम्मेवादी सौंपी जाएगी परंतु परिस्थितियों तथा विकल्प को ध्यान में रखते हुए ही इसे लागू किया जाएगा।
- संगठन के प्रत्येक सदस्य को निर्वाचित होने, निर्वाचित करने व विभिन्न स्तरों पर अपने विचार व्यक्त करने का अधिकार होगा परन्तु मतभेद होने पर बहुमत के निर्णय को लागू करने की जिम्मेवारी निभानी होगी। अन्यथा संबंधित सदस्य के खिलाफ अनुशासनात्मक कार्यवाही की जाएगी।

- संगठन में सर्वसम्मति या उसके अभाव में बहुमत की राय से निर्णय लिए जाऐंगे। उच्चतर इकाइयों के निर्णयों को निचली इकाइयों को मानना होगा।
- संगठन में यदि किसी पदाधिकारी की अस्वस्थता अथवा पारिवारिक परिस्थितियों के कारण संगठन का कार्य प्रभावित हो रहा हो तो उस स्थिति में परिषद/कार्यकारिणी द्वारा किसी अन्य सदस्य को यह जिम्मेवारी अल्पावधि के लिए सौंपी जा सकती है।
- यदि कोई पर रिक्त हो तो परिषद/कार्यकारिणी उस स्थान को भरने के लिए अधिकृत होगी।

Index